SWEET & SAVAGE

THE WORLD THROUGH THE
MONDO FILM LENS

Mark Goodall

HEADPRESS

CONTENTS

Foreword 4

An Exhibition of Atrocities — J G Ballard on mondo films 6

Introduction — Autopsia: the act of seeing with one's own eyes....................9

CHAPTER 1
Mondo as Document...17
   Mondo Cane...22
   Mondo Cane 2000 (This is America 3)..29
   Des Morts (Of the Dead) 32

CHAPTER 2
Mondo and Shock Cinema 36
   Brutes and Savages..39
   Mondo Candido 42
   Mr. Mike's Mondo Video 47
   Mondo di Notte Oggi 50

CHAPTER 3
Voyeurism and Sexuality in the Mondo Film 54
   La Donna nel Mondo (Women of the World)..57
   Mille Peccati... Nessuna Virtù (Wages of Sin) 61
   Svezia, Inferno e Paradiso (Sweden Heaven and Hell) 64
   Mondo Freudo 68
   I Malamondo 72
   L'Occhio Selvaggio (The Wild Eye)..75
   Sexy Magico 79
   Primitive London 82

CHAPTER 4
Anti-narrative in Mondo..85
   Il Pelo nel Mondo (Go! Go! Go! World)...91
   Europa di Notte 94
   Mondo di Notte 3 (Ecco) 97
   Realtà romanzesca (Realities around the World) 101
   Addio Zio Tom..104
   Australia After Dark 111

CHAPTER 5
The Frame of Mondo 114
   Africa Addio 119

2

CONTENTS

CHAPTER 6
Animals in Mondo Film...128
    Ultime Grida dalla Savana (Savage Man... Savage Beast).....................136
    Savana Violenta (This Violent World).....................................141
    Dolce e Selvaggio (Sweet and Savage)......................................146
    Faces of Death..150
    America Cosi Nuda, Cosi Violenta (Naked and Violent)......................155

CHAPTER 7
Mondo Magic and Ritual..158
    Angeli Bianchi... Angeli Neri (Witchcraft '70) 163
    Magia Nuda (Mondo Magic) 167
    Nuova Guinea, L'Isola del Cannibali (Guinea Ama).........................172

APPENDIX I
Interviews with the Jacopetti/Prosperi team
    Gualtiero Jacopetti 176
    Franco Prosperi 183
    Stanis Nievo 195
    Riz Ortolani 203
    Giampaolo Lomi 207

APPENDIX II
The Mondo Soundtrack 211
    Riz Ortolani 212
    Piero Umiliani 214
    Piero Piccioni 215
    Angelo Francesco Lavagnino 216
    Bruno Nicolai 216
    Guido and Maurizio De Angelis...217
    Carlo Savina 218
    Ennio Morricone..218

APPENDIX III
Considerations on the Documentary Film *by* Gualtiero Jacopetti.................220

Acknowledgements 229

Bibliography 230

Selected Filmography 233

Index...237

About this book...244

3

City of the Living Dead

FOREWORD

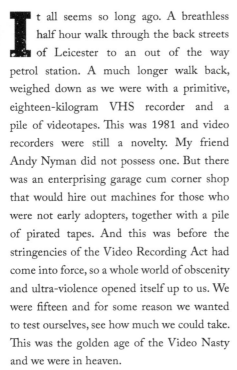

It all seems so long ago. A breathless half hour walk through the back streets of Leicester to an out of the way petrol station. A much longer walk back, weighed down as we were with a primitive, eighteen-kilogram VHS recorder and a pile of videotapes. This was 1981 and video recorders were still a novelty. My friend Andy Nyman did not possess one. But there was an enterprising garage cum corner shop that would hire out machines for those who were not early adopters, together with a pile of pirated tapes. And this was before the stringencies of the Video Recording Act had come into force, so a whole world of obscenity and ultra-violence opened itself up to us. We were fifteen and for some reason we wanted to test ourselves, see how much we could take. This was the golden age of the Video Nasty and we were in heaven.

We sought the thrill of the forbidden. Not pornography, although the stuff we watched was akin to it in a way. It provided a sharp thrill, a jolt, a shock. There was an electric pleasure in testing our limits, provoking a visceral response. These were Italian horror movies — directed by the likes of Lucio Fulci, Umberto Lenzi and Ruggero Deodato. They contained ghoulish acts of bloodshed depicted in stomach churning detail — beheadings, gougings, eviscerations and the like. Their titles had already written themselves into a kind of mythology:

"Have you seen *City of the Living Dead*?"

"No."

"Oh you've got to see it. A girl sicks up her own intestines."

"What about *Cannibal Ferox*? They make a man eat his own eyes."

A few years later, long after these films were banned, the mythology had grown into a cult of the taboo. The movies were discussed

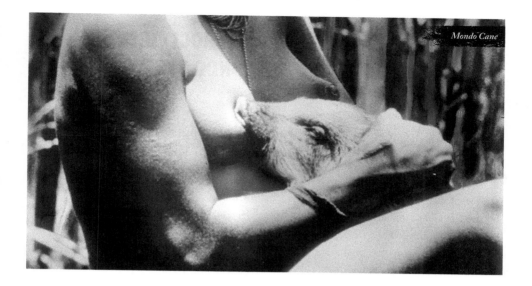

Mondo Cane

with a reverence and in semi-academic terms in specialist magazines such as *Shock Xpress* and *Eyeball: the European Sex and Horror Review*. Mingled amongst the lurid examples that were familiar were other even more mysterious and exotic titles, including one that recurred frequently: *Mondo Cane*.

I assumed at first that it referred to a character — pronounced 'Kane', as in *Citizen Kane* by Orson Welles. 'Mondo' seemed redolent of 'Mongo', the brutish half-wit in *Blazing Saddles*. Consequently I created a vivid image of a lumpen, feral giant pulling people to pieces. Later I discovered these films — for there was a series of them — were something else entirely. A kind of shock documentary with weird and bizarre things recorded all around the world, a Latinate 'Ripley's Believe it or not' with a nihilistic twist. I still had yet

to see one when we recorded the first series of *The League of Gentlemen*. In this the character of Tubbs is seen briefly suckling a piglet. I was shocked, not long after the program was transmitted, to finally see *Mondo Cane* and discover that it contained exactly the same image — Tubbs being replaced by an African Tribeswoman. Life truly is stranger than fiction. But then that is the point of the Mondo film.

For the uninitiated, or for the fan, I cannot think of a better, more erudite guide than my old friend Mark Goodall. He has devoted the better part of the last decade to researching this fascinating and bizarre subject and here are the fruits of his labours. So turn the page and find out why it truly is a world of dogs.

— Jeremy Dyson, *London, April 2005*

Jeremy Dyson is a writer of television and film comedy and drama. He is a co-writer of BBC comedy series *The League of Gentlemen* and is also the author of *The Essex Files, Never Trust a Rabbit, Bright Darkness: the lost art of the supernatural film* and *Still*.

FOREWORD

AN EXHIBITION OF ATROCITIES: J G BALLARD ON MONDO FILMS

Interview by Mark Goodall

J G Ballard, born in 1930 in Shanghai, was one of the foremost chroniclers of the modern and postmodern world.

His work comprised science fiction novels such as *The Drowned World* (1962), dystopian fantasies *Crash* (1973) and *High-Rise* (1975), autobiographical best-sellers *Empire of the Sun* (1984) and *Miracles of Life* (2008), and the prescient *Cocaine Nights* (1996) and *Super-Cannes* (2000) about super-rich elites. An enthusiastic supporter of the mondo film, he first incorporated them into his fiction through the pages of the quarterly *Ambit* magazine. His column 'Plan for the Assassination of Jacqueline Kennedy' was made up of a collage of descriptions of murder footage, assassination fantasies and the blurring of sex and death and reality and fantasy he saw evident in the late twentieth century media landscape. These texts were later collected into an anti-novel *The Atrocity Exhibition* (1970) where Jacopetti and his style of film-making was specifically name-checked.

In this interview, Ballard makes clear his pleasure that a Jacopetti retrospective took place in the UK*, the country whose absurdities most strongly influenced his work.

This interview was conducted in late 2003 and early 2004 by letter correspondence.

J.G. Ballard died in 2009.

J G BALLARD: I was a great admirer of *Mondo Cane* and the two sequels, though if I remember they became more and more faked, though that was part of their charm. We, the 1960s audiences, needed the real and authentic (executions, flagellant's processions, autopsies etc.) and it didn't matter if they were faked — a more or less convincing simulation of the real was enough and even preferred. Also, the more tacky and obviously exploitative style appealed to an audience just waiting to be corrupted — the Vietnam newsreels on TV were authentically real, but that wasn't 'real' enough. Jacopetti filled an important gap in all sorts of ways — game playing was coming in. Also they were quite stylistically made and featured good photography, unlike some of the ghastly compilation atrocity footage I've been sent. It is lovely to think that he had his retrospective in a British university (as in *The Atrocity Exhibition*, which is *not* set in the US, as some think).*

I think that Jacopetti was genuinely important, and opened a door into what some call postmodernism and I call boredom. Screen the JFK assassination enough times and the audience will laugh.

MARK GOODALL: What were your initial impressions of the films of Gualtiero Jacopetti (*Mondo Cane, Mondo Cane 2, Women of the World, Africa Addio* etc.); where did you see them; what was the audience like?

JGB: I was very impressed by Jacopetti's films — I saw all of them from 1964 or so onwards — they were shown in small cinemas in the West End, and to full or more or less full houses, and my impression is that the audiences completely got the "point". As far as I remember, the response of the people sitting around me was strong and positive. I think there was comparatively little sex in the first *Mondo Cane*, and I can't recall even one dirty raincoat. The audience was the usual crew of rootless inner Londoners (the best audience in the world) drawn to an intriguing new phenomenon. At the time, some twenty years had gone by since the war's end, and everyone had seen the World War II newsreels — Belsen, corpses being bulldozed, dead Japanese on Pacific Islands and so on. All grimly real, but safely distanced from the audiences by a sign that said "horrors of war". What the *Mondo Cane* audiences wanted was the horrors of peace, yes, but they also wanted to be reminded of their own complicity in the slightly dubious process of documenting these wayward examples of human misbehaviour. I may be wrong, but I think that the early *Mondo Cane* films concentrated on bizarre customs rather than horrors, though the gruesome content grew fairly rapidly, certainly in the imitator's films.

But the audiences were fully aware that they were collaborating with the films, and this explains why they weren't upset when what seemed to be faked sequences (they might have been real in fact) started to appear in the later films — there was almost the sense that they needed to appear "faked" to underline the audience's awareness of what was going on — both on-screen and inside their own heads.

We needed violence and violent imagery to drive the social (and political) revolution that was taking place in the mid-1960s — violence and sensation, more or less openly embraced, were pulling down the old temples. We needed our "tastes" to be corrupted — Jacopetti's films were part of an elective psychopathy that would change the world (so we hoped, naively). Incidentally, all this was missing from the way audiences (in the Curzon cinema I think) saw another 1960s shockumentary — *The Savage Eye* (directed by Joseph Strick) — when I saw it I, like the audience, shuddered but felt no complicity at all. A fine film.

MG: Can you recall any critical or other 'professional' reactions to Jacopetti's films when they were released?

JGB: I remember the critical/respectable reaction to the Jacopetti films was uniformly hostile and dismissive. As always, this confirmed their originality and importance.

MG: Jacopetti has distanced himself from the films that later copied *Mondo Cane* labelling them "counterfeit". What were/are your impressions of the copies of his films?

"I fear that you will never persuade the Americans to like Jacopetti — they hate moral ambiguity and their black and white Protestantism clashes head on into the Catholic relativism built into every frame of the *Mondo Cane* films."
J G BALLARD

JGB: I can't remember any specific imitations, though I must have seen one or two. They were too obvious, ignoring the delicate balance between "documentary" footage on the one hand, and on the other the need to remind the audience of its role in watching the films, and that without its intrigued response the films wouldn't function at all. The balance between the "real" and the ironic simulation of the real had to be walked like a tightrope.

MG: How did mondo films influence your own work/ideas/ thought processes (in particular *The Atrocity Exhibition*)?

JGB: For me, the *Mondo Cane* films were an important key to what was going on in the media landscape of the 1960s, especially post the JFK assassination. Nothing was true, and nothing was untrue (*The Atrocity Exhibition* tried to find a new sense in what had become a kind of morally virtual world) — "which lies are true?"

MG: What in your view was important about Jacopetti's films? Do you think the films have any relevance to the present day, or to the future?

JGB: I suspect they're very much of their time, but that isn't a fault, necessarily. But there are many resonance's today as in the Bush/Blair war in Iraq — complete confusion of the simulated, the real and the unreal, and the acceptance of this by the electorate. Reality is constantly redefining itself, and the electorate/audience seems to like this — a Prime Minister, religiously sincere, lies to himself and we accept his self-delusions. There's a strong sense today that we prefer a partly fictionalised reality onto which we can map our own dreams and obsessions. The *Mondo Cane* films were among the first attempts to provide the collusive fictions that constitute reality today. Wartime propaganda, and the *Believe it or Not* (Ripley) comic strip of bizarre facts in the 1930s, were assumed to be largely true, but no one today thinks the same of the official information flowing out of Iraq — or out of 10 Downing Street and the Pentagon and significantly this doesn't unsettle us.

* A Gualtiero Jacopetti retrospective occurred as part of the 2003 National Museum of Photography Film and Television's Bradford International Film Festival. The retrospective was collaboration between the festival and the department of postgraduate studies at the School of Art and Design, Bradford College.

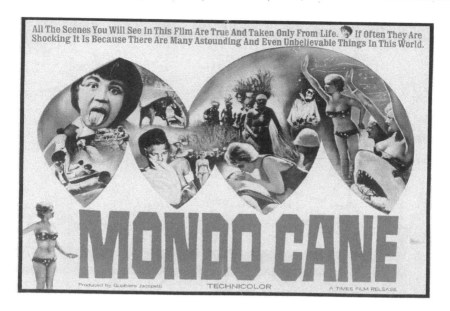

All The Scenes You Will See In This Film Are True And Taken Only From Life. If Often They Are Shocking It Is Because There Are Many Astounding And Even Unbelievable Things In This World.

MONDO CANE

Produced by Gualtiero Jacopetti   TECHNICOLOR   A TIMES FILM RELEASE

INTRODUCTION

Autopsia: the act of seeing with one's own eyes

Traces of the mondo film, one of the most controversial and overlooked genres in cinematic history can be found in a bewildering array of contemporary mass media products. The cable and satellite TV shows depicting 'the world's worst'; the voyeurism and surveillance of 'reality TV'; the anti-narrative fictions of J G Ballard and Patrick McCabe; the wordless melancholy of Godfrey Reggio and Ron Fricke's 'cinema of looking'; the ironic mockery of *Eurotrash*; the infantile sick-making of *Bizarre* magazine; the global photo-imaging of *National Geographic*, which still promotes a voyeuristic agenda and *New Internationalist* which promotes a social one. Benetton's *Colors* magazine is a mondo film in print form. Meanwhile most contemporary news reportage owe in part their aesthetic and political form to the films made in the late twentieth century whose radical take on the documentary film became known as mondo. The story of this cinematic genre is a story that has remained buried and forgotten. The most extensive search for traces of mondo history will uncover only the sparsest of nebulous details centred around predictable examples from which the imagination of what

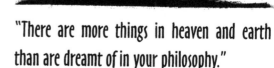

"There are more things in heaven and earth than are dreamt of in your philosophy."
HAMLET

mondo means has been shaped (in his book based on his innovative televison series, *The Incredible Film Show*, Jonathan Ross dismisses mondo as a "short-lived craze"). Common opinion states that the mondo film began at the inception of cinema, in fact as soon as film cameras were pointed at things, and there are photographic examples of pre-mondo activity dating back even further. But the mondo film truthfully began in the early 1960s when an Italian film based on a Tuscan colloquial expression called *Mondo Cane* directed by Gualtiero Jacopetti, Franco Prosperi and Paolo Cavara was released. The trail of mondo films begins properly with this film because it is beautifully crafted, mesmerising and unique; there had been nothing like it before. But the genre of mondo, what one reviewer called "the Jacopetti school", has got uglier, nastier and more derivative right up to the arrival of the 'compilation tape' (an underground homemade collection of unpleasant film and video images) by way of gory natural inquiry films and the infamous and once banned *Faces of Death* franchise. Largely because of this

conception of morbidity the reaction to mondo films has been thus fixed: most individuals that engage with the films sense vulgarity, shock, violence, and dishonesty as the most immediate traits. Others feel this too, but are also mesmerised — the impact on seeing the films is permanent, addictive, and irresistible. The powerful jolt reaction experienced by the mondo devotee is arguably deeper than the shock or disgust provoked by the contemporary horror film in that the 'horrors' presented in mondo films are, if not always steeped in vérité, mimetic representations of a form of real lived experience (as opposed to the hyper-reality of modern horror). The art of the mondo film is thus elusive but thrilling and this book tries to illustrate some of the secrets of this aesthetic and emotional tornado while attempting to bring some cohesion and rational examination to a history of the art of the mondo film. It is not an attempt at chronicling every filmic or televisual example of mondo activity. There is already a body of obsessive lists of mondo films (including those submitted by *Psychotronic Video* magazine in

1989, and those available on the web sites the Internet Mondo Movie Database and So Sweet So Perverse which all gamely try and decode the infuriating multiple titles for most mondo films). It is rather an attempt at defining, through focus on those films most 'significant' to the genre, the magical power of the mondo aesthetic. Kerekes and Slater's monumental study *Killing for Culture: death in film from mondo to snuff* vividly exorcised the most unpleasant aspects of the mondo film, extrapolating the death aesthetic of the extreme mondos to that of the snuff movie and beyond. Their book places the mondo film into a meaningful and worrying context (as does Joel Black's more recent essay on real[ist] horror where a similar link between the death film and mondo is made). But this is only one, albeit fascinating, context. So the intention of this book is to complement rather than challenge such theses and to focus on some of the key films in more analytical detail than previous authors have been able to do. The book will encourage three notions:

1. That mondo films are a powerful and important aspect of film history.
2. That much of today's media output owe a debt to the aesthetics and politics of the mondo film.
3. That mondo films belong to the 'high' genres of documentary and the practices of the avant garde as much as they do to exploitation, trash and shock cinema.

The intentions of the creators of the most exceptional mondo films were entirely serious and artful and should be respected as such (see Jacopetti's *Considerations on the Documentary Film*). Such films were often not conceived to 'exploit' audiences — although many mondo films later did this; they were not made to 'break the taboos' of societies or to agitate for any meaningful socio-cultural or political change, but some did this too; they were not intended to be pornographic, although many exhibited and encouraged voyeuristic tendencies. These films were created as cinematic, poetic and useful commentaries on human behaviour in some of its wildest and weirdest formations. The supreme mondos were, unlike many of their offspring, created with great skill and craft supported by not insignificant budgetary foundations. The most noteworthy mondo films were films that certainly changed forever the way the world was viewed and reported on through a lens. Mondo was a global phenomenon: there were examples from France (Claude LeLouch's *La Femme Spectacle* (*Paris in the Raw*), Germany (Manfred Durniok's *Welt Ohne Scham* (*Mondo Bizarre*), Scandinavia (*Naked North*) and the USA (*Mondo Mod*). Even Britain enjoyed a mini mondo flurry: Norman Cohen's *The London Nobody Knows*, Edward Stuart Abraham's *Our Incredible World*, and Arnold Louis Miller's *Primitive London/London in the Raw* all offered shockumentary thrills to Europe's staidest audience. The universal scope of the mondo film, through its form, content and prefix envisaged the global village to come. This book is about the way these films were made and the way in which audiences and critics have received them.

It is notable that most of the texts on mondo films so far have emphasised the works as misanthropic, cynical or negative representations of twentieth century global cultures. Indeed *Mondo Cane* begins (in a publicity statement for the film) with the remark that "of all living creatures man is the only one born crying". This mournful observation crystallises the ideological 'readings' that are etched into the formless history of mondo so far. Yet if we read on to the end of the same proposal we find that "though this is a world which has gone to the dogs, it is also a world in which we are happy to live" — hence the mondo paradox writ large from the outset. This type of conceptual contradiction has arguably done a disservice to the critical record of the genre over the years and yet it is these very contradictions that make mondo films so fascinating and prescient.

Mondo and Documentary

In his book *Introduction to Documentary* Bill Nichols defines mondo films' relationship with documentary as that of being a "cabaret of curiosities (which) is often an embarrassing fellow traveller more than a central element". In this he does not deviate from the received wisdom that in the documentary tradition mondo films are at best pseudo-documentary films, at worst sensations contrary to all that is known as actuality (that is if the films are mentioned at all). Even Peter Bondanella's exhaustive study, *Italian Cinema*, makes only cursory reference to the mondo genre (despite mondo being an Italian invention). Kim Newman's history of Italian exploitation film, *Thirty Years in Another Town*, at least acknowledges this: that the mondo genre, part of the Italian trend for what Paul Rotha called "neo-exoticism", was an original and authentic movement in a postwar Italian film industry dominated otherwise by an avalanche of Anglo-Saxon counterfeits. There are clear stylistic and ideological reasons as to why mondo films have been kept out of

documentary film history and the 'distancing' effect engendered by this response is relevant to an understanding of how and why mondo films have been so wilfully ignored. Firstly, the trend in documentary film in the 1960s (especially in the UK/US) was for 'observational' or 'participatory' documentary film modes, the former constructed film documents out of blank record; the latter utilised interview and interaction between filmmaker and subject and use of archive and testimony. Clearly and immediately mondo films transgress these 'cardinal rules' offering a perversion of these modes. The 'participatory' mode crucially assumes an 'anthropological' approach to the presentation of 'real' events. This sociological and academic approach leads the viewer to expect to "witness the historical world as represented by someone who actively engages with, rather than unobtrusively observes, poetically reconfigures, or argumentatively assembles the world" (Bill Nichols). Although the mid-late mondo films of Angelo and Alfredo Castiglioni were constructed with the filmmakers participation in the cultures of the film, resulting in a "scientific approach", many examples of mondo film ignore the notion of empirical delivery, if not through the distance created by the edit process (where time/space/geography is collapsed) than by that most powerful and essential of mondo 'tools' the voice-over. Notwithstanding the patronising tone of many voice-overs the numerous attempts at convincing the viewer that the camera crew had been engaging intimately with the people they were capturing on film are often negated by the proliferation of 'secret' filming using 'hidden cameras', a peep show mode of recording. Mondo films further eschew participatory notions such

Mondo Cane

as the notion of the filmmaker as a "social actor" or as leaving a "bodily presence" (Bill Nichols) with their insistence on aerial shots (the helicopter is a favourite methodology) and by use of acquired footage from outside sources. Similarly the notion of observational filmmaking was subverted in mondo films (despite the ironic fact that the tools of the observational documentary film — lightweight Arriflex cameras, for example, were critical in the development of mondo films). In a review of *Mondo Cane* the British *Monthly Film Bulletin*'s damning critique of the film was topped by the argument that if the film had been made instead by Jean Rouch (French exponent of the documentary film) it would have been a lot better, and more truthful. This and other reviews simply reflect the trend of film criticism of the time for an engagement with authenticity, realism and fidelity in documentary practice. Thus in ways in which we shall discover, and despite fulfilling Michael Renov's notion of documentary as "a discourse... of delirium", the mondo film continues to have a

problematic, if inextricable, relationship with the notion of the documentary film.

Mondo and exploitation

It is noticeable how most of the meagre entries for mondo films in film indexes are indifferent to the genre, describing the style and approach of the mondo film as either "repellent" (*The Oxford Companion to Film*), "lurid" (*The Macmillan International Film Encyclopaedia*), "emetic and glib" (*Halliwell's Film Guide*). The conceptualisation of mondo films as exploitation films has been well established and is still the realm within which they are most frequently located (particularly in Anglo-Saxon countries). The engagement with mondo films in the underground press has emphasised the 'shock' value of the films, as these are the values most coherent with the ideologies of the various 'paracinematic' publishing exercises. Such fanzines tendency to present a sensationalist angle on the mondo aesthetic reflects the desire for such magazines to celebrate the transgressive, the weird and the taboo. Bill Landis' *Sleazoid Express* has,

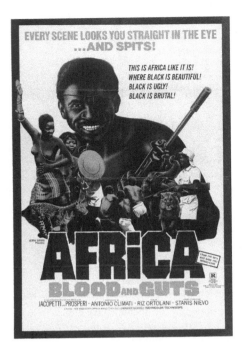

EVERY SCENE LOOKS YOU STRAIGHT IN THE EYE ...AND SPITS!

THIS IS AFRICA LIKE IT IS! WHERE BLACK IS BEAUTIFUL! BLACK IS UGLY! BLACK IS BRUTAL!

AFRiCA
BLOOD AND GUTS

JACOPETTI · PROSPERI · ANTONIO CLIMATI · RIZ ORTOLANI · STANIS NIEVO

Africa Addio as *Africa Blood and Guts* where the techniques of exploitation reached new heights (or lows).

Mondo and art film

"A closer examination of the mondo film reveals a cultural critique of otherness in its appropriation and exploitation of western concepts of primitivism, modernism, authenticity, representation, gender, class, race and identity. The mondo film extracts, shuffles and reinserts others back in to the mainstream of western popular culture and imagination. Unconcerned with holism, context, and authenticity (the mondo film) relies on fragmentation, jump-cuts, decontextualisation and fakery to create its product."

— Amy J Staples

for example, published a tabloid-style account of the work of Jacopetti and Prosperi in both magazine and book form; the Italian horror fanzines *Nocturno* and *Amarcord* have published articles devoted to the gore elements in mondo films (again linking mondo with snuff movies). One publication, Charles Kilgore's *Ecco*, is structured around the 'cinema of attractions' and Kilgore's love of mondo movies defines the ideology of the magazine. However it is perhaps not surprising that American engagement with mondo films is largely devoted to the field of exploitation; this after all is the place where the notion of film as a spectacle and commercial tool has been refined most successfully. American producers were some of the quickest to capitalise on the success of *Mondo Cane* and are mostly responsible for creating the genre as an exploitation strand. Perhaps the most grotesque example of this was producer Jerry Gross' re-launch of Jacopetti and Prosperi's

So mondo films are avant garde? Links have been made already between mondo in general, and *Mondo Cane* in particular, as expressions of experimental art cinema. Perhaps rightly so, as to examine the identity and ideology of the 'avant garde film' is to enter a cinematic arena where shock, confusion, sensory assault, contrast/ juxtaposition, sex and violence are plentiful. In an interview with Nico Panigutti, Jacopetti defined in his own words the importance of the confrontational edit process (the "shock cut") to the language of the mondo film. Such 'shock cuts' appear regularly and most spectacularly in the films of Jacopetti and Prosperi and were applied in subsequent mondo films. A use of montage to create traumatic and critical meanings worthy of Eisenstein. Similarly the avant garde technique of deconstruction is critical in the mondo aesthetic, where extensive use of freeze-frames, rapid zooms, and extreme close-ups drive the energy and breathlessness of the films (much to the abhorrence, as noted above, of documentary advocates). The more recent development of the 'compilation tape' (*Amok Assault Video* and others) — a collage of disparate footage — can be seen as the result of the cut and paste methodology afforded by cheap VCR copying devices and clearly, if brutally, reworks mondo stylistics. It is this reflexive quality of the mondo film that creates the most transgressive moments which when refracted through a postmodern aesthetic continues to shock and surprise.

The most notable films of the avant garde to be associated with *Mondo Cane* have been Georges Franju's *Le Sang des Bêtes* (*Blood of the Beasts*) and Stan Brakhage's *The Act of Seeing with One's Own Eyes*. Brakhage made his infamous autopsy film based on the doctrine of seeing, taken directly from the origins of the meaning of the word 'autopsis' ("an eyewitness observation", "any critical analysis"). Although Brakhage directly avoided loading his film with metaphor (despite earlier planning to weave other shots between the autopsy scenes) this definition of the word and action clearly lives on in the mondo aesthetic. Brakhage's "drive towards the creation of an aesthetic", through a desire to "keep it clean, go spare, go clear", is echoed in Jacopetti's conception of the "total film". Franju meanwhile conceived his abattoir film as a revealing of truth through the camera lens where even shocking images, "the heart of the atrocious", must not spare the viewer in an attack on societal hypocrisy. In construction the film prefigures mondo aesthetics, not just in its nightmarish, disturbing imagery and use of the amoral metaphor, but also in the way that Franju employs a light, popular song of the time (Charles Trenet's La Mer) as a jolting effect (critic Raymond Durgnat called this "nihilistic anarchism" and labelled both Franju and Jacopetti "poet-tourists").

So, mondo films engage with the notion of the avant garde through the construction of the filmic image-sound. But they also engage with the notion of the avant garde via a critique of the practices of high art. One of the most famous scenes from *Mondo Cane* is a mocking representation of the French artist Yves Klein. In *Mondo Cane No.2* a Greek avant garde artist with a technique of paintings consisting of vomited-up pigments is also mocked. The film ends with a further parody of performance art in a sequence of a concert where the tune is rendered via slaps across the performers' faces. Vale and Juno have argued that 'incredibly strange films' (which they have indicated includes mondo film) can be subversive and 'critical' in the way that is expected of most avant garde filmmaking processes: "(Incredibly Strange Films) often present unpopular — even radical — views addressing social, political, racial or sexual inequalities, hypocrisy in religion or government; or in other ways they assault taboos related to the presentation of sexuality, violence and other mores". British author J G Ballard was so enthralled by mondo films that he dedicated his novel *The Atrocity Exhibition* to the aesthetics and politics of mondo ("radical declensions of violence"); the notion of violent media as

"All the scenes you will see in this film are true and are taken only from life. If often they are shocking, it is because there are many shocking things in this world."
MONDO CANE

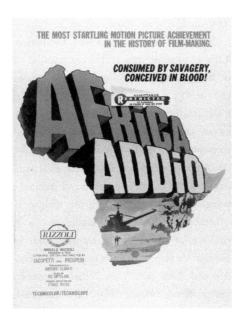

THE MOST STARTLING MOTION PICTURE ACHIEVEMENT
IN THE HISTORY OF FILM-MAKING.

CONSUMED BY SAVAGERY,
CONCEIVED IN BLOOD!

AFRICA
ADDio

RIZZOLI

pleasurable entertainment is the key to the book. The situating of Godfrey Reggio's Qatsi trilogy into an avant garde context resonates with the mondo film too — both in the sense of filmic scenarios and the language of film aiding a spiritual awareness — a journey, but also with the presentation of the shock of the real (the first film of the trilogy *Koyaanisqatsi* has been labelled a 'modern-day mondo film'). Finally, questions of 'authorship' informing discussions of the filmmaker as a unique creator of a work of art, likening experimental filmmakers to the creators of books or paintings, are significant in any discussion of film as art. The presence of Jacopetti as producer, editor, director emphasising his role as an 'author' (an auteur) is an image that Jacopetti has cultivated somewhat over the years.

Such considerations will inform the examination of mondo films in this book and try to aid a better understanding of mondo filmmaking and its nebulous influence. To this end the text on the films is book-ended with

two important pieces. The first is an interview with the author J G Ballard exploring his fascination with mondo films. The second is the reproduction of an essay, never before published, written by Gualtiero Jacopetti outlining his personal and polemical approach to documentary filmmaking.

The goal of this book is to agitate for a greater appreciation of the mondo aesthetic and of certain mondo films in particular. It is likely, however, that advocates of documentary filmmaking will remain resistant to the mondo genre; that the avant garde remain distant to it and that fans of "sleazy mindless movies" have already moved on to 'better/worse' audiovisual entertainment. To paraphrase *Mondo Cane* this book 'will not make judgements or pretend to moralise'. As always it will be the reader, and the viewer, that will decide.

As I write, the wounds of American slavery are being reopened with the History Channel's remake of *Roots* (the 1970s American television miniseries based on Alex Hailey's bestselling novel of the same name) together with recent films about slavery in America including *Birth of a Nation*, *12 Years a Slave* and *Django Unchained*. In Zimbabwe the process of black Africans, driven by a distorted ideology, are violently reclaiming land from white 'settlers'. Jacopetti showed such acts over forty years ago. Meanwhile in the Darfur region of the Sudan, rape, torture, ethnic cleansing and genocide are being carried out for revenge and for punishment, a hideous scenario that has been dubbed the 'new Rwanda'. But the 'old' Rwanda we have already seen, in *Africa Addio*, and the awful legacy of these and other shockumentary film images, and our failure to act on them, haunts us still.

CHAPTER 1
"SEE THE WORLD IN THE RAW"

Mondo as Document

Given the plethora of exploitation/trash material now lurking under the mondo banner it's easy to forget that *Mondo Cane* was at first a new and unique type of documentary film, albeit a film acting as a direct riposte to what up until that point had been known as 'documentary' practice. In the Anglo-Saxon world the meaning of documentary had been shaped by leading theorists Grierson, Flaherty etc (Jacopetti acknowledges this in his *Considerations…*) whose work in turn influenced neo-realism which emerged in the postwar period led by Italian directors Rossellini, Visconti, De Sica and screenwriters such as Zavattini. The films that emerged as part of this were driven by an aim for authenticity and/or to express a clearly identifiable 'argument'. In documentary film this resulted in what Bill Nichols calls the 'expository' and 'observational' modes where the director/filmmaker imparts information/posits argument or merely observes what is happening in front of the camera lens, without intervention or comment: either a propagandist tool or a puritanical notion of film production as an exercise in factual record. Grierson's agenda for documentary was reformist positioned from the democratic left and with a strong enlightenment aim (docu-theorist Brian Winston later showed how Grierson's agenda was, in fact, untenable, his films commissioned as they were by British Conservative administrations). Jacopetti and Prosperi's contra-methodology, funded privately by Italian publisher Angelo Rizzoli, was adopted by French filmmaker Jean Rouch who himself moved away from expository/observational modes and was criticised, much as Jacopetti would be, for problematising the way in which documentary films are "still bound to reason, to words, to Baconian plain style" (Paul Stoller) and negating through their work Grierson's Calvinist notion of evidence (although ironically Grierson famously defined documentary as a "creative treatment of actuality"). In the same way that Rouch's poeticism and 'indirect language' was not rebuffed by European and North American academics so too the work of Jacopetti suffered from its unusual and striking approach to documentary filmmaking (British reviews of *Mondo Cane* when it was released did align Jacopetti's technique to Rouch but as a lesser variant of the conception of documentary being creative as well as reportative, a duality John Corner calls "the art of record"). Jacopetti

"For me… there is almost no boundary between documentary film and films of fiction. The cinema, the art of the double, is already a transition from the real world to the imaginary world."
JEAN ROUCH

mistrusted the 'authentic' truth of neo-realism — the way in which fictional films were presented, visually and ideologically, as fact — rejecting the idea that the indexical function of (cinema) photography is 'truthful' or 'evidential'. Jacopetti and Prosperi's 'realism' owes as much to the tradition of representing reality through literary "mimetics" (Eric Auerbach) found in the work of compatriots Boccacio and Dante, the art of the commedia where grotesque comedy can be intrinsic to the notion of realism. Jacopetti not only shares this poetic approach to documentary with these compatriots and with Rouch, but also with another French director Barbet Schroeder, whose more honest approach to documentary film production is clearly articulated through the practice of putting "some fiction into documentary and some documentary into fiction" (Schroeder's *Idi Amin Dada: a Self Portrait* contains odd poetic narration intrusions;

his bizarre *La Valée*, a fictional film concerning a group of western hippies embarking on a journey into an unknown zone of Papua New Guinea on a quest for transcendental and spiritual reawakening is a surreal trip where the 'action' is augmented by documentary sequences representing real 'primitive' practices and rituals). Schroeder, like Jacopetti, has also made clear the importance of the edit process in the creation of the film art as well as a similar concern with the use of colour processes for effect. In celebrating the art of the edit Jacopetti again breaks with formal documentary modes which do not avoid the edit process but will minimise or limit the amount of cuts made as this draws attention to the artificiality of the film process and thus destroys any notion of truth or realism, or "lived experience" (Nichols). This observational authenticity found its fullest expression in the direct cinema of the US and Free Cinema in the UK while ethnographic directors such as David MacDougall make great play of the lived experience they locate within the rushes, unedited film as it was shot, as opposed to the lost vitality of edited film sequences. Editing for MacDougall "Centres particular meanings" for him, which was a negative or problematic function. For Jacopetti it seems the very essence of his film art. Renov meanwhile outlines four tendencies in documentary practice: to record, reveal, or preserve; to persuade or promote; to analyse or interrogate; to express, tendencies which we are expected to locate with varying degrees within documentary film works. Another theorist, Heider, proposed "attributes" which a film could be measured against to affirm its documentary status. The remarkable thing about mondo films is that they manage to collapse these tendencies into one unique practice.

Yet Jacopetti goes beyond description and evidence in his documentary style, instead forging unique 'documentary poetics' imbuing the material recorded by the camera with his own personal and researched take on the events. This documentary-poetic work of Jacopetti and other mondo films conforms rather to David Bordwell's notion of poetics as a "conceptual framework within which particular questions about films' composition and effects can be posed" and it is this that makes it so fascinating.

Fakes

Mondo films, and the material they present to the world as 'actualities' have commonly been labelled fake, while the more exploitative mondo films were clearly conceived with a 'flexible' approach to evidence-based film. When applied to the work of Jacopetti and Prosperi such accusations appear harsh whose 'integrity' is upset by these accusations and whose 'honest' approach to documentary filmmaking has been clearly and regularly stated (particularly by Jacopetti; Prosperi seems at times to be more ambivalent). The words 'fake' and 'documentary' are uncomfortable and always create controversy whenever they are matched (see for example the controversy over German filmmaker Michael Born's fake documentaries and the UK Carlton Television Colombian drug cartels debacle). Arguments in documentary theory have consistently engaged in the question of where 'creative treatment' of actuality becomes 'fiction'. The structural criticism of the 1970s argued for a purist notion of documentary, exposing works with artistic or creative pretensions as inauthentic coupled with a fear that some of the leading theorists (Grierson) had too much 'faith in film'. Reflecting back on this now it seems that the theoretical ideas developed by Jacopetti were correct in asserting the 'honesty' of the director, the author, above any attempt at pure 'objectivity'. While clearly some scenes, even in the most convincing mondo films were necessarily 'mocked up', it is perhaps the intentions of the authors that are more important than the fidelity (the scenes depicting the ritual protest suicide of a Buddhist monk in *Mondo Cane No.2* have been dissected by Kerekes and Slater and more recently the directors have owned up, claiming that their job is to "make cinema" as well as

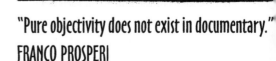

"Pure objectivity does not exist in documentary."
FRANCO PROSPERI

19

documentary). The notion of documentary as a true representation is challenged by such activity but a retelling of events in certain instances may be permissible.

Travelogue

A curious parallel can be drawn between literary approaches to exploration and the mondo film aesthetics. In analysing travel writing of the colonial period Mary Louise Pratt posits three strategies taken by 'Imperial' travel writers in recording 'other' territories: 'estheticisation' (description of the landscape); 'density of meaning' (application of semantic discourse — exposition); 'mastery' (control over the seen by the seer). In documentary film terms there can be a relation between these strategies and documentary modes of practice: estheticisation (opening shots of landscape); density of meaning (exposition of narrative content); mastery (power of the documentaries to control and shape the story) and in particular the way in which mondo films are constructed. The mode of the travelogue embodies many of the principles of the travel writer and this again is something that many mondo scenes relate to. The final manifestation of the link between travel writing/travelogue modes of representation and mondo are the writings of Alberto Moravia who, as well as penning travel books, provided the scripts for *Magia Nuda* and *Ultime grida dalla savana*. Moravia's travel writing was modernist in style and more 'real' but still operated within the strategies outlined above, and was 'authoritative' — so was ideally integrated into the mondo aesthetic. Indeed Pratt's analysis of the impulse of such writings "to condemn what they see, to trivialise it, and disassociate themselves utterly from it" rings true as a description of the mondo mode.

In this world landscapes and people are still primitive, or spoilt by the encroachment of 'civilising' influences (the "white man's lament"), the voice is unequivocal and forceful. The accusations levelled at Moravia's "coding of the third world" in Pratt's work, its "rhetoric of triviality, dehumanisation and rejection" is mirrored in the stinging critiques that Jacopetti and Prosperi endured upon the release of *Africa Addio*. The notion of presenting an overarching critique on a subject is a mondo feature and runs throughout many mondo films — the logical extension of the 'I see all' perspective on global events and customs. It is a powerful and commanding position, as a documentarist' to be in and it demands respect. Pratt notes that travel writers are not able to possess the scenes they witness (they can evaluate) but documentary filmmakers move nearer to ownership of their representations working in the cinematic mode where the meaning is created in the edit and postproduction process back in the comfort of their own environment with all the tools of the cinematic art as their disposal.

The Voice of God

As we have noted some documentary modes have suppressed the voice of God narration as an intrusive, prescriptive communication tool. But in the mondo aesthetic the narration and script are central to the creation of meaning in the film and here after opening up the meaning of the scenes begins to develop a mastery over the subject. The mondo film employed some of the finest exponents of narration, many of them the most famous voices in film history (George Sanders, Edmund Purdom, Peter Ustinov, Vincent Price). Narration in mondo occupies a magical space in film art, that between the sounds which naturally belong to the world on-screen and those which do not. The latter Ralph Stephenson defines as the commentative — in mondo films the disembodied commentary of an outside observer. There are some specific manifestations of film sound in mondo that relate to the narration and its power: while disembodied voices occur in documentary many mondo films exploit the notion of the narrated as remarking ironically on the action after the event (Jacopetti and Prosperi's *Women of the World*, for example, is described as being "viewed" by the English language narrator Peter Ustinov). Ustinov is famous, in his own work, for the wry, sometimes racist observations he makes on global cultures and customs. In an interview with *Shock Cinema* Purdom meanwhile posited the opposite stance: that for him, the many narrations of mondo films he delivered were done without reference to the visual cues ("I took very little interest in the content of these documentaries"). Instead Purdom read the script out in isolation. Needless to say, both of these alienating effects would be despised by conventional documentary practitioners (Heider's purist ethnographic attributes deplores any "overly wordy", "banal" narration). Ironic contrasts, counterpoint, is a significant mondo device played through violent juxtaposition in the compiling, but no less so in structure of the narration. Often the pomposity or pretentiousness of human activity will be undercut either by droll narrative comment, patronising mockery or racist abuse — sometimes all of these at once. "Narration is what you do when you fail" Robert Drew once claimed, speaking of documentary. Yet without this ever-present, sneering, mocking companion, the mondo films would not properly exist.

The other important aspect of Italian

mondo films was the fact that all Italian films of this period were made with post-synchronous sound. This extended even into mainstream, 'serious' drama features where the provincial accents of Italian actors were dubbed by studios into conventional Roman dialect. Therefore with this practice commonplace the fragmentary effect of the sound and visual relationship was exploited as a feature of mondo. Stam and Shohat define this as an oppressive inauthentic gesture of ideology; for mondo directors it aided the weirdness of the finished film. Any calls for restraint were loudly ignored as some of the more hysterical commentaries testify.

So the mondo film enjoys a troubled relationship with that of the documentary genre. It exits both as part of the documentary tradition, but is estranged profoundly from it. The films examined in this chapter will serve to illustrate this further.

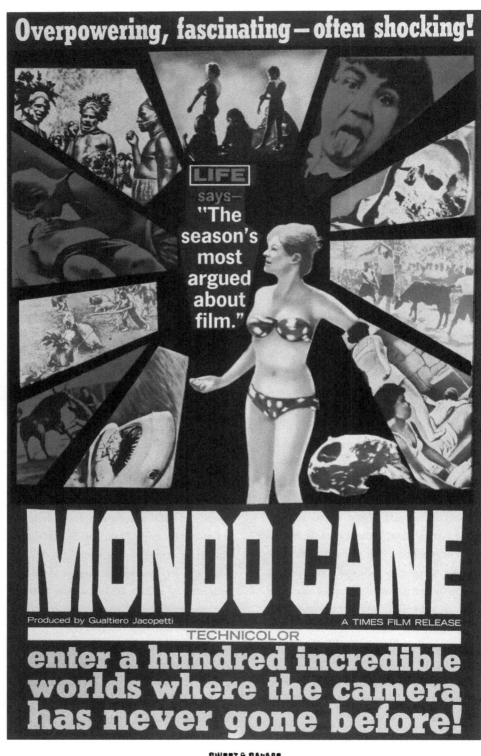

22

SWEET & SAVAGE

MONDO CANE

Directed by Gualtiero Jacopetti, Franco Prosperi, Paolo Cavara
(Italy, 1962)

Given the plethora of films dedicated to the proposition that the world is full of strange things, and that such things need to be shown to paying audiences, it is justifiably hard now to appreciate the impact of the original shockumentary film. While many commentators have argued that the art of the shockumentary began long before Gualtiero Jacopetti decided to create the feature length newsreel that became *Mondo Cane*, a close examination of the film reveals that this perception is false and that Jacopetti was right to claim the film as "a one off, an original".

Mondo Cane was conceived with, and still exhibits, a uniquely Italian sensibility: a potent combination of postwar liberalism (a radical position in a staunchly Catholic country protected by conservative Christian political parties), journalistic tendencies (Jacopetti began as a reporter under the tutelage of Indro Montanelli, the godfather of radical Italian newspaper journalism, while key cinematographer Antonio Climati was trained as a news-cameraman. The ethnographic/anthropological research — Prosperi and location manager Stanis Nievo began as marine biologists, albeit thrill-seeking ones). The film was conceived as a violent repudiation of the postwar Italian obsession with neo-realism which, in its attempts at representing a form of gritty actuality through location shooting,

deployment of non-professional actors, and use of monochrome film stock, which Jacopetti found unconvincingly staged — "artificial". He headed in the opposite direction producing a surreal, thrilling Technicolor version of the staid cinema newsreel, commonly shown in theatres to 'educate' the population about world events. Jacopetti developed a reputation for the controversial, both private (legend has it that Fellini wanted to consult Jacopetti for advice on the orgy scene in *La Dolce Vita*) and professional, and as his newsreels were underwritten by the producer and publishing mogul Angelo Rizzoli, thus evading state doctrine, Jacopetti had somewhat of a free hand. His previous work with Alessandro Blasetti on *Europa di Notte* (see chapter four) had opened up the possibility of showing the bizarre and the shocking and the real in the documentary sphere.

In addition to documentary attributes, *Mondo Cane* is shot through with a macabre sense of grisly black humour especially in

"In my opinion there is no difference between journalism that is written and journalism that is cinematographic."
GUALTIERO JACOPETTI

MONDO AS DOCUMENT

Mondo Cane

relation to the rituals and practices of the western world, a rarity at the time and one since acknowledged as being important and original. Erik Barnouw, for example, in his classic text *Documentary*, noted that the western documentary tendency for "colonialist predilections, by which white men buttressed assumptions of superiority" was uniquely overturned by *Mondo Cane*, which responded to the question "were weird practices not available to filmmakers elsewhere — in Europe and America for example?" with considerable vigour. *Mondo Cane* transgresses many boundaries and received practices and its contradictory/contrasting attributes have ensured that the reaction to the film has always been accordingly confused. The film rapidly became a talking point across a range of cultural spheres. The film's moral ambiguity

and lack of what the *Monthly Film Bulletin* (*MFB*) described as a "precisely defined attitude towards its material" made it 'problematic' for some. *Mondo Cane* featured in Haskell Wexler's *Medium Cool*, a critique of shock journalistic practices. Wexler was himself a trained news-cameraman (he had shot Joseph Strick's proto-mondo *The Savage Eye*) and reflected the troubled ethics of his trade in this film. At one point the main character discusses the questionable morals of filming 'reality', in this instance social tensions in 1968 Chicago, citing *Mondo Cane* as an exemplar of journalistic controversy ("how should I know what their motives were: they were Italian!" he cries). The *MFB* called the film a "catalogue of horrors" a "hymn to death and mutilation embellished with a shrug and a giggle". Other reviews criticised the film's lack of 'objectivity'. Yet in his survey of 'Classics of the Foreign Film', Parker Tyler aligns it with Georges Franju's surrealist abattoir shockumentary *Le Sang des Bêtes* (*Blood of the Beasts*), locating the film within the realm of art documentary, and describing the film's attitude to its material (positively) as "hysteria", a film which "tangles our optical nerves within a continuous snarl of global boundary lines". "Jacopetti's colour cameras are voracious and frank in what they see," noted Bosley Crowther in the *New York Times* while *Life* magazine described the film as a travelogue with "a diabolical nerve shattering difference... depicted in blood-curdling Technicolor". Some reviews eventually incorporated the ambiguity of the film into their assessments: Judith Crist writing in the *American Herald Tribune* described it as "Intelligent and repellent... cultured and coarse... its artistic aspirations brought low by its vulgar venality, its fascinating truths obscured by prurient practices". There is, in fact, contrary to the negative comments, an exact preciseness in the way that *Mondo Cane* was conceived, clearly evident in the various juxtapositions of the 'modern' and the 'primitive' but also thematically — a feat never again achieved in the mondo canon, and one which estranges *Mondo Cane* from the weak imitations trailing in its wake: thus Jacopetti's journalistic sensibilities, the search for weird stories, were an important ingredient in the creation of the film.

All of the components of what we now know as mondo were forged in this film and these became the often distorted blueprint for all other mondo style cinematic works. These include depictions of: the bizarre rituals of world cultures and religions; man's cruelty towards animals; the encroachment of technological 'development' onto the 'natural world'; sex and death in the modern epoch together with the combination of visual savagery with audio sweetness. The ambitious sprawling nature of the film is what has always made it so exciting even if some of the 'shocking' aspects of the film seem tame by today's brutal standards.

Much has also been made of the compilation aspect of *Mondo Cane* and the accusation that Jacopetti and Prosperi 'bought in' footage from other sources (the 'evidence' for this being the list of collaborators at the end). This is another specious aspect of the film's legend: *Mondo Cane* was strongly financed by the wealthy producer Rizzoli and is clearly filmed in what became the trademark Jacopetti/Climati style — fantastic use of intrusive, wide-angled lens close-ups, hand-held movement towards scenarios, exquisite framing and composition. Jacopetti has claimed that the team "shot almost two million feet of film": this is buttressed, separately, by Prosperi who recently explained how they efficiently shot masses of material in one location to leave them enough for a sequel, and more. The film is brilliantly edited by Jacopetti setting standards unreachable for most mondo mimics. One sequence in particular illustrates the virtuosity of this

"Warning: See *Mondo Cane* on an empty stomach. Money-back guarantee: after seeing it, you'll pass up the pâté."
PETER BUNZEL

technique: in Singapore the terminally ill are left in a 'house of death' to slowly wither away while a ritual feast and wild dance is held by their relatives nearby. These two scenarios are cleverly and precisely intertwined, the contrasts between the sadness of death and the joy of living depicted in increasingly rapid cuts (and musical synchrony). The life traces in the faces of the dying appear to fade before our eyes. Notwithstanding the power of this scene Jacopetti recently told me that given the opportunity he would edit the sequence differently and "half the length of it". Despite this the cuts in *Mondo Cane* are always lively and quick and it is through this that Jacopetti and Prosperi created the 'shock cut' — the jarring movement without warning from one scene to another. "To keep the audience's interest alive there needs to be a contrast of images", Jacopetti claimed. Within this area of technique however there were different approaches: the famous 'shock cut' at the start of the film, a sharp jump from a close-up of the breasts of girls parading to attract American sailors along the French Riviera to the breast of a New Guinea native suckling an orphan pig is shocking, emphasised with a violent dramatic chord by the composers of the film's music Riz Ortolani and Nino Oliviero. The cut between dog worship at the Pasadena Pet Cemetery and dog eating on the island of Formosa is similarly startling. The cut between shots of discarded automobiles into a section on the absurdities of contemporary art are gentler and the brutal sacrifice of a Ghurkha ritual (a cow is beheaded) leads into Portuguese *Forcada* (bull running) by a freeze-frame shot of the animal. The originality of the film resides in its still amusing portrayal of the rituals of the so-called developed world. While the film contains its share of typical mondo 'primitive' ritual (tribal pig feast in New Guinea, Malaysian fishermen meting out bitter revenge on the sharks that have amputated their limbs, brides of the Bismarck Archipelago stuffed and held in cages, Cargo Cults) it is perhaps the examples of civilised brutality that are the most eye-catching. These range from the silly (female Australian lifeguards 'practising' their kiss of life drill on the willing local male population, an exclusive New York restaurant serving ants, stuffed beetles, muskrat, roasted worms, the rites of drunken Germans in Hamburg), the dangerous (Portuguese bull running where participants are gored and tossed about) to the macabre (children polish the bones of the dead in a Roman cemetery). One of the most intriguing sequences is on a religious ritual of Calabrian peasants, *I Vatienti*, who on Good Friday lacerate their legs with shards of glass before running through the streets in a simulation of the sufferings of Christ. For affluent filmmakers of the Italian (and European) North these scenes appear 'primitive' and echo a commonly held derision in Italy towards the south, which embodies the concept of *la miseria*, a resistance to modernisation and a retreat into ancient ritual. The sequence is made unforgettably morbid by the sombre musical accompaniment, a simple organ fugue that begins slowly, increases tempo and then ends ominously. The sequence starts with a shock freeze-frame of one of the genuflecting participants. The garish violence of the film (particularly the colour) is still entrancing, the artificiality of Jacopetti and Prosperi's interpretation of documentary one of the film's notable aspects.

Mondo Cane — A performance of Yves Klein's *Anthropométries*

This freeform approach is highlighted in the sequence on the French conceptual artist Yves Klein — an ideal mondo subject as his performances, dubbed *Anthropométries*, incorporate elements of burlesque (the models are daubed in blue paint and pressed on to the canvas), spiritualism/mysticism (Klein was a Rosicrucian), nudity (the models are attractive young naked women). Klein's obsession with the colour blue, a version of which he later patented as 'International Klein Blue' (IKB), represents the sky and the globe and the theorist of his *Les Nouveaux Réalistes* movement, Pierre Restany, who went on to create his own 'mondo style' publication on global art, culture and ritual *Planète*. Paolo Cavara was dispatched to Paris to shoot the sequence that Klein imagined would be a tribute to his art. Jacopetti however used the shots as an attack on the egomania, delusion and pomposity of modern art replacing Klein's specially composed *Monotone Symphony* with a lush, instrumental version of the *Mondo Cane* theme (in some versions of the film this is the vocal version sung by Katyna Ranieri) and supplying some derisory narration. When Klein visited the Cannes Film Festival to view the finished film the artist was so furious that, according to myth, he induced one of the heart attacks that were to later kill him (he is referred to in the film as "Czechoslovakian" which may have made his blood boil). Given this collage of weird and wonderful scenarios it is easy to forget the starkness of the film's remarkable opening images: simple hand-held point of view (POV) shots of a dog being led reluctantly into a compound. There is no narration (in the original Italian film; the English version has the narrator read the text out, pointlessly

Mondo Cane – Feast in New Guinea

and incorrectly) only the desperate barking of the dogs, as the opening statement of intent fades into view. It is worth noting that the narration in the original Italian, by Stefano Sibaldi, one of the best dubbing voices in Italy, is quiet and understated, rather than hysterical and pompous, creating a sense of cynicism rather than mockery. Another of the successful aspects of the film was its musical score, in particular the theme tune which, when supplemented with English lyrics by Norman Newell, became the song More, one of the most successful songs ever written notching up over a thousand versions and seven million broadcast performances.

The film ends with the sombre portrayal of the 'Cargo Cult', a ritual practice held by Aboriginal natives who mistake the cargo planes that fly into Port Moresby airport for objects from paradise bearing gifts from their dead ancestors and the airport as a trap the white man has devised to capture these gifts. The natives have constructed their own rickety wooden plane to try and lure the cargo planes towards them instead. This is such a moving and fitting end to the film because it defines the essence of mondo dogma: the destruction of natural habitat and ancient customs by capitalist technologies and the attempts by natives to adapt to these changes, a world "gone to the dogs" perhaps, but one which *Mondo Cane*'s sangfroid viewpoint is happy to offer up.

A sequel to the film *Mondo Cane No.2* (*Mondo Pazzo*) was issued by Cineriz. The sequel utilised footage left-over from the original project and whilst fascinating is more akin to the cash-ins that avalanched after the massive success of *Mondo Cane*. Jacopetti, despite his name being credited against the film, has always claimed it to be the work of others, carried out as a contractual requirement. It is the only film directed by Jacopetti and Prosperi without Riz Ortolani's music.

MONDO CANE 2000 (THIS IS AMERICA 3)

Directed by Gabriele Crisanti
(Italy, 1988)

There is a huge difference between the early 1960s shockumentary innovator *Mondo Cane*, and the late eighties melted plastic edifice that is Gabriele Crisanti's *Mondo Cane 2000*. The English language title for the film, *This is America 3*, immediately gives the game away demonstrating vividly the barrel-scraping depths to which the mondo film had plummeted by the end of the twentieth century. Not only is Crisanti's mondo horror unoriginal but it is a very poorly made documentary film. The *mise en scène* is ugly and lacks the cinematographic finesse of Climati, Frattari and Ruzzolini, while Claudio Cimpanelli's music, ridiculously fast electro drum rolls and incredibly tinny synthesizer envelopes, would have been outdated before the film was two years old (Cimpanelli was also recruited by Stelvio Massi for his mondo nadir *Mondo Cane Oggi: L'Orrore Continua* (*Mondo Cane No.3*). Crisanti was already known as a producer of standard-quality Italian genre films such as the thriller *Giallo a Venezia* and horrors *Malabimba* and *Zombi Horror*.

Yet the intentions of the film are noble, and one which many directors and critics have indicated a desire to see rendered, namely, the application of mondo aesthetics to the postmodern world and its hideous, ugly face. Crisanti's premise, outlined in the opening diatribe about the 'the primitive' being encroached upon and destroyed by technology

and the values of global capitalism, is laudable, critical even. "This is what we call mondo cane," narrator David Traylor pontificates; "mysterious, uncontaminated — a paradise lost." The image of an unspoilt (probably South American) dreamland, where 'noble savages' ("people excluded from modern civilisation") go about their simple, natural everyday activities is briefly evoked. "These people are regarded by outsiders as exhibits in a zoo" the narrator continues, seemingly unaware of the irony that comes from a genre infamous for gawping at the world's peoples that this statement produces. In preparation for the images to come we are posed with the conundrum: "But is this the real mondo cane, or a parallel world?"…

Crisanti then introduces us to the repulsive, vicious world of "blind materialism", through images of the city most likely to represent this concept: New York. The title sequence montage of gesticulating black preachers, body popping hip-hop dancers, blank-zombiefied city workers supported by an hopelessly outdated electro-synth soundtrack (this annoying and incessant beat quickly unsettles the viewer, provoking a similar feeling to that of a dentist's drill probing an abscess!). A series of cheap and tacky scenarios unfold beginning with the unintentionally hilarious depiction of a man who fulfils his "kink" by trashing scrapped police cars. The sight of a masked man in a cheap suit wearing a Stetson, piecing together his assembly kit sledgehammer before launching into a slow-motion assault into car windows, bonnets and doors beggars belief, as does the voice-over: "Is he a closet anarchist?" Ridiculous.

Modern-day variants on the old theme of vice-for-sale are offered: porno-taxis (riders can enjoy hard core sex videos while travelling to the office); prostitution and drug dealing in Central Park (shot with infrared cameras, a trick copied without advancement from *Mondo Freudo*); child prostitution (degradation fuelled by "unrestrained consumerism"); group sex "image therapy" and music-driven autoeroticism (explicitly shown and shamelessly pornographic); masochistic massage (an excuse for further tit and bum close-ups); mail-order sex toys and catalogue photo-shoots (medium close-up shot: a penis flops out of its pouch — "talk about letting it all hang out"); arse art: sculptures of female body parts ("a well rounded business capacity"); food shaped like genitals ("porno pastries" — a curiously beautiful piano waltz augments this scene: why?) and so on. A brief foray into 'alternative' drugs taken within rituals is presented in the Andes where a drug called Tibodio, forged from burnt cocoa leaves, acts as "the God himself". Tibodio also features as part of an Amazonian fertility rite but any sense of anthropological/ethnographic insight disintegrates into cheap exploitation when shock cuts between the priest, the infertile woman and the bludgeoning to death of a cow are shoddily delivered. Then we are presented with a freeze-frame filled record of the hallucinogenic, tarantella-like effects of the piato drug ("Is this the mondo cane god?"). Transgressions are routinely mocked, as ever: a transvestite is described as a "gay girl guy" (or was it "gay girl guide"?). "Hey, did someone say gay!" the narrator smirks, warming to the theme, and we are transported into the middle of a gay pride march in New York (the variety of homosexuals involved are all attributed mock characteristics, "spaghetti gays" being my personal favourite). Horrific, ultra gory pathologist photos of homophobic murders and bloody mutilation shots are suddenly shoved in our faces abruptly quashing any warm emotions one may have felt at seeing human beings allowed to celebrate their 'difference' freely and openly. Meanwhile the filmmakers find some 'punk hairstyles' shaped like male and female genitalia particularly amusing. The sex obsessions only cease when we are treated to some of the gravest portrayals of late twentieth century science and medicine in the contemporary world: the surgical removal of a monkey's pulsing heart; the removal of a monkey's testicles for 'medical research'; a cadaver whose eyes have been removed and sold. The sickening fascist proposition by one Leonard Bailey to use 'mentally deficient' childrens' organs for transplants is critiqued in a typically sensationalist manner: "think about it!" we are ordered. Whether fabricated or not these scenes are always grim, depressing and ultimately hopeless.

Almost as relentless as the techno beats are the references to the "plague of the year 2000" — AIDS. The undisguised fear of the disease is perhaps explained by the timing of the film's production occurring as it did at the high point of paranoia of the phenomenon. Scenes relating to the disease, including children condemned by their parents' infectiousness are indeed thought

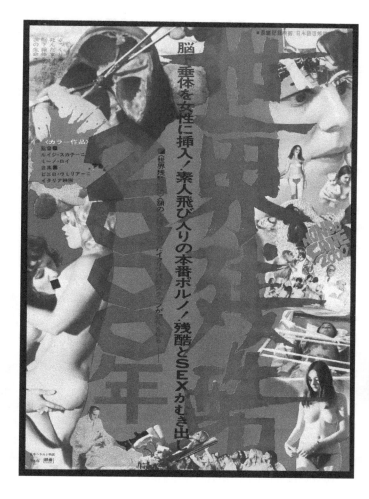

provoking. Yet being a mondo film the sneers are inevitable, a group of campaigners for AIDS awareness are labelled a "deadly serious group". Hmmm… The film ends with a grave warning about the "madness and horror of the year 2000". A special effects door opens and we are back again in the pan-pipe drenched world of the 'real' mondo cane. A retreat from the present and future into the past from which many have not returned?

At one point, during a sequence on a project producing videos made from secret footage of public toilets, the voice-over describes the director's feeling that his work was like "Fellini, Lucas and Spielberg all rolled into one". Clearly a laughably misguided notion, but one that causes the viewer to wonder (listening to the moralising tone evident in films like *Mondo Cane 2000*) as to whether some mondo filmmakers actually share this viewpoint. It is no surprise, given how far this film and many of those before it have stretched the concept of 'documentary', that even Jacopetti felt moved to denounce such motley and unwelcome subscribers to the genre he invented.

DES MORTS (OF THE DEAD)

Directed by Jean-Pol Ferbus, Dominique Garny, Thierry Zeno
(Belgium, 1979)

I n his book, *Film as a Subversive Art*, Amos Vogel lamented on the lack of filmed material concerned with one of the last visual taboos — "the ultimate secret" — real death. Vogel wrote "that this entire area... [which] simply does not exist in contemporary cinema, reveals taboo in its purest form". This was in 1974. Five years later the Belgium team of Ferbus, Garny and Zeno provided a direct riposte to Vogel's laments — their film *Des Morts*, arguably still the most powerful film on the subject of mortality ever envisaged. (Zeno, who died in June 2017, has his name appear last in the direction credits but it would be uncontroversial to say that he, as producer, cinematographer and editor was the principal force behind the film.)

Mostly the film is constructed with a deep sense of gravitas and sensitively articulates a vision of 'real' death in the modern world. As a serious documentary film it steadily progresses through an account of what death and dying is like 'in reality'. Shots in the film are generally conceived in the manner of ethnographic/anthropological film studies: expositions are shot from a flat, square, even ugly perspective and there are few 'special effects' such as the use of elliptical lenses or obtuse compositional devices. There is no narration in the film and almost the only sound we hear is that of the synchronised voices of interviewees, diegetic music, or natural sounds emanating from

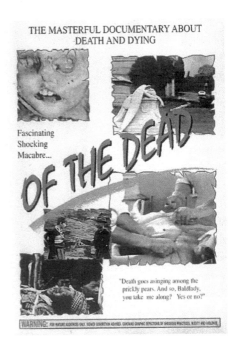

THE MASTERFUL DOCUMENTARY ABOUT DEATH AND DYING

Fascinating
Shocking
Macabre...

OF THE DEAD

"Death goes asinging among the prickly pears. And so, Baldilady, you take me along? Yes or no?"

WARNING: FOR MATURE AUDIENCES ONLY. VIEWER DISCRETION ADVISED. CONTAINS GRAPHIC DEPICTIONS OF SHOCKING PRACTICES, NUDITY AND VIOLENCE.

the *mise en scène*. Additional information is conveyed via block capital subtitles (as in ethnographic 'classics' such as Robert Gardner and Hilary Harris' *The Nuer*). All of which is a style that Zeno perfected elsewhere in his film career (a review, for example, of his 1987 film *Eugène Ionesco, Voix et Silences* in the Belgian journal *La Libre Belgique* notes that "the director succeeds by playing down his own role" acts as a reminder of his observational approach). Thus *Des Morts* is a contemplative film that appears to sit uncomfortably in the realm of the mondo film.

The film begins simply and starkly with a medium-shot of a young American mortician beginning to describe the post-mortem procedures common to 'civilised' funeral directorships, namely the pathological cleansing of dead bodies, in this case fingernails (the title of the film appears on the screen). The film then cuts to a long sequence on a funeral rite in Thailand (one of two such scenes book ending the film, the other is set in South Korea). A mother who has died is laid out and mourned over, being subjected to sung and played laments, ritual fanning with palm leaves, rifle and crossbow salutes. A feast is prepared from five slaughtered cattle (killed violently, if carefully, so that they fall onto their left side) before she is finally laid to rest in a coffin. Again the sequence is shot in an ethnographic mode: unobtrusive fixed camerawork, simple titles locating place and date, location sound, even translations of the conversations taking place between the

native peoples. The access given to the crew, in order to secure such powerful and intimate pictures (the rite takes place over several days) is also that of the ethnographic filmmaker, securing the trust of the people for scientific anthropological purposes and becoming profoundly ensnared in the ritual itself. This sequence is inter-cut with shots of an American funeral where the actions are carried out quickly and efficiently, and by machines. The only music heard here is a loud and meaningless blast of nondescript rock emitting from the hearse driver's radio. The contrast is emphasised when we note that in opposition to the mechanistic lowering of the American coffin by crane, the hand-made Thai coffin has been made way too narrow and the corpse must be wedged in sideways. Further solemn documentary/ethnographic sequences appear: Catholic funerals held under grey Northern European skies (notably those of the directors' homeland); testimonies of terminal muscular

dystrophy sufferers and a woman who replays a tape of her dying (now dead) husband to bring him 'back to life'; unique footage inside a cremation chamber of the body's reluctance to become completely immaterial; glaringly lit emergency ward footage of dying and critically wounded Mexican knife victims. The post-mortem footage of a man we have just witnessed dying on-screen (Mario Sanchez Fernandez, according to the tape stuck across his chest), harsh, unflinching shots of his head and torso being wrenched open and then crudely sewn back up again, recall the blank, shocking images created by Stan Brakhage in his silent autopsy document *The Act of Seeing With One's Own Eyes*: very serious, very considered and very moving.

And yet *Des Morts* is also a mondo film.

Whereas Brakhage simply let the camera roll for his film, trying to record as "cleanly" and "sparely" what he saw, Zeno's cutting and shaping of the images in his film resorts to shock and surprise. The first such 'shock cut' of the film, the leap from Eastern to Western funerals, is read at first viewing simply as a defectively rendered montage. But looking again we discover that Zeno actually uses the shock cut to accentuate the jarring differences between attitudes to the act of death. Creative use of the art of the film edit services to convey complex metaphysical ideas. The powerful use of non-diegetic music is spare (as would be required of a textbook documentary portrait), yet the slow haunting theme created by Alain Pierre takes the already heart-wrenching images to another level. His application, particularly of electronic cues (used as an accompaniment for a sequence on a modern American cortege, and as an eerie accompaniment to a frightening account of cryogenic facilities, where the surreal experiments in freezing corpses for an eventual cure for mortality is treated to spooky electro doodlings) is pleasurably incongruous. 'Lyrical' shots, not slickly convincing but still eerily beautiful, such as the twilight cemetery panorama at the end of the film add a gothic ambience to the mood and extra emotion to the already sombre subject of the film. The calm ethnographic dispatch of large portions of the film is also shattered during the cryogenics sequence. The use of still colour photographs to illustrate the frightful process is conventional enough, but suddenly the interviewee appears as a circular insert to these images. Even for the late 1970s this is a cheesy effect, although arguably fitting for the absurd nature of the subject matter. Even the mondo predilection for animal slaughter is incorporated. The closing bloody moments of a Mexican bullfight (the animal suffers multiple skewerings) is inter-cut with a shop butchering chickens and calves on-site (the severed calf's head is shown still convulsing). The window outside displays the legend *"muerto"*. Zeno is unable to resist some rapid mondo style cutting when a bell tolls to herald a Mexican rite urging souls back from the dead. A man in a black hooded robe explains the significance of the ritual through a yellowing towel wrapped over his mouth. Mondo pazzo indeed.

The final mondo attribute is the way in which the filmmakers mockingly represent America and the twisted and estranged manner in which western capitalism encompasses mortality. As well as the creepiness of the mortuary assistant (who appears at regular interviews throughout the film), like an automaton Norman Bates with a nervous laugh, there are the people of Sierra Dawn and their trailer park existence, coded as weirdly disturbing (why do domestic home organs seemingly evoke the work of the devil?) and an enterprising businessman describes how he now conducts the scattering of cremated ashes over the Golden Gate Bridge in San Francisco on a "volume basis" (i.e. more than one scattered at any one flight means higher profits). The familiar mondo fixation with Californian pet cemeteries is revisited too. The inclusion of a sequence identified as a "television archive document" featuring an execution of a Philippine rebel informant by his 'comrades', his still-twitching body dumped into a shallow grave (predating a similar sequence in the British 1990s mondo *Executions*), is, with its sudden appearance in the film's narrative and introduction via an oddly contrived radio report heard over the feeding of the muscular dystrophy sufferers, pure mondo. There is even, in the final moments, an acknowledgement of the inevitable prying role of the filmmaker: a rerun of key scenes in the film over the closing musical passage cleverly and disconcertingly shows the characters we have 'enjoyed' watching turning to look, at times inquisitively, others despairingly straight at the camera, at us. This is a brilliant device which seals the work as an unsensational shockumentary classic and a bitter reminder of the uncomfortable work necessary for the successful acquisition of such unforgettable poignant moments in the history of the human condition, living or dead.

Des Morts is not one of the most shocking mondo films but it is certainly one of the most memorable. Its 'mondo-ness' is understated and cleverly manipulated by a master film poet. The quiet elegance of *Des Morts* (Vogel once worried, correctly, that Zeno would be "written out of official film history") ensured that the film troubled society's moral guardians significantly less than the terror of their first widely banned feature *Vase de Noces* (*Wedding Trough*), a film about a man screwing, killing and then eating his pet pig.

Le Sang des Bêtes

CHAPTER 2
"EVERY SCENE LOOKS YOU IN THE EYE — AND SPITS"

Mondo and Shock Cinema

In their book, *Cinema as Art* Ralph Stephenson and J R Debrix, in discussing the work of French director Georges Franju, noted that "the brutality of *Le Sang des Bêtes* would have been unbearable if the film had been in colour". If film is capable of delivering shocks more cruelly depending on the use of the chromatic, then the mondo film seeks to make the unbearable a vivid and amplified form of exotic film art. It was astute of Stuart Swezey (in his *Amok Journal*) to call Jacopetti a "master technician of shock in the human organism"; the work

of Jacopetti and other mondo directors explores the effect of visceral shock on the cinematic audience and it is such mechanics of shock cinema that this chapter hopes to examine, illustrate and explain. Swezey called *Mondo Cane* a true "experiment in terror" and contrasted the powerful churning effects of the mondo film, unfavourably, with that of the more renowned genres of film shock — slasher movies, zombie and cannibal films, video nasties. There are however links that can be made between the emergence of the Italian mondo film and the aesthetics of

Italian horror and exploitation film: what Antonio Tentori and Antonio Bruschini call the "pseudo-mondo film" (Palmieri and Mistretta refer to mondo as "horror's mad cousin"). So the ways in which mondo helped to legitimise shock in popular film is fascinating and important too. The very fact that mondo films are termed 'shockumentaries' states the acceptance of cinema shock as an essential ingredient of the genre. Tellingly it is the shock element of mondo which has filtered through into the shocks of the contemporary TV age — viewing designed to hit the viewer in the face "like a ton of bricks". The French writer and surrealist Antonin Artaud, amongst others, considered 'theatre' as an assault on the audience ("the cinema is a direct and rapid language which has no need for a slow and ponderous logic"), a process mondo films sometimes attempt to conform to. The Jacopettian self-defined device of the "shock cut" makes powerful and long-lasting use of the film splice, the edit. Examples will illustrate this but for now it is enough to define this methodology as an affront to the conventional 'laws' of cinematic art — to hide the cut from audiences (Bazin called this "invisible cutting"). In mondo films the cut is up-fronted, experimental, crude, abrupt, startling... shocking and this mostly occurs as a deliberately coded effect. In an attempt to explain the validity of shock cuts in documentary Jacopetti argued that "Brusque passages are life. Soft passages are history, they're not the daily experience". So in mondo the shock aesthetic represents the recording of events and rituals as 'reality'; a reality to be experienced — not rationalised — by the viewer. This is the value and use of shock in mondo.

Ado Kyrou, whose essays on surrealism and the cinema are still widely quoted, stated that in film "nowhere else does the ugly come so close to the sublime... the uncanny" and the mondo film has always excelled at utilising shock to illustrate difficult aspects of world culture as entertainment. Amos Vogel states that "however irrational, the taboo image reflects subconscious realities still operative in men". In this way shock and provocation hold much more than a simply visceral effect on the viewer and their senses, they act on the subconscious desires and thoughts to leave a marked effect. The size of the cinematic image contributes greatly to this shock effect; Vogel is not the only critic to have observed the powerful effects of the cinema/theatre space on the film effect "in flinching from or in reverential complicity with the taboo image, we elevate a reflection of moving light patterns to the statues of truth".

Shock has featured as an essential aspect of 1960s and 1970s Italian film whether at the low end of the cinematic hierarchy (the horror and giallo cycles) or at the so-called high (Cavani's *Beyond Evil*, Pasolini's *Salò*) where

"I don't think there is much hope for the future of the cinema. Shortly, if not already, it will no longer be possible to enter a movie house because the mere fact of stepping into it, apart from the film actually showing, may mean entering an indecent place, a brothel for maniacs."
CLAUDIO SORGI

"Shock, from the beginning. I always look for this. It's inside of me. It's life. Life is a continuous passage from one feeling to another."
GUALTIERO JACOPETTI

shock is utilised as a polemical device to jolt audiences out of any calm complacency upon entering the cinema space. *Salò* was once called "perhaps the most successful representation of physical cruelty in the history of cinema", a film that makes brilliant and troubling use of ritualised tableaux. The cinematic apparatus itself — especially in the documentary film — exerts a form of assault on the object filmed, the camera eye positions adopted by the camera perfect for the cold thrill of horror but also that of the mondo film. Clover calls this "assaultive gazing" — the ways in which the film camera penetrates the subject through a variety of means. There may be differing degrees of this 'assault' (Clover is interested in a deep penetration) but in a film like Jacopetti's *Zio Tom* the assault is an idealised voyeuristic 'I-camera' attack perfected by highly developed use of shockumentary techniques. The audience is drawn in to the shock moments and becomes ensnared in images of sexual possession and repulsive sadism. Mondo films are always inviting us, the audience, to look and be repelled by what we see — an ideal horror aesthetic.

The Italian cinema produced in its golden age of exploitation and cult films a wealth of directors and technicians capable of utilising the tools of cinematography for shock effect. The work of Lucio Fulci and Sergio Martino, to name but two, is renowned for expressionistic use of the hand-held camera, pans, zooms, tilts with rapid clean cutting being a feature of Italian film that bled into many of the best mondo works.

The links between mondo and horror can be epitomised by Ruggero Deodato's 1979 film *Cannibal Holocaust*, a notorious critique of shockumentary methodologies that the director called "a clear and straightforward denunciation of the 'journalistic approach'". Ever since the release of this film the world conflates 'mondo' with 'horror', 'cruelty' and 'snuff'.

Away from the realm of horror the aesthetics of shock appeared in avant garde experimental groups such as the Vienna Action Group whose filmed performances shocked the senses in the late 1960s/ early 1970s. These films were conceived as Artaudian blows to the audiences' perceptions and rationalities whilst illustrating a further Freudian dimension to the notion of shock images in cinema. Intriguingly these art films share with horror the central motif of blood and its uses/misuses. Hermann Nitsch, one of the principle Vienna Action Group artists claims his art tries to bring the senses close to the response of disgust, yet art critic Adrian Searle stated "art cannot imagine how disgusting life can be", at least film is the art form that brings such raw cycles of life closer. Mondo films are often 'disgusting'.

Overall, the mondo film delivers more visceral shocks than the conventional horror film as its root in the (sur)reality of global spaces and the numbness of witnessing real violence, death, tragedy unleashes power as yet untapped or neutered by contemporary art and culture.

BRUTES AND SAVAGES

Directed by Arthur Davis
(USA, 1978)

The mondo director has long been criticised for his narcissistic approach to the art of the documentary film record and its ill-fated subjects. The mechanics of the mondo film, imbued as they commonly are with a strong sense of individualistic words, thoughts and deeds, encourage such criticism — more perhaps than any other kind of filmmaking enterprise. Yet even against such a background the remarkable contribution of Arthur Davis to mondo reveals the most monstrous, untamed ego in the entire history of the subgenre. Davis' crazed film, *Brutes and Savages*, is one of the most astonishing, disingenuous and disgusting of all mondo films, standing as a testament to the worst excesses of the shockumentary condition. Due to this alone the film is worthy of closer examination. The film, *Brutes and Savages*, is crowded by Davis' ridiculous presence but his book of the film, a thin facsimile of John Cohen's *Africa Addio* account, is also notable for excesses of self-promotion, where he modestly describes himself as an "author, world traveller, motion picture producer and director". In fact, Davis was renowned as an exploitation film distributor and a showman in the grand burlesque tradition, and so his infamous mondo production is merely the ill-advised public face of his self-overindulgence. The *Brutes and Savages* book weakly posits an entirely

spurious 'anthropological' motive for the making of the film, a pretence that slips away almost as soon as the film has begun. Davis' talk of the "tantalising beauty" and "fascination of '*Brutes and Savages*'" quickly gives way to homoerotic, voyeuristic, humans-as-animals accounts of tribal ritualistic activity. Davis' approach mirrors the worst excesses of mondo filmmaking where the subjects are there to be exploited and humiliated or at best (secretly) recorded and documented (in his reflections on the project Davis expresses regret that his

Brutes & Savages

crew were unable to capture some "adventures", being refused permission by tribal chiefs to photograph, and could "find no subterfuge or tactic to overcome this handicap"). After witnessing one alleged display of 'magic' Davis muses "what could Madison Avenue do with a man like this?" In the first pages of his account of the making of the film, Davis claims dramatically that it was filmed in secret with (telescopic) cameras "hidden" in dense foliage or up tall trees. However any cursory viewing of the film reveals the dishonesty of these claims: most sequences are professionally shot, with clear and varied perspectives often via tripods. The technical skill involved in the shock film process are also acclaimed, Davis stating in his text: "It took human hands, trained eyes, and creative skills to have brought the fantastic, unusual pictures and exotic sounds of *Brutes and Savages* into significant reality."

Brutes and Savages claims some form of ethnographic/documentary honesty in the project from the outset, firstly by presenting a

(red text on black screen) caption, "A Factual Report." Secondly, by noting that the film was made with the support of 'The Institute of Primitive Arts and Cultures', an organisation which may or may not exist. Any sense that the viewer be at all convinced by the scientific basis of these claims is promptly dispelled by the next caption which affirms that "all scenes, whether actual or simulated, represent actual truth". A mondo style voice-over invites the viewer to "join the blood and the beauty of the Arthur Davis expedition and his hidden cameras... promoting life in the raw where you can decide who are the brutes and who are the savages now".

In terms of film style, *Brutes and Savages* remains one of the most psychedelic of the mondo films due in part to its lurid colour schemata (blood is always vibrant crimson) and bewildering use of musical score provided by mondo maestro Riz Ortolani. His accompaniment to this exotic exploration is a funked up, percussive disco beat that lends an even more disjointed and surreal feel to the action. Many of the scenes veer into hallucination, aided by the sporadic appearance of Davis himself, bedecked in a series of increasingly camp and ridiculous outfits. Davis is a 'filmmaker' happy to appear in front of the camera dressed in an Armand Denis-style colonial safari outfit if for no other reason than to underline the film's subtitle, "The Arthur Davis Expedition." This is a visual parody, the imagined representation of a 'mondo film director' and so any pretence of authenticity is dispelled as soon as Davis addresses one Nuba chief at length in English.

The sexploitation of mondo makes a spectacular appearance when tribal mating rituals are presented as pornographic spectacle, the camera encroaching perversely upon body after body. Erotic moans and sighs are added to the soundtrack of certain scenes for smutty effect, accompanied further by slow and steamy 'wah-wah' funk slithers in the background. Ancient rituals are turned into hypnotic blood and gore spectacles, the mondo proficiency for alchemising gold into excrement. The decapitation of a goat is intensified by Ortolani's rising bongo mayhem on the soundtrack then the animal's sliced-off head is shaken gleefully in front of the lens. Afterwards, young girls of the tribe shake to a *Shaft*-style disco-funk workout. Astounding.

The claims to 'realism' in the film are made truly ridiculous by a scene depicting a Juba manhood initiation ceremony where fifteen-year-old boys must safely cross a crocodile infested river. The first boy makes it over safely but predictably the second is attacked and eaten by crocodiles. "This cursed place smelled of death. It hung in the air like a stagnant pool of putrefied human flesh... the water was as dark as a witch's sinister brew," Davis wrote

of the prelude to this scene. After the attack he observed: "Cut! I told the cameraman. I was sick to my stomach." These remarks are sadly undercut by the fact the scene presented is one of the most obviously fabricated mondo sequences committed to celluloid. It is obvious that most of the close-up shots of the attack have been filmed in a water tank with dummies. The floating limbs are fifth-rate Tom Savini and the denouement when the reptile emerges with a head clasped in its jaws, rather than invoking sharp shock and horror, instead hurtle the viewer into derision and incredulity. Many of the ritualised fights presented in Africa and South America are poorly staged and terribly acted.

The truly shocking and notorious moments of an otherwise absurd film are centred on the numerous animal killings — by both human hands and non-human. The brutality of these rituals is clear and disturbing: Llamas have their throats cut and hearts ripped out (still pulsating long after they have been removed) and are chopped into pieces as a ritualised event. Convincing scenes of eagle attacks on muskrats, crocodiles on a jaguar, and a lioness pouncing on a rabbit turn the stomach of hardened shock film devotees. Yet the ultimate effect is to make the staged, fake parts of the film even more absurd. Arthur Davis concludes: "my ventures with these tribes impressed upon my consciousness that modernised man should better understand these people. That is the purpose of *Brutes and Savages*." Alas a statement scarcely no one believes.

Davis, seemingly unaware of the offensive philosophy of his film, is a fraudster and his film (and his book) a silly charade — one of the most ridiculous and shocking and amusing mondo films of all time.

MONDO CANDIDO

BLUTIGES MÄRCHEN

CHRISTOPHER BROWN • MICHELLE MILLER • JACQUES HERLIN • JOSE' QUAGLIO • RICHARD DOMPHE • GIANFRANCO D'ANGELO

musiche scritte e dirette da RIZ ORTOLANI • direttore della fotografia GIUSEPPE RUZZOLINI • scenografia FRANCO VANORIO • costumi FRANCO CARRETTI

montaggio FRANCO LETTI • una Produzione PERUGIA CINEMATOGRAFICA S.P.A realizzato da CAMILLO TETI • TECHNICOLOR - TECHNISCOPE

LA MUSICA DEL FILM É INCISA SU DISCO CBS-SUGAR N. 90652

SWEET & SAVAGE

MONDO CANDIDO

Directed by Gualtiero Jacopetti and Franco Prosperi
(Italy, 1975)

For years Jacopetti and Prosperi faced accusations of cynicism and destructiveness, their films condemned by most critics for their alleged savage brutality, misanthropy and negativity. Strangely *Mondo Candido*, to date Jacopetti's final film, is an attempt at refuting such allegations, instead demonstrating Jacopetti's ideology to be the 'optimist' of French author Voltaire's legendary satire of the philosophy of determinism. The film had an unhappy history and production, the result of which Jacopetti and Prosperi became estranged and remained so thereafter (this stems from the fact that external production constraints applied by the producers compromised Jacopetti's methods and he left Prosperi to finish the film). Riz Ortolani was in place and produced one of his finest 'mondo' scores, the lush romanticism elevating the sometimes ponderous action to a new level. For the first time the cinematography lacked the input of Antonio Climati and Benito Frattari. Although the TechniScope camera work was solid and rendered with the appropriate levels of spectacularity by one of the greats of Italian film history, Giuseppe Ruzzolini (director of photography for films as varied and important as Steno's *Piedone a Hong Kong* and Damiano Damiani's *Trinity Is Back Again* [both 1975], Pasolini's *Teorema* aka *Theorem* [1968] and *A Thousand and One Nights* [1974], Polanski's *What?* [1972].

Leone's *Giù la testa* aka *A Fistful of Dynamite* [1971], Pontecorvo's *Queimada* aka *Burn!* [1969], Cavani's *Francesco d'Assisi* aka *Francis of Assisi* [1966]), Climati's intrusive, fluid multidimensional traits were absent. Jacopetti relinquished control of the film's edit and his beautiful, jarring, shock technique is absent from the smoother exposition of the film as it stands. At first *Mondo Candido* looks like a competent period reconstruction of Voltaire's 1758 story of a naïve innocent blundering through the worst life has to offer. The film opens at the spectacular location of the French medieval Château de Pierrefonds and continues to romp through the Rabelaisian narrative with some nice attention to detail. Yet soon the vaguely titillating contemplation of a medieval romp gives way to a freeform, surrealist, Felliniesque cascade through historical conflict delivered in a mesmerising collage of film shocks and surprises.

Mondo Candido marks a departure from the documentary style of *Mondo Cane* and *Africa Addio* and the quasi-documentary style of *Zio Tom* to a carefully calculated reinterpretation of Voltaire's philosophical and political standpoints. As ever Jacopetti and Prosperi synthesise complex ideas and concepts into surreal film set ups and retell the original stories in their own parodic and sensational way. The eighteenth century historical moments littering Candide's life-

43

Mondo Candido

spanning narrative are morphed into present day parallel concerns and events; as with *Zio Tom* Jacopetti and Prosperi bring the past into the present and the future, albeit with less of a robust, violent political stance than with the earlier film. It should be no surprise in a way that Jacopetti turned to Voltaire for inspiration as the art of satire, of which *Candide* is the pre-eminent text, has always been essential to his adventures in film and even further back with his newsreels for Rizzoli's scandalised Italy. Despite this the more explicit, even conventional satire of *Candide* fails considerably more than Jacopetti and Prosperi's earlier films, a fact acknowledged now by everyone who worked on the film. It was never released in the UK or the US.

The film starts with all the requisite signifiers of a romp: servants with wobbling cleavages; a naked statue of Atlas who asks Candido (played by English actor Christopher Brown, who also appeared in TV vet drama *All Creatures Great and Small*) to hold the globe for him while he stretches ("how beautiful you are!" rhapsodises Candido), and a tableaux of picnickers in the form of Manet's *Le Déjeuner sur L'herbe*. A parade of the principal characters: the Baron, Baroness, and their daughter Cunegonde, the love of Candido's life and Pangloss the philosopher and mentor to Candido. Pangloss rehearses Voltaire's words that "this is the best of all possible worlds", an ideological mantra repeated throughout the film (and the book). Amongst the disgusting foods at a grand feast, a collection of grotesque characters emerge: a handmaid with three breasts, a midget chef inside a larger chef's apron pocket, each recalling the excessive world of Fellini's most fantastical cinematic moments. For this, writers Jacopetti and Prosperi's lyrical skills have never deserted them and even here, in their least successful film experiment, moments of genuine tenderness emerge amongst the horror, carnage and death. The portrayal of cherubic Cunegonde, played by British actress Michelle Miller, veers into slow-motion, soft focus reverie, she swings through the air whilst consuming a symbol-of-love apple to Ortolani's beautiful, lush, slow orchestration. This technique recalls, albeit deployed for different means, the equally dreamy Cape Town beach scene from *Africa Addio*. At such moments the old rascals of shockumentary betray their romanticism. Voltaire's original narrative is surreal enough and Jacopetti and Prosperi here use the stylistic straits of contemporary art to create a mystic, otherworldly landscape. Candido's abrupt expulsion form the Thunder-ten-Tronckh castle sees him circle in bewilderment at the wind swept, desert location he has been dumped into, a scene that could be straight out of Jodorowsky's hugely influential (at the time) *El Topo*. This landscape re-emerges twice, firstly in a scene with martyr angels (one of whom looks uncannily like the former Liverpool defender Alan Hansen), and again at the film's denouement, this time filled with the world's outcasts.

It is at this point that *Mondo Candido* veers into deeper hallucination. A Bulgarian medieval battle turns queer when the opposing army are revealed to be equipped with twentieth century armaments and their victims transform, upon death, into *Alice in Wonderland*-style packs of flat cards. After a skirmish with an ogre the narrative leaps into an insane version of the Spanish Inquisition, a ghastly perverted tableaux of violence and torture. A 'mach pagan' machine crushes bodies which are then pasted into a giant book; nuns are stripped of all but their coifs and are masturbated en masse along a long greasy pole. Some are sealed into sacks with live dogs and cats — the resulting pain is presented as excruciatingly orgasmic. As Candido is being inexplicably spanked by a bunch of old hags, Cunegonde appears, surveying the scene with some satisfaction before clicking her fingers along to the organ-pop beat that fills the background. The beat group performing this music catch her eye, in particular the singer/bassist 'Attila'. Cunegonde then recognises Candido's bare arse. As before, Jacopetti and Prosperi extrapolate the historical into the fantastical, accentuating the perversion and violence of the imaginary sites through incredible control of the *mise en scène*. The appearance of Cacombo, a black slave, reminds viewers of the ridiculous racial types of *Zio Tom* and once Candido has helped him escape the gallows he becomes a trusted if absurd friend. This is not a racist portrayal but another element within a conveyor belt of unreal absurdities running through the entire film. The sexual degradation of Cunegonde in Voltaire's original novel is re-imagined through the bizarre representation of a rock group who gang-rape her. Cunegonde reveals to Candido that she is no longer virginal and his naïve image of female purity is destroyed. Cunegonde's memories of these vile acts are presented in flashback (Attila the guitarist having sex with her in a top-only 'suit' of armour). Phallic spikes protruding from his outfit are fondled by Cunegonde and she then sits on a mini drawbridge which has dropped from over his groin. Puerile and vulgar but totally in keeping with the transgression of the original text? The powerful cinematic motif of the broken mirrors is revisited (see the climax to *Enter the Dragon*) when Candido and Attila's fight results in wholesale destruction of the glass — and of themselves.

Jacopetti once stated he would have liked to make a film about America. We can

Mondo Candido – Candido feels his way in the world

only fantasise about how this would have looked, but in *Mondo Candido* some scenes present a glimpse of what this may have been like. Candido and Cacombo escape to the promised land of America, boarding a ship together with a parade of US heroes past and present (Cristofo Colombo, Uncle Sam, Davy Crockett, Al Capone, Marilyn Monroe, Henry Kissinger) as the narrative swings, once again, seemingly untroubled between the past and the present. At Columbus Day celebrations in New York, Pangloss appears again, this time in the guise of a TV director. His continued pronouncements that "this is still the best of all possible words" resonate with unintentional chill poignancy as we see over his words a long pan of the Manhattan skyline. Topical (for the mid-1970s) conflicts such as the Northern Irish troubles and the war in the Middle East between Israelis and Palestinians are evoked in cartoon fashion

(this is the "end of religion" Pangloss states as a car bomb explodes in front of Candido and Carambo). The infamous section from *La Donna nel Mondo* picturing the female regiments of the Israeli army is recalled in a truly stunning scene which begins with sexploitation (women having naked showers) and ends in Peckinpah-style violence as they are gunned down in bloody slow-motion by Attila's Arab militia, who are in turn killed amidst agonising, gory carnage. Freeze-frames of these female soldiers depicted in violent pornographic death were used to promote the film.

The utterly surreal finale to the film occurs when all of the characters are reunited (including a now wizened, haggard Cunegonde) in an icy, sand swept wasteland seeking the truth of life from a mysterious guru — the Dervishu. Candido asks him "why does man exist" to which the acousmetric character replies "get stuffed".

Candido has travelled a long way.

After seeing a younger, innocent mirror-image of himself on the opposite bank of the river Candido implores him(self) "No! — don't go that way" but then realises he must let go. He skips off back to the castle and we are back where we started on his metaphysical journey, older if not wiser.

Although considered a failure, artistically and conceptually, *Mondo Candido* still enjoys a strange allure. There are still glimpses of the Jacopetti and Prosperi spirit in this unforgettable overblown, Technicolor indulgence. Many things about the film are indeed gross but as Fellini's corpulent obsessions have somehow withstood the test of time, perhaps Jacopetti and Prosperi's are due a reappraisal.

MR. MIKE'S MONDO VIDEO

Directed by Michael O'Donoghue
(USA, 1979)

It is not uncommon for Michael O'Donoghue's shockumentary spoof, *Mr Mike's Mondo Video*, to be described as one of the worst films ever made. And yet this bizarre addendum to the mondo canon clearly demonstrates a deep, if not profound, understanding of the aesthetics and motivations of mondo filmmaking. O'Donoghue was a writer for the American satire magazine *National Lampoon* before becoming one of the founder members of the legendary TV show that gave birth to a generation of American comics *Saturday Night Live* (O'Donoghue in fact is credited with uttering the first ever words on the first ever edition of the show). *Mr Mike's Mondo Video* is a satire in the reckless spirit of the aforementioned comedy origins and one suspects the criticism of the film largely stems from the rough, emetic ethos of the entire production. The film is part celebration of mondo and part critique — albeit a critique as tasteless as one might expect from an alternative comedy veteran studded with cameos from the director's peers (Dan Ackroyd, Bill Murray, Deborah Harry and Carrie Fisher). O'Donoghue intensifies the more dubious aspects of mondo filmmaking to sick proportions always refracted through a comedic lens.

The celebratory and homage style quality of the film is clear from the outset. The by

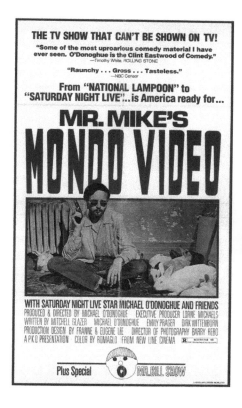

THE TV SHOW THAT CAN'T BE SHOWN ON TV!

"Some of the most uproarious comedy material I have ever seen. O'Donoghue is the Clint Eastwood of Comedy."
—Timothy White, ROLLING STONE

"Raunchy . . . Gross . . . Tasteless."
—NBC Censor

From "NATIONAL LAMPOON" to "SATURDAY NIGHT LIVE"... is America ready for...

MR. MIKE'S MONDO VIDEO

WITH SATURDAY NIGHT LIVE STAR MICHAEL O'DONOGHUE AND FRIENDS
PRODUCED & DIRECTED BY MICHAEL O'DONOGHUE   EXECUTIVE PRODUCER LORNE MICHAELS
WRITTEN BY MITCHELL GLAZER   MICHAEL O'DONOGHUE   EMILY PRAGER   DIRK WITTENBORN
PRODUCTION DESIGN BY FRANNE & EUGENE LEE   DIRECTOR OF PHOTOGRAPHY BARRY REBO
A P.K.O. PRESENTATION   COLOR BY ROMAGLO   FROM NEW LINE CINEMA [R] RESTRICTED

Plus Special   MR. BILL SHOW

now familiar pre-credit rolling, white-on-black text screen exposition/warning, in this instance states that:

"The film you are about to see is shocking and repugnant beyond belief. It contains scenes of disturbing sexual practices and mindless violence. If older people with heart conditions are watching, or persons under psychiatric care, make them sit close so they won't miss anything. Do not allow children of an impressionable age

47

Michael O'Donoghue in *Mr. Mike's Mondo Video*

to leave the room. If they are sleeping wake them up, slap them. Give them hot coffee."

The images that accompany the subsequent sequence are similarly parodic, featuring a rapid montage of shock shots intertwined with sexual images, an inventory of which jolts the recall of any serious mondo aficionado: tribal ritual dances, disrobing women, stoned rockers, transgressives, Japanese women with parasols, a chicken (it turns out that these scenes are taken from the sequences of the film itself). The music meanwhile is a mordant, ugly synth drone in the style of Ortolani's 'savage rite' cue from the *Cannibal Holocaust* score. All of this in reply to the voice-over query: "What is Mondo?"

After a brief introduction by Mr. Mike himself ("welcome to a world where the bizarre is commonplace and the commonplace is bizarre"), Joe Meek's haunting Telstar melody appears accompanied by a set of ridiculous joke lyrics sung partly in Italian (allegedly) by Italian-America crooner Julius LaRosa (singer of novelty hit Eh, Cumpari), presenting us with a daft, if near perfect, pastiche of the mondo predilection for sentimental musical framing. The film effectively incorporates key mondo traits such as the use of a swinging sixties underscore to herald a new location, the suggested (and usually simulated) use of hidden cameras to film illicit scenes (in this case a joke about Italian cinejournalists), insertion of grainy and shaky 8mm footage to represent 'reality', the inclusion of fluxus-style 'art film' segments as a subject for ridicule, scenes 'deleted by network' and even a 'cargo cult' parody at the climax of the film (where the natives collect the discarded waste of American popular culture) which just predates Jamie Uys' *The Gods Must be Crazy* (1980) and doubles the viewer's mondo kicks by mimicking the bloody POV decapitation conclusion to *Cannibal Holocaust*. Even the *Mondo Cane* font is replicated for the end

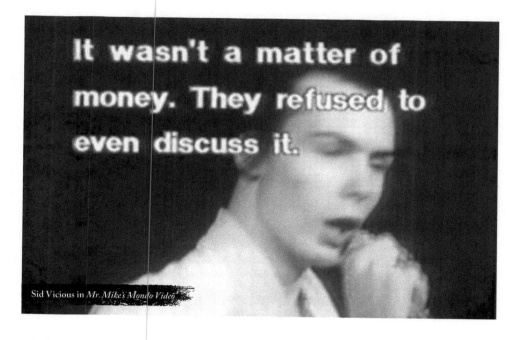

Sid Vicious in *Mr. Mike's Mondo Video*

title frames. The freeform nature of *Saturday Night Live* occasionally emerges to shatter any mondo ethic and reveals a peculiarly American translation of the Italian mondo film style. In this take on shockumentary the inclusion of any punk subcultural activity is worthy of being described as 'mondo' and so we witness the surreal performance of Klaus Nomi, who mimes to an aria from Saint-Saëns' opera *Samson and Delilah* dressed as a space mutant, Sid Vicious' rendition of My Way is screened (without the sound as permission was refused by Paul Anka's licensing company): Vicious, who had just died of a heroin overdose, is described by O'Donoghue as a "mondo kind of guy", Root Boy Slim and the Sex Change Band in full flow, and so on.

Even weirder is the random inclusion of 'out there' art in the form of short and cheap animation sequences; some found footage of an early nudie CineArt featurette *Uncle Si and the Sirens*; the Thomas Edison footage of the electrocution of an elephant, infamous as an early example of shockumentary footage. The inclusion of a failed film sequence Crowd Scene, Take One, where the mechanics of trying to construct an elaborate cinematic scenario are laid bare, is equally odd.

To be truthful, the shocks in *Mr Mike's Mondo Video*, after the troubling opening segment on an Amsterdam 'Swimming Club for Cats' (where cats are actually launched into a swimming pool and left to desperately scramble back to the side) are puerile and tame in comparison with the genuine shocks of the more extreme examples in this chapter. Nevertheless, O'Donoghue, who died of a cerebral haemorrhage in 1994, has captured some of the mondo spirit effectively and with some humour. In its celebration of the freaky, gross and the sleazy *Mr Mike's Mondo Video* neatly summarises the place mondo films occupy in American cinema history: the trashcan.

49

UN FILM DI
GIANNI PROIA

MONDO DI NOTTE OGGI

SWEET & SAVAGE

MONDO DI NOTTE OGGI

Directed by Gianni Proia
(Italy, 1975)

In this strange and disturbing film Gianni Proia, creator of the *Mondo di Notte* series, revisits the mondo oeuvre with one of most reflexive, postmodern contributions to the genre. After a ten year absence from the subgenre, Proia's return to the mondo film also marks the return of some of the key figures in his earlier trilogy, most notably the French cabaret/burlesque star Coccinelle who opens the film with a modern interview in her 'dressing room'. She is now a flabby, faded ex-star (who was never a recognised star to begin with) being confined to appearances in second-rate cinematic burlesques, her jaded remarks and sad attempts at exuding a whiff of glamour standing as a metaphor for the decline of the entertainment tradition of which she was once part. The decline of the burlesque is perhaps the overarching message of this film, although it is unlikely that Proia originally intended this. If the film was conceived in the grand mondo tradition of celebrating the shocking and the bizarre, then that is not how it can be read today (the inclusion of weak TV variety act Rod Hull and Emu, for British viewers particularly, illustrates how desperate the search for shocks had become). *Mondo di Notte Oggi* includes a parade of modernist night entertainments, some of which are vaguely interesting, but the overall impression left by the film is that this particular approach to mondo filmmaking had now run its course.

At least that is how it looks today.

The film offers a reflexive (film about filmmaking) approach to mondo from the outset as we open with a rerun of the footage from the earlier *Mondo di Notte* series of Coccinelle crooning in French. This cuts, cruelly (and certainly without her knowing) to shots of her now bearing a striking resemblance to a homogenised version of the later, and grotesque, incarnations of Diana Dors or Anita Ekberg: deluded, over made-up and bitter. Proia's camera (provided by mondo great Benito Frattari) travels over her body, lingering on her breasts just as it did ten years previously but any eroticism is lost. "Ce'st la merde" Coccinelle remarks of the 'mondo di notte oggi', at the point in which the liberation and excitement of the cultural and social revolutions of the 1960s, turned ugly, violent and depraved.

There then follows a brilliant, freaky title sequence where footage from the original *Notte* films is filtered through psychedelic posterisations, various strippers and singers such as the American troupe the Platters, morph into scorched abstraction, in the same way things got scary in *Doctor Who*, the picture careered into inversion. The colour schemata is wonderful, lurid and exciting, while the music provided by Gianni Oddi (an Italian sax legend responsible for the riffs on films as diverse as *Last Tango in Paris* and *The*

Legend of 1900) runs from gentle soft bossa and jazz vibes to the original *Notte* theme, An Old Cow Hand, delivered in the style of the Mike Sammes' Singers. The whole sequence is a kaleidoscope of distant memories updated for the hallucinogenic epoch, misguided, weird and unforgettable. It's arguably the best moment in the film.

The cynical, reactionary attitude towards social progression (particularly Northern European) that is found sprinkled throughout the classic period Italian mondos, is continued and exacerbated manifold. In fact the film opens properly in Sweden, a country still, ten years later, the target for attacks on any over-liberal approach to modern living. A serious-looking (hence stereotypical) Swedish family 'unit' tuck into a meal while pornographic scenes flicker away on the family TV screen behind. Eventually the boy leaves the table to sit and take in the scenes. Neither his parents, nor grandparents seem remotely concerned and carry on eating. The theorem, that Scandinavian liberalism still reaches irresponsible levels, is undercut when the porn is interrupted by Rod Hull and Emu delivering a ridiculous innuendo filled 'comic sketch', enough to evaporate the fiercest libido and more redolent of the British neurosis over sexuality and eroticism. Much of the film is devoted to the more unusual sex bars of North America, firstly heterosexual entertainments, then homosexual variants, bondage, sado-masochism and fisting, the clichéd, conservative image of gay living. The exhibitionist display of New York dance clubs of this era caught Proia's imagination, in particular those sights where nudity, sex and drugs played out with hedonistic (pre-AIDS) abandon ("keep it in your pants" one sign asks), propelled by the fast,

disco soundtrack of Gloria Gaynor and Esther Phillips. Interviews, always hilarious, with moustachioed club owners punctuate the vista of wicked abandonment, their mercenary, free-market philosophising strangely worrying; one can almost smell the burn out. The film manages to cram in possibly more nudity than any other 'proper' mondo film, reflecting an era when even 'high' art stage performances, in one instance ballet, were filled with bare flesh. A pointless piece of Parisian 'theatre', depicting a man's sex obsessions and frustrations end up with full nudity and simulated sex acts. The attitude towards sex in the film is unremittingly puerile and the viewer is left to decide whether this reflects childish Latin immaturity or a satire on warped Anglo-Saxon repression. Few would argue that the entertainments on offer at the Nevada resort of Las Vegas amply fulfil mondo credentials, the disturbing eeriness of a supposed palace of fun poorly masking the ugly face of capitalism run riot. There are many scenes of Vegas acts from erotic fanciness (naked women in water tanks with dolphins, nude full-scale MGM musical tributes), to disturbing circus simulations: trapeze, dog shows and the monstrously camp Siegfried and Roy (where an urge to witness real death-by-lion is almost excruciating). The slickness of the Vegas productions and that of Stockholm impresario Ulrich Geismar's 'lesbian' mirror act contrasts violently with porn baron Paul Raymond's totally un-sexy London farce *Pyjama Tops*. This stultifying combination of men in blazers and dirty old men cavorting with naked young girls in a middle class split-level apartment merely stimulates a desire to nod off. Throughout the entire film we are transported back to the ghosts of the original *Notte* cycle, the effect of which is

Mondo di Notte Oggi

usually to reinforce the notion that nocturnal enticements have become more sordid and desperate. But one contrast between the 'old' and 'new' startles: the memorable and disturbing Shinto manhood ritual, where a throbbing mass of young Japanese men compete violently and dangerously for a stick symbolising their passage towards masculinity, is replaced with a tender and erotic massage by first one and then several young women as a route for the more modern Japanese male towards sexual fulfilment. To compound how times have changed from the all-male ritual of *Ecco*, a woman is shown enjoying the attentions of two male masseurs. From the sacred to the profane by way of the orgasm. Proia attempts a lighter ending by inserting a Benny Hill-style scene around a 'fountain of desire' where a man wishes his wife away to be replaced by a sexy girl, who then wishes away the man for a hunk, who then takes a fancy

for the man before and the wife returns again (recalling Proia's earlier bizarre quasi-mondo feature *Realtà romanzesca*), but this fails to lift the now jaded spirits of the viewer.

Reflexivity makes another appearance as a silly act, where a piano player narrates the story of a young man's search for love in a new city, beginning with slide-show illustrations of his encounters and ends with the couple emerging on the stage before making love on a bed 'for real'. But *Mondo di Notte Oggi* is far from a conceptual art film. Rather it is a gloriously grotesque update of mondo from the age of innocence to the age of contempt, the film's sadness, perversity and ugliness resembles a signpost to the horror-show mondos of the 1980s. Proia is a very good mondo filmmaker and he may have intended this. With mondo one never knows. Whatever, *Mondo do Notte Oggi* offers up a vision of a future haunted by the past.

Peeping Tom

CHAPTER 3
"HE USED A CAMERA LIKE MOST MEN USE A WOMAN"

Voyeurism and Sexuality in the Mondo Film

V oyeurism — the pleasure of watching others perform acts — has long been an important aspect of the mondo aesthetic. From the earliest incarnations of the 'classic' period (1959–1975), where directors offered audiences a 'peepshow' on nightclub and burlesque acts, to the hunting and cannibal mondos that came later, where what we see through the camera-gun becomes pathological.

The deployment of the camera lens serving as a gateway to the forbidden and the taboo has been critical. While the association between cinematic apparatus and voyeurism is as old as cinema itself, in fact deeply enshrined within the basic act of recording things as they happen, it is within the mondo genre that this association

finds one of its richest manifestations. Certain other genres have exploited voyeurism effectively: horror being the most notable, knowingly using voyeurism to potent effect; whereas others, such as ethnographic filmmaking, employ voyeurism accidentally. Perhaps significantly well known feature films dealing with voyeurism (*Psycho*, *Peeping Tom*, *Blowup*) emerged together with the golden age of mondo (it would be hard for Antonioni, being at the forefront of an Italian new wave, to have ignored the impact of the probing eye of the shockumentary trend). The greater flexibility offered by new lightweight cameras with powerful zoom lenses and vivid colour processes was then aligned with an explosion of experimentation and creativity.

Thus the 'golden age' of European cinema was that of mondo too. Mondo films become the visual manifestation of our worst fears and desires.

The etymology of voyeurism is simply that of the French verb *voir* (to see). Yet manifestations of voyeurism (particularly in cinematic terms) cannot be separated from sexuality and its expression through eroticism and pornography. In many ways mondo films amplify the message of better known and respected discourses (see above) on the voyeurism of the male gaze and have often been used to exemplify the troubling relationship between the power of the active watcher (male) and powerlessness of the passive watched (female). Susan Keppeler in her book *The Pornography of Representation* talks about the "women-zoo peep show", where women are visually represented by cameras as animals were in the past. Keppeler notes that "the reproduction of women in images makes woman-images ever more exotic and remote", certainly a crucial element of mondo 'sexys' such as *La Donna nel Mondo*, *Mondo Oscenita* and the *Mondo di Notte* series. Her statement that "the cultural space of women, captured and framed in images is one big show world", could easily be mutated into a tag-line for a mondo film. Inevitably a concern for feminist writers and critics, cinematic voyeurism reproduces a patriarchal society where this pleasure in looking (made by men for a male audience) appears in a most lucid and powerful way. Laura Mulvey, in her very famous essay on the visual pleasures of film, whilst noting in *Blowup* the importance of the main character's abilities as a photojournalist ("a maker of stories, a captor of images") observes that film's multiperspective look makes it more effective than "striptease, theatre shows etc" and so accidentally articulates

a key mondo aesthetic. The voyeuristic tendency of mondo has been likened to that of a peepshow with all of the grubby associations that form of visual entertainment offers. In the book, *Grindhouse*, Eddie Muller and Daniel Faris describe the "hidden camera" as a "vital element" of mondo films but go further to evidence this as being a key aspect of the "fakery" of many mondo sequences. The eroticism of mondo where strippers and sexy nightclub acts are recorded and displayed is thus pseudo-eroticism — a form of porno-kitsch; the viewer's curiosity for the forbidden is being exploited by the mondo director (or more often producer) in grand guignol style. Thus the uneasy POV gaze of mondo films contributes negatively to parity in representation. As if to reinforce the link between shockumentary film and sex, mondo films featured heavily in adult film magazines of the era (most notably *Cinema X* and *Continental Cinema*) where nudity and sex where permissible as part of a liberatory ideology.

La Donna nel Mondo

Cultural attitudes to voyeurism and sexuality, as we shall see, mean that this titillating dimension of mondo films is one of the most derided aspects. Yet these negative associations are countered by Amos Vogel, for whom voyeurism is an integral, even subversive, aspect of film form. For Vogel "the primitive taboo remains with us... as we watch scenes of death, intercourse or birth in reverential abandon, our silence is witness to the thrilling guilt of the voyeur/transgressor (to see what one has no right to see), coupled with fear and punishment". Vogel acknowledges the powerful effects of voyeurism in cinema as a way to confront and explore taboos. In his examination of these taboos Vogel articulates, again accidentally, or at least subconsciously, the mondo aesthetic. When he notes that "particularly traumatic are sudden and unexpected transitions from innocuous to taboo images" for example he could be beautifully describing the Jacopetti effect. Such 'trauma' is

precisely what Jacopetti was aiming for through his selection process and editing style — the 'shock cut' as he called it. Another American critic, Parker Tyler, reinforces the association between voyeurism and taboo in the creative act: "the whole concept of voyeurism implies that reality contains certain taboo spheres — and especially where the naked eye is concerned; where seeing is the same as believing... there is nothing like the naked eye for satisfying both curiosity about facts and the sense of pleasure". These critiques value voyeurism as an essential part of a cinema that challenges and threatens to be located within both underground film and commercial cinema. The voyeuristic tendency is thus elevated from that of 'guilty pleasures' to 'subversive act'. Therefore, although mondo films are not often featured in discussions of cinematic voyeurism, a closer examination of some key examples reveals that they are in fact luminous exemplars of this important aspect of film art.

LA DONNA NEL MONDO (WOMEN OF THE WORLD)

Directed by Gualtiero Jacopetti, Paolo Cavara, Franco Prosperi
(Italy, 1962)

At first glance Gualtiero Jacopetti and Franco Prosperi's third feature looks like the ultimate voyeuristic cine-voyage. The film was marketed, particularly in the UK and US (the home of sexploitation kitsch) as a kaleidoscope of saucy pin-up views of the numerous manifestations of 'women of the world' and the concept today looks tired and sexist. Jacopetti later tried to disown or dismiss the project, claiming that the studio and his producer (Angelo Rizzoli) tied him and Prosperi to it as part of a three picture deal. To make matters worse the film was haunted with personal misfortune, indifference and bad vibes, ample reasons for all involved to try and disregard the project. Yet behind the sleaze and misjudgements was a serious journalistic project — at least in its inception. The initial idea for the project dates back some years before *Mondo Cane* when Prosperi devised the notion for a film documentary about 'love in the world'. Although this was never realised the concept came alive again when Rizzoli tried to create a film project in collaboration with controversial Italian feminist journalist and writer Oriana Fallaci. Fallaci had written an account, based on travels with the photographer Duiolio Pallottelli, of the changing role of women across Asia and the Far East, the Pacific Islands and North America. As both Jacopetti and Fallaci are famed for their extrovert personalities a collaborative film project was never likely to succeed; indeed a meeting with Rizzoli at Cannes was aborted. So Prosperi's original scheme was resurrected to become *La Donna nel Mondo*. It's easy to assume that the film would have been less squalid, more 'feminist' had Fallaci remained onboard. Yet certain sections of the film do bear a resemblance to reportage and are at least admirable for Jacopetti and Prosperi's trademark filmic talents: sardonic-poetic commentary; clever editing, beautiful cinematography; gorgeous use of music (Ortolani and Oliviero again). Moreover, Fallaci's own book about 'women of the world', *The Useless Sex*, now seems almost as dated. The sexual politics of the book that contains the notion, for example, of a Miss Universe competition being a liberating concept, are ill-conceived by today's standards (Fallaci's dislike of Muslim traditions, recently scandalously unearthed in books and articles published in Italy, makes an early appearance in the book). Fallaci's own observations about women are privileged and frequently ornamental. In addition the concept of the roving camera eye was to be developed in more offensive and lame ways by American mondo directors (see *Mondo Freudo*). All of this is not to defend a largely unsuccessful film. It is drawn out and the sequences are not paced as astutely

57

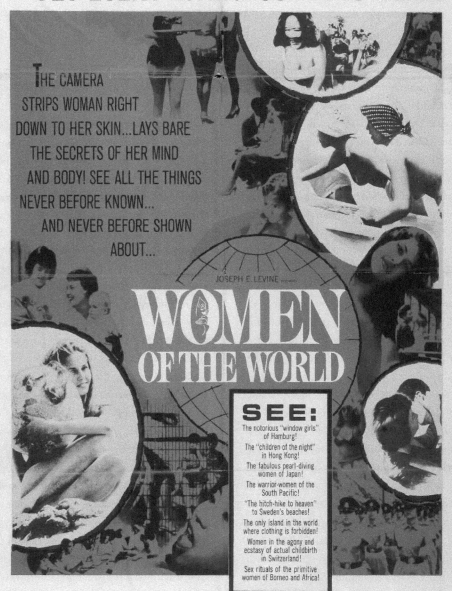

as the team's other efforts. The principal problem was that most of the material in the film was outtakes from *Mondo Cane*. This is made abundantly clear when a sequence on Chinese women covering in white clothes to avoid turning "bright yellow" in the sun can be recognised in publicity material for *Mondo Cane*. The concept is thinner — indeed most mondos that divert from the global concept struggle to be engaging. One would expect the infamous (to Northern Europeans) Italian notion of the *bella figura* to be more prominent in the film but its appearance is relatively modest. In fact the sexism of the film is exaggerated in the English language versions, particularly the version where the voice-over was provided by Peter Ustinov, famed for his 'wit' in parodying peoples of the world excused by way of the fact that he declared on many occasions to be 'one of them'. Innuendo too, a British speciality, emerges often in Ustinov's telling of the film. The credit sequence for the Ustinov version of the film features a camera monitoring a woman's behind as she hurries through an airport lounge, stating that we are about to see women of the world "as viewed by Peter Ustinov". As if to emphasise the leering nature of this the on-screen titles then sashay in rhythm with the woman's rear movements; a brilliant and innovative piece of kinetic film sexism.

The rest of the above mentioned credit sequence is cleverly devised. Set in an airport lounge in the early sixties, a site of great promise, liberation and multiculturalism (we see this illustrated with a parade of ethnically diverse women: Japanese, Indian, African; an Hawaiian woman greets the passengers of one flight with a carefully staged dance).

Some female film stars appear, including Sophie Loren (edited out of the English version). As the SAS plane (a Jacopetti/Prosperi favourite) becomes air bound it suddenly freezes and some text informs us that the film is dedicated to Belinda Lee, the British actress and companion of Jacopetti who helped shape his image as a jet-setting playboy and Latin Lover par excellence (this too is missing from the English version). The scene is set then for a Philleas Fogg-style foray into the mysteries of the female species. There is plenty of 'of-its-time' voyeurism in *La Donna nel Mondo*: we peek at members of a female regiment of the Israeli army undressing after harsh training. The titillation fears of the preceding sequence in which a Roman military corps is distracted from its march by girls in the crowd (their sideways looks are frozen on-screen) are evidently justified. The real efforts of some of the female soldiers are slyly mocked: when one of them stutters over a climbing structure the music stutters with her and from being militaristic in tone becomes 'feminine' sounding.

European sexual behaviour is also derided, especially the various Riviera cults that have emerged: all-naked beaches and the Cannes Film Festival featuring prominently (we are presented with an inspired moment at Cannes when we see the reflected image of a curvy would-be starlet reflected in a man's sunglasses). In California girls try to eke out a living pumping gas (to a man who looks remarkably like Franco Prosperi) while they wait to be discovered by movie moguls. Jacopetti warns, "that's the law of the cinema," as we visit Milton Green's photo studio "chop up 100 women just to create one". There are the usual lyrical moments:

lovers in cars on a Californian coastline remind you how the cinematography for the Jacopetti-Prosperi pictures is at times beautiful.

The peep show hidden camera is shown several times and for disparate rationale: Firstly, to aid authenticity: in the 'women in the windows' of Hamburg (the camera is hidden in a laundry van); the Bedouin women who scramble to recover used artillery shells in battles on the Moroccan/Algerian border (we see Climati behind the enormous tele-lens and Prosperi issuing orders); the promiscuity of co-eds in a Stockholm apartment block is spied upon *Rear Window*-style from a fortuitous "observation post" ; meanwhile the illegitimate children born out of these loose sexual morals are photographed thanks again to "our telephoto lens"; then the Thalidomide case of Belgian Suzanne Vanderput who killed her baby out of sympathy. Here the crew are seen trying to find "some shadow in her face that betrays her true state of mind". Secondly, as comment: in Tokyo a naked girl can be photographed by tourists from any angle. The scopophilic irony of us watching them, via the film camera, watching her is not lost on the directors. Finally, for amusement: we see Frattari filming the Chinese beach-bathing girls hiding in a turret swinging an enormous phallic telephoto.

The real social strides and achievements made by women are treated with a certain amount of disrespect. Jacopetti and Prosperi, unlike Fallaci, compare the running of large corporations in the US by women (the treasury, the Bank of New York) to the running of a domestic home (such an

ideology was exemplified by the Thatcherism project in 1980s Britain). Likewise, moves towards homosexuality, in the shape of Parisian lesbian and gay bars are dismissed as "a pathetic parody of men one can only view with sadness" and a "ridiculous attempt at negating women".

The shocks, despite Jacopetti and Prosperi's reputation, are few in this film. The most notable is a clever cut from a girl being ritually tattooed in Borneo to plastic surgery in the west where women have the skin on their faces 'removed' so that a fresher, younger face can emerge later. The women's faces, as they recover in the beds of the private clinic, are a bloody mess. This sequence looks fake but the jolt between the two scenes, aided by a sudden superfast avant-jazz burst is real enough.

Jacopetti and Prosperi are masters of the mordant finale. This time we are at Lourdes where thousands sacrifice everything to come and be cured by the 'White Lady'. The spiritual and emotional intensity, the assemblage of which is a true and difficult cinematic art, whilst at odds with the majority of the rest of the film, is moving and thought provoking. An interesting insertion is the record of a town in Southern Italy where traditional sexual values are still enforced by, according to the local gravestone inscriptions, penalty of death.

Mondo films, particularly the sexual aspect of them, arguably generated a particular kind of sensibility, which paved the way for changing this kind of strict Catholic morality. The sexual freedoms, urged on by an interest in Freudian models, were accelerated by the acceptance of films like *La Donna nel Mondo*. Whatever its other faults this, for liberals at least, redeems the film.

MILLE PECCATI... NESSUNA VIRTÙ (WAGES OF SIN)

Directed by Sergio Martino
(Italy, 1969)

The main thrust behind Sergio Martino's mangled contribution to the mondo canon *Mille Peccati... Nessuna Virtù* is exemplified brilliantly by its English title — *Wages of Sin* (*Mondo Sex* is the other, cruder, alternative title). The film is narrated by mondo stalwart Edmund Purdom and his voice-over is a superb, at times hilarious, exhibition of mondo moralising. The main premise of the film is sound enough: to critically analyse, via the documentary film mode, the rapidly increasing exploitation of sexuality in modern consumer capitalism. The concept of 'love' under market economics,

the director points out, has become devalued, mechanised, standardised and estranged from real human experience. Hence 'a thousand sins... no virtues'. The film presents the standard forty or so sequences of evidence to answer this question posed by the narrator at the beginning: "does love pay?" Martino made several contributions to the mondo and pseudo-mondo canons including *America Cosi Nuda Violenta* (1970) and *La Montagna del Dio Cannibale* (1978) but was better known for the creation of giallo thrillers and erotic comedies. *Mille Peccati...* was his first feature film. Working with the same excellent

Mille Peccati... Nessuna Virtù

cinematographer Floriano Trenker, who does a passable mimic of Antonio Climati's intrusive and pushy style, Martino's skill in the depiction of sexualised images is clear from the offset. For the credit sequence the camera circles around a naked and painted female dancer flexing her body in a drug-induced hypnosis while a throbbing psychedelic beat accentuates the scene. The familiar ambiguity of mondo sexuality is thus 'laid bare'— the film is simultaneously a celebration and a critique of the cinematic sexualised image — both titillating and terrifying. The moral confusion of the piece is emphasised by the way in which we are directed from, on the one hand, scenes roundly condemning the commoditisation of sex (via factories producing sex aids, sex shops, sex clubs, hostessing) to other scenes 'anthropologically' observing changing sexual behaviour (gay marriages, homosexual clubs, free sex, love relationships within the church). Martino expects audiences to marvel at the social and cultural shifts he has recorded whilst at the same time lamenting the decadence of such practices and phenomenon.

Despite this some of the segments arguing against the commodification of sexuality are well executed. One scene describing the development of a Swedish club for the hiring of young men by middle-aged females ends with the tart observation that "the woman always pays". The exploding Swedish sex industry is a regular target in this film. As the narrator laments that "love is indeed dead" the practices of a factory producing and supplying sex aids by mail-order is described as "eternal love-making — churned out over and over again". The notion of the production of seven-inch vinyl records of sex sounds — 'pornophones' (these also appear in Scattini's *Svezia, inferno e paradiso*) and the hi-tech match-making of an electric dating machine are similarly despised. The film is apparently an examination of sin, and so gluttony is portrayed in true mondo gastro-style with close-up shots of fat people stuffing food into their faces accompanied by a soundtrack of burps, belches and gurgles. Modern art meanwhile — a long-standing mondo target — also contributes to these 'wages of sin' as German painter Kurt Rumbhild (a made-up name) creates paintings by pouring pigment onto his canvases while his model couples have sex — "it's productivity that counts" remarks Purdom. At the end of the sequence, as two women enter the studio, we are informed, although not shown, that Rumbhild is about to create "his widely acclaimed 'Sapphic Love'". Mondo modesty anyone?

Perhaps unsurprisingly given the age of the creators of this film (Martino was thirty-one when he made it) the strongest condemnation is reserved for the practices of European youth cultures — in particular those which are anti-conformist. In these sequences sex and drugs are 'problems' and those groups dedicated to alternative lifestyles are rounded upon with particular venom. The conservatism of this stance becomes apparent when communal living, free love and drug taking are mapped against so-called 'normal' existences. Young couples, for example, starring in porno films to earn money, are presented as being incapable of answering the narrator's question "what's the difference between a prostitute and what you do?" To

ensure that the point is not lost the voices of the characters are dubbed in a 'thick' *Eurotrash* style. "Here, then, is the point reached by the generation of today," he despairs as we finally exit the scene. The narrator similarly describes the practices of German "morphine" addicts as being a "shortcut to happiness; a slow suicide which kills the taste for life long before the brain flakes into imbecility". "The masses" on the other hand "have the courage to make something of their lives". Meanwhile over scenes of an avant garde "nude-in" at the Amsterdam Paradiso theatre the narrator observes that "the naked ape has always been a vaudeville attraction". The deeply pessimistic ending to the film circles around a British family who openly share pot and are said to be seeking the space where "dream reality and living reality interfuse". Prophecies of doom are thrown back onto the audience with the challenge: "do they care? do you? think about it children: we are all in your hands". The family disappear into the grey London morning.

Mille Peccati... is like many 'classic' era Italian mondo films, well executed, colourful, crisply edited and entertaining. The film is an important contribution to the sexual aspect of the mondo film, rendered with much greater gusto than the American efforts in this sphere (see *Mondo Freudo*). One can see from this why Purdom was favoured so much as the voice of English mondo. His range is hugely varied, expressive and, like Ustinov, delights in 'admiring' pretty young girls and aping the accents of foreigners; here Germans, French and British are mimicked with a shocking lack of respect. The moral ambiguity of mondo films was never more evident. And this, depending on your view, is either inspiring or idiotic.

UN FILM DI

LUIGI SCATTINI

FOTOGRAFIA DI

CLAUDIO RACCA

SWEET & SAVAGE

SVEZIA, INFERNO E PARADISO
(SWEDEN HEAVEN AND HELL)

Directed by Luigi Scattini
(Italy, 1967)

Vilgot Sjöman, the director of *I Am Curious* — his controversial portrayal of late 1960s Sweden — once explained that his intention in making the film was to "puzzle a foreign audience with it [Sweden], saying, at once, that it is both very active and open, but that you still find a lot of sexual difficulties". This paradox lies at the heart of Luigi Scattini's less arty but no less powerful mondo portrait of the Scandinavian country and is expressed in the film's title: *Sweden Heaven and Hell*. The film is unusual in that it focuses on the behaviours of one nation only; mondo films up until that point had almost always suggested a global view on events. So why did Scattini choose Sweden? He, after all, had completed several more conventional mondo films before embarking upon *Svezia*... these being *L'Amore Primitivo* (1964) and *Sexy Magico* (1963) and would go on later to produce (under a pseudonym) *Vizi Segreti della Donna nel Mondo* with Jacopetti's other lensman Benito Frattari, *Questo Sporco Mondo Meraviglioso* (both 1971) and the witchcraft/magic mondo classic *Angeli Bianchi... Angeli Neri* (see chapter seven) — an output that easily makes him one of the most productive mondo directors. Scattini elected Sweden because for most non-Scandinavian Europeans (and Northern Americans), Sweden in the late 1960s embodied a nation

practically and intimately engaged with various liberal socio-cultural revolutions in the psychological and sexual sphere. Many of the new freedoms of this epoch were represented vividly in the film. The sleeve notes for the original soundtrack LP remarks: "The documentary tries to compare the two most evident aspects of current Swedish society: prosperity and the inner anxiety which ensues from it." Thus Sweden, for an Italian shock director, offered a great many rich psycho-sexual audiovisual opportunities — a desirable and debatable vision of the future for less advanced Europeans. Scattini, moreover, is a highly skilled director and the pace and breadth of the images created for *Svezia*... though lurid is impressive and engaging, building impressively on Enrico Altavilla's original collection of newspaper articles-turned-book. The soundtrack by Piero Umiliani is masterful; an essential feature of the film's identity, with its unique blend of jazz, pop and song (see appendix ii). The narration by legendary Italian actor Enrico Maria Salerno, no stranger to contemporary cinematic sexuality, is modest yet expressive — a rival to Sibaldi (see *Mondo Cane*). These qualities are sadly lost in the cheap video dupes circulating today. The film opens with the by now common 'statement of authenticity'. Except here Scattini is candid

Svezia, Inferno e Paradiso.

abrupt contrast between the 'new' and the 'old' could not be better realised. This central paradoxical theme of the film is underlined towards the end when a sequence depicting a labyrinthine underground atomic bunker complete with firestorm practice runs — 'Hell' — cuts into idealised images of Swedish girls sunbathing naked in a lagoon filmed by a hidden camera — the 'Heaven' of the title. These fake and softly pornographic scenes illustrate very well the mondo predilection for images of women standing for an idyllic fantasy — youthful female heterosexuality as liberating, intoxicating and democratic. Scattini, like Proia, is not averse to employing sexploitation to fire-up his films. A scene depicting a group of sadistic bikers, driven by a minimal, repetitive guitar riff ends with the gang-rape of a young girl. We watch this from a POV from her skirt before moving up to a close-up of her blank face. The audience very easily becomes complicit in her exploitation. A haunting freeze-frame on her left eye ends with a remark about what this has borne witness to. Voyeurism is not devoted to female sexuality though. A striking, and according to the LP sleeve notes, "difficult to pull off," scene involving illicit alcohol and drug taking is shot through blurry trees, monitoring the passing backwards and forwards of the bottle. Occasionally the men involved spot the camera and unsteadily wave it away. During a sequence regarding the way in which affluent Swedes' second (often derelict) country homes are used by male vagrants, the camera 'chances' upon them in the dark. The torch beam blasts them full in the face and they try to turn away. The tone towards the subjects of the film, with regard to examples of youth culture, is less moralising than other mondos (at least

with the audience: "all of the scenes in this film were taken from real-life or are based on real events," a more honest reworking of the famous opening statement from *Mondo Cane*. Scattini, like Jacopetti is a brilliant film editor. The forty or so scenes in *Svezia...* mostly end abruptly, but not so that the viewer is distracted. This technique, only valid in the most skilled mondo directors, effectively aids the notion of cruising from one contrasting element to another but also provides the 'shock' element critical to the best mondo moments, whether for humour or for shock purposes (and befits a director of more than a dozen giallo film works). Examples of this are abundant: a 'lesbian' club in Stockholm ends with two women embracing in an erotic kiss. As the camera closes in voyeuristically we are jolted with a sudden and extreme close-up of an ageing Salvation Army volunteer. The cold shock of the image juxtaposition is augmented by the synchronised switch from a pulsating, sexy beat groove to the jaunty but staid waltz of an accordion. The

Biker rape in *Sweden Heaven & Hell*

in the original Italian); pity would be a better description of the quiet narration. It appears evident that Scattini has learned well from Jacopetti. The narrator asks a group of young drug takers of the Stockholm strip "why do you do it?", to which the replies are incoherent. "It's terrible…," he mutters disconsolately, and the scene tails off. Mondo films often contain scenes of detached amusement at some 'crazy' aspect of 'modern' living — the cinematic version of the parental head-shake. This occurs in *Svezia…* when the decline of the Latin/Italian lover is attributed to the increasing interest by Swedish girls for black men (from the "third world" we are told), a theme later reworked fictionally by compatriot Tinto Brass in *Nerosubianco* (1969). The lothario now has to resort to becoming 'hip', frequenting groovy bars where topless girl bands play blaring psycho beat music, surely the inspiration for Russ Meyer's 'Carrie Nations' in *Beyond the Valley of the Dolls*. One of the most bizarre

and avant garde parts of the film occurs at the climax of a scene on loneliness and depression amongst the abandoned — the flip side of a rapidly developing, modern consumer culture. In desperation a young girl tries to telephone a priest for help; but he is already conversing with someone else. Her frustration is expressed through an odd montage of still images of cold empty streets. These are inter-cut with her face until finally we 'jump-cut' to a bridge and her suicide leap. This is all achieved through the shock of severe montage, almost amateurishly rendered but horrifying and vivid. Effects are employed again as the film ends with a freeze-frame close-up on a blonde Swedish girl's face; heaven or hell? The Italians are, as always, ambiguous. This presumably has been the fascination for such a feature length study. *Svezia, inferno e paradiso* is less 'real' than Sjöman's film, but no less puzzling and intriguing for non-Scandinavians as a colourful portrait of a culture in conflict.

MONDO FREUDO

Directed by R Lee Frost
(USA, 1966)

It is true that Austrian psychoanalyst Sigmund Freud first developed the notion of scopophilia. In his *Three Essays on the Theory of Sexuality*, Freud identified scopophilic behaviour as that which takes other people as objects and subjects them to a controlling and curious gaze. Freud later extended this practice to a sexualised pattern of pleasure seeking, which in its extreme forms becomes perverted, such as the activities of the 'peeping tom'. True, Freud developed this; yet it is unlikely that he ever envisaged his complex hypothesis being used as a justification for selling cheap voyeuristic exploitation movies to jaded American film audiences. *Mondo Freudo* is the most blatant manifestation of the cinematic peep show; a film fashioned almost entirely out of sexualised 'hidden camera' and 'secret filming' moments. The film was compiled by American sexploitation producer Robert 'Bob' Cresse (*Love Camp 7*, 1968) and distributed through his company Olympic International Films, a purveyor of much grindhouse entertainment that flooded American cinema screens in the postwar period. 'Mondo' was merely the latest vehicle for such material. The film both depicts sexual acts through representational processes, and is at the same time a sexual act in itself — precisely a scopophilic one.

From the outset, *Mondo Freudo* is frank about its motives. The scene opens on a beach in Southern California, a sunny Saturday afternoon when people are relaxing, swimming and playing. We see a camera operator fixing an enormous protruding lens onto the front of a film camera. A voice-over outlines the technical specifications of the lens ("a telescopic... 1000 millimetre... with telebar") and then the camera ("an Arriflex eleven 'B' 35

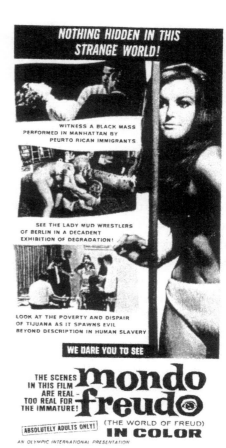

69

millimetre") before assuring the viewer that these mechanisms will "give you a long, close-up look at our society... and... will be your eye onto the Freudian world". Now the camera closes in on the sunbathers and begins to pick out individuals as the credits and music appear, a demonstration of the powerful capabilities of the film camera and its apparatus to objectify human behaviour for sexual pleasure. As if to reinforce this act of voyeurism, and to impress the viewer further with the capabilities of the kit, the scene switches to night time and we now look at the beach through an infrared filter and lights "developed by the US military" that allow us to see what young couples are up to in the dark "without them being aware of the light". Aside from the avalanche of technical information, the narrator offers a few behavioural observations of his own: "Sex under the sun is not for the civilised... only the night can wash away their modesty." The shots of semi-naked couples rolling around in the sand are rendered through a red haze. The shots are so close up to naked breasts and thighs and the spotlight so intensely focused that they become fragmented and abstracted, inappropriately reminiscent of parts of Stan Brakhage's *The Act of Seeing With One's Own Eyes* (1971). The scene is a clear studio set, a fake that only adds to the surreal aura of the segment. The film then switches to b&w (for reasons which are never made clear) and we are at a "watusi club" on the Sunset Strip in Hollywood, then to a burlesque set up from *Hollywood's World of Flesh*. From here the film follows a familiar pattern; sequences purportedly showing the plethora of sexualised nightclub acts and routines of this "Freudian

World" unfold. Private and public clubs in England are visited, the crucial difference being that in private clubs full nudity is allowed. A succession of strippers demonstrates this as a sombre faced audience look on. A man diverts his eyes at the final naked moment. The audience applaud modestly. The pseudo-documentary pretence is maintained when the crew trace (fake looking) prostitute cards displayed on a wall to two 'lesbians'. The director interviews the girls and offers to pay them to perform for him. They begin to do this but request that the camera be turned off as they could be arrested... and so the scene ends. A "topless watusi" club is lingered over as girls, one black and one white, shake on caged podiums to riffs from house band the Duvals. Other sequences show a female slave market in Tijuana (where genitals are 'scratched out') and a ludicrous portrayal of a Puerto Rican black mass, patently assembled in a studio, and crammed with as much fetishist extreme close-ups of naked breast swinging, crotch shots and chicken blood made from red paint as the producers could stretch to. The regular mondo diversion into modern art takes place: we witness two painters, Thor and Lorenzo, who respectively use naked women as canvases (à la Piero Manzoni) or to paint with (à la Yves Klein).

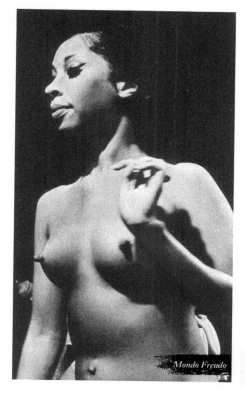

Mondo Freudo

Frost and Cresse, despite some occasionally competent cinematography, are not good filmmakers. The narration is mock professorial, silly and, like most of the scenes, slow and contrived. A sunset strip "girlesque" sequence (filmed again in b&w to spuriously connote 'realism') of a live sex floor show omits the sex act itself by the crude device of having the back of a member of the audience's head obscure their "hidden camera". If a "Freudian

world" consists almost entirely of the breasts of young women bobbling, swaying, bouncing, probing, jiggling, flopping and rising in front or above of a large camera lens then *Mondo Freudo* is a vérité film masterpiece (or a Russ Meyer flick). It doesn't, and the American predilection for this artless burlesque form of filmmaking, which in the English-speaking world represents mondo, adds nothing to the credibility of the genre. The producers of this film prominently display a large poster for the Italian pre-mondo *Sexy Proibito*, made some four years earlier, on the walls of one of their 'nightclubs' which only confirms, despite their boast that *Mondo Freudo* is "the first documentary to examine the hidden world of sex", how tired this variant had become.

I MALAMONDO

Directed by Paolo Cavara
(Italy, 1963)

Cavara, who collaborated with Jacopetti and Prosperi on *Mondo Cane* and directed some of the famous scenes of that film, can be regarded as a filmmaker intimately engaged with the concept of the 'camera eye'. That is not to claim that *I Malamondo* (simply *Malamondo* in English), Cavara's first solo movie after the Jacopetti and Prosperi collaborations, is a masterpiece of film art, or even of mondo film art: the camera work is not as vibrant and engaging as in other mondos and is occasionally out of focus; the emphasis of the film is to portray the sex and danger of early 1960s youth culture, acknowledged openly as Cavara's personal vision, is at times conservative, simplistic and even moralising in tone. The direction (assisted by Franco Giraldi, later the maker of many 'spaghetti westerns') lacks a unifying structure of purpose. It is often flat and if anything more like tired reportage. For Italian critics Antonio Bruschini and Antonio Tentori, in fact, it is only the great score by Ennio Morricone that distinguishes it from other mondos of the period — a not unreasonable observation. Yet Cavara's understanding of the power of the camera eye, developed on *Mondo Cane* and later realised most effectively in *L'Occhio Selvaggio* (see below), was processed through the making of this film and lies at the

THE THRILL GENERATION..

THE ECCENTRICS, THE ANGUISHED, THE CONFUSED TAKING A RIDE ON THIS WIDE, WILD WORLD...

MARSHALL NAIFY PRESENTS

MALaMONDO

EastmanCOLOR

Produced by GOFFREDO LOMBARDO · Directed by PAOLO CAVARA
Music by ENNIO MORRICONE
Released by MAGNA PICTURES DISTRIBUTION CORPORATION

THRILL TO THESE HIT TUNES!
'FUNNY WORLD' · 'SAD SATURDAY NIGHT'
Sung by CATHERINE SPAAK   Sung by ADRIANO CELENTANO

Malamondo

heart of his film philosophy. The first scenes of the film demonstrate this succinctly. As the theme song Funny World ends we emerge on an extreme close-up of a pair of rheumy eyes. A slow zoom out reveals the eyes to be those of the philosopher Bertrand Russell who is lecturing a group of students on how to live life effectively and to avoid "repeating the errors of the past". These young people, we are informed, "do not want to be part of mass society." Suddenly we have left Russell's stuffy academic retreat and are confronted with a shock-cut montage of young faces, all of them fixed with restless contempt. This quick-fire burst of adolescent aggression is heightened by Morricone's discordant score: a mess of blaring trumpets, machine gun drum rolls (part of his score for *Battle of Algiers* is a reprisal of this) and rising vocal refrains. The sequence ends with a woman scornfully

laughing at the camera — and at us. Thus the voices of modern authority are neglected in preference to wild and free existential living. The perceived alarming effects of this are the heart of *Malamondo*. The boredom of youth — regularly identified in mondo as the cause of social problems — is exemplified as a group of young, postwar-rich Italians "who don't dig anything" and are driven by apathy to slaughter a pig, after which the participants all look numb and sickened; "no one is hungry now" intones the narrator — the futility of youthful excess. Scenes at the Dachau concentration camp, which is now a museum, are shown and young Germans are warned of the dangers apathy can instigate. Again their expressions, as a former prisoner painfully relates the horrors he witnessed, are profoundly numb. Two sequences then depict the violence of youth: the first, a barely credible biker's game called 'Conquering Hero' is held in the English town of Leicester, in which the first motorcyclist to circle the town before a jukebox record ends 'gets the girl'. This climaxes when the leader skids through a red light into a truck and is found with blood trickling out of his mouth. This race is set to a fine variation of one of Morricone's spaghetti themes — the wild East Midlands anyone? The second features a French game of 'Chicken' in which two participants must stand atop a rising elevator until it hits the skylight and one of them loses their nerve and yells out. Bizarre student rituals are filmed: a Prussian military school, where duel scars were once proudly acquired through swordsmanship must now, due to restrictions, be obtained via a barber's razor. Blood drips obscenely through the shaving foam; a Dutch form of hazing where heads of new students are shaved before they are humiliated; Cambridge University students stage an anti-war protest on Remembrance Day. Sex and horror are important in *Malamondo*: students in Nottingham are said to live out life in the spirit of the town's most famous son, D H Lawrence, by indulging in wild sex parties (held in terraced houses); northern Italian students gather on the beach for a striptease; a group of necrophilliacs meet for an orgy of drink and sex across the gravestones of the dead — "the tenants downstairs don't complain" quips the narrator. A number of oddities flesh out the film: a mixed race marriage in Sweden is observed before the comment is made that in Scandinavia "the Latin Lover has given way to the appeal of the African Lover". The "civilisation" of the Swedish girls in doing this is praised (this scene was reprised in Luigi Scattini's *Svezia, inferno e paradiso*);

Cavara, recalling his famous shoot of Yves Klein for *Mondo Cane*, has a dig at a French performance artist having an "intellectual orgy" where the concept of flinging paint at a rapidly spinning canvas is first displayed (later to be copied by Brit artist Damien Hirst). The naked-girl-on-a-child's-toy-truck image emblazoned across the publicity for the film occurs here; Italian rocker Adriano Celentano and his group compose and perform a new hit in a Roman piazza.

The only youngsters to be admired by the filmmakers are a group of Royal Ballet School students who "unlike most of their generation... don't cultivate violence, they let themselves be cultivated".

The film ends with a warning as to the effect this "frantic, irrational and absurdity" as Sweden, which has "the worlds highest suicide rate" is revisited. A girl, ensconced in a bed-sit, contemplates suicide whilst listening to a version of one of the film's theme tunes sung by Belgian Catherine Spaak; but in Sweden there is a helpline to a minister who can "save her soul". The final caption of a giant yellow question marks heralds the usual mondo mixed-message, half-hearted empathy tinged with admonishments. "Are they any farther out than the youth of the past?" asks the narrator. "Whom do they hurt... mostly themselves and the ones they love."

The voyeurism of *Malamondo* is modest by mondo standards and largely based around an attempt at explaining youth culture to an older audience (nudity and violence were played out more in the advertising campaign for the film). Cavara realised after making the film that there were 'issues' with the inherent voyeurism of mondo. His next film fought against this.

HE USED A CAMERA like MOST MEN USE a WOMAN

...and a woman like something you'd keep locked up in a cage! See the strange secret world of the 'Mondo Movie' makers in...

GEORGES MARCI presents a film by PAOLO CAVARA

PHILIPPE LEROY
DELIA BOCCARDO

THE WILD EYE

GABRIELE TINTI · GIORGIO GARGIULLO · LARS BLOCH
GEORGES MARCI · PAOLO CAVARA · GIANNI MARCHETTI

IN COLORSCOPE BY PERFECT
AN AMERICAN INTERNATIONAL RELEASE

L'OCCHIO SELVAGGIO (THE WILD EYE)

Directed by Paolo Cavara
(Italy, 1967)

L'*Occhio Selvaggio* — *The Wild Eye* — is not, despite its thematic and directorial credentials, a mondo film. And yet it is one of the most important film documents in any history, no matter how selective or minute, of the shockumentary genre. The reason for this is that the film offers an effective, snarling, bitter critique of mondo ethics and was the first to do so — a year before Haskell Wexler's *Medium Cool* and a decade before Ruggero Deodato's infamous mondo-shock deconstruction

Cannibal Holocaust. Cavara was there first and the film has the crucial authority of a director intimately involved in the creation, at the inception of the 'classic' mondo style. Almost every frame of *L'Occhio Selvaggio* resonates with the practices, techniques, experiences and moral questions, those real, and those imagined by critics, of the genre developed by the *Mondo Cane* team of which Cavara was an integral founding member. Cavara's involvement in the creation of mondo films is today forgotten, despite the fact that in 1951 he engaged in a film expedition with Franco Prosperi and Carlo Gregoretti (see *Africa Addio*) and made films for Italian television.

The experience of producing *Mondo Cane* and his own mondo feature *I Malamondo* a year or so after, had evidently troubled Cavara. Thus, in this film he turned the prying eye of the documentary camera away from the subject/object and onto the protagonist — in this case his alter-ego 'Paolo' (Philippe Leroy), an unscrupulous director of shock documentary scenes, in order to comment on the psychological and emotional effects he had experienced as a sensation-seeking journalist. It's a bold move; the horrible protagonist of the film not only shares Cavara's first name but his physical appearance (despite this Cavara tried to deny that Paolo was modelled on himself). The result of this catharsis of his role in the production of mondo documentaries was that afterwards Cavara abandoned documentary films in favour of more 'honest' fiction comic and thriller films. If not an outright rejection of documentary Cavara at least wanted audiences to accept documentary as a mere translation of reality — a personal, as opposed to didactic statement on the world. Paolo too trades in the production of cinematically induced emotions and his theories on the production of films are expunged throughout the narrative, theories dedicated to "truth sacrificed to the requirements of the show".

The film stars Italian Gabriele Tinti, and Frenchman Philippe Leroy, both stalwarts of European popular cinema. (Tinti appeared in cult-pop offerings such as Marco Vicario's *Il Grande Colpo dei Sette Uomini D'Oro* [1966] and several of the '*Emanuelle Nera*' series including *Emanuelle e gli Ultimi Canninbali*

[1977]; Leroy, by appearing in films such as *Femina Ridens* [1969], *Roma Bene* [1971], *Il Sandokan* [1976] and *Il Gatto* [1978] bestrides a complete history of Italian cult cinema.) Delia Boccardo plays Barbara, Paolo's muse and desire object. The film follows the attempts of this group to produce a sensational documentary film of horrible events based largely in the Far East with the Vietnam War as a backdrop. Paolo is a ruthless individual who will stop at nothing to get good, sellable pictures.

His meditations on the art of the shockumentary are hideously cynical. He says to Barbara at one point, after she has confronted him about the morality of his techniques: "audiences are masochistic and sadistic. A pretty girl with a rifle arouses their masochism; the same girl is helpless and unarmed by their sadism. There are no good or bad films. There are just those with or without the occasional stimulation that makes the public digest the rest of the film." To illustrate this Cavara inserts, in true mondo style, some light moments around Paolo and Barbara's romance and love-making, travelogue scenes poeticised by Gianni Marchetti's great lounge-jazz score. Paolo constantly attempts to construct scenarios that will heighten the reality kick. He tries to persuade a Buddhist monk to set himself on fire in front of a sacred statue while Barbara and he make love. Later, in a Saigon bar, he asks two Viet Cong informers to find him monks that are prepared to be sacrificed in the same way. Both of these requests fail but he does succeed in bribing the owner of a rehabilitation home for opium addicts (after being disappointed with the 'reality' of the home; "there's not much movie-wise") to let

Vietnamese execution in *L'Occhio Selvaggio*

him film them being beaten as part of their treatment. He also films Barbara's disgust as she watches this scene unfold (Deodato lifted this concept for *Cannibal Holocaust*). A faded deposed sultan allows Paolo to film his destitution in a series of humiliating set ups which Paolo takes great care to make look aesthetically pleasing (butterflies — hired in — drop through the shafts of temple light while the sultan is forced to catch and then eat them). As if to authenticate the message of *L'Occhio Selvaggio*, Cavara draws on real-life incidents and also from his mondo world. These include the capture, arrest and beating by the Viet Cong of Paolo, his cameraman Valentino (Tinti), and producer, as they try to film rebel positions. "We're Italian journalists!" Paolo protests in a clear reference to the incidence of Jacopetti's arrest in *Africa Addio*. Back at the hotel after he has been released he asks Valentino "did you get any film of me being beaten?", another tangible

dig at his ex-colleague (Cavara, who was one of the Italian-based editors of the rushes for *Africa Addio*, is alleged to have instigated accusations of staging after seeing the footage of that film). The spirit of Jacopetti rears up again when Paolo and Valentino get to film a rebel execution but persuade the officers to move the prisoner so that the light is better (these were accusations — thrown out of court — levelled at Jacopetti and Prosperi over *Africa Addio*). Even the opening of the film, the crew hunting a gazelle across an open plain, refers to the zebra hunt in the same film. The first truly voyeuristic sequence in the film starts with a wide-angled shot of

"He used a camera like most men used a woman — and a woman like something you'd keep in a cage!"

VOYEURISM AND SEXUALITY IN THE MONDO FILM

L'Occhio Selvaggio

Valentino looking through the viewfinder back at us, a dual-scopophilic moment. It is revealed they are filming deaf and dumb prostitutes. As Cavara had also worked on *La Donna nel Mondo*, the exploitation of women by mondo directors is clearly an issue. The strap line for the film in the US illustrated this beautifully and the threat that the wild eye "sees things you wouldn't dare look at!" is the garish language of the peep show. "We are all objects," Paolo says to Barbara and he is constantly seen closely watching her: at dinner, on the boat, in the cinema.

L'Occhio Selvaggio, shot in Techniscope with high production values, is a powerful and disturbing insight into the mind of a mondo director. The existential angst of a filmmaker beginning to question his motives and methods was improved by the additional script work of Italian novelist and travel writer Alberto Moravia (see also *Ultime grida dalla savana* and *Magia Nuda*). At the end, after Paolo has filmed the bombing of an American nightclub in Saigon, his delight in getting the pictures is halted when he discovers Barbara has been killed by the collapsing ceiling. As he kneels next to her corpse he urges Valentino to "get me on film". He stares down the lens of the only thing he has left — his camera. The frame freezes.

"Reality is boring — lies are entertaining," Paolo once stated, as if to exactly articulate the mantra of mondo cinema. Have we learned from this?

SEXY MAGICO

Directed by Mino Loy and Luigi Scattini
(Italy, 1963)

A classic example of the 'sexy' mondo, from the 1960s. Of course, all mondo films contain sex, but these early films, especially the Italian specimens, took special delight in capturing the changing attitudes of sexuality and the expression of such in the changing postwar world of 'la dolce vita'.

Replete with an excellent and highly sought after sleazy jazz soundtrack by Marcello Gigante and captivating visuals shot by Jacopetti and Prosperi's cinematographer Benito Frattari, *Sexy Magico* tours virtual hot spots of the world in search of female flesh.

Loy and Scattini were both hack directors, but of some skill, who would go on to contribute significantly to the popular Italian genre film.

The title sequence is one the most captivating sections of the film, being a carefully and somewhat skilfully choreographed scene of six girls in brightly coloured attire lounging on leopard-print baroque chairs gradually emerging from the darkness, each spot-lit, while a series of exotic dancers in leotards of varying shades parade in front of them. A slinky jazz tune plays out over the images.

Nanà, who became famous for the striptease in Fellini's *La Dolce Vita*. This incongruity hits straight away as the exotic title sequence described above cuts straight into scenes of African landscapes and the picturesque if fly-infested black "victims of white colonial rule", accompanied by exotic pipe music and various tamburi drum rhythms. The images could have been lifted straight from *Mondo Cane*. By way of setting the tone, the Masai tribe are said by the narrator to offer a cultural experience that is both "traditional and savage".

Yet *Sexy Magico* is important because it offers portraits of the Italian adventure into colonialism, a phenomenon mysteriously left out of all the other Italian mondo films, which focused on British, Portuguese and French Africa. The tribeswomen of the former Italian colony of Ethiopia, for example, who seem to do most of the work, are contrasted with Ethiopian air hostesses dressed in the manner of western fashion culture, represented of course by shots of their bottoms wiggling up a plane gangway. This is the university-educated modern African woman beloved of mondo filmmakers.

This African opening is in turn abruptly interrupted by an incongruous striptease by a black dancer, dressed like the models on the posters for the later *Africa Addio* in a blonde wig. This is either a witty parody of racial

As significant part of the mondo modus operandi is that the films switch between scenes of the 'primitive' south and the 'civilised' north, or contrast and complement one ancient ritual or another with others more modern. What is bizarre about *Sexy Magico* is that there are basically two halves to the film stitched crudely together: one part consisting of documentary sections on African culture and wildlife; the other various stripteases with thematic narratives, mostly one suspects, faked in Roman sound studios. I say this because the strips feature recognisable glamour dancers/strippers of the time such as Italian Rosa Fumetto, Parisian Jessica Rubicon and Lebanese actress Aichè

expectations in an emerging postmodern world, or a crass and racist slur. The music for this strip begins with a smattering of bland afro-jazz before switching to a more tribal (if incongruously Brazilian) offering when the girl casts aside her blonde wig to become a "black eve". At the climax of the dance she sits astride the conga drum and writhes erotically.

We also see bits of Somalia, also (partially) an Italian colony in the nineteenth century. Here, modern Somalis demonstrate their contemporaneity by doing the twist. The next striptease features a girl tormented in her sleep by dreams of primitive passions and a mysterious unnamed book. The performance is accompanied by the song No, All'amore ('No, don't speak of love') sung by Anita Sol.

Further incongruity occurs when the climax of this nude performance cuts to a ritual sacrifice of a goat in Africa followed by a relatively impressive nightclub act, 'The Devil and the Virgin,' in Nairobi where a woman is possessed by an evil spirit, the stripper playing both characters at the same time. A stripper from London — Miss Violet — puts on a show for the white minority of Kenya. This "scientific occult" performance incorporates tricks of the film camera (she disappears into thin air at the end) and so clearly evidences the fraud behind these sequences. At least *Mondo Cane* had pretence of reality about it. Next, a comic nightclub act consists of a jazz pianist who attempts to prepare and consume a lunch in-between bars of the tune he is supposed to be performing. The odd diversion to look at the natural wonders of the African landscape, such as Balancing Rocks in Southern Rhodesia (now Zimbabwe), fails to lift the mood.

If the point of *Sexy Magico* is to satirise the degeneration of European culture while at the same time showing how Africa is moving forward into the future, then that would be good. However, the nature of the structure of this film makes that somewhat uncertain. Ultimately, if anything, the film is about the exploitation of women the world over, and the exploitation of the exotic as titillation for western culture. Conversely, Gigante's excellent score was later used for a sequence in fellow Italian Gillo Pontecorvo's classic *Battle of Algiers* (1965) where French police plan a bombing atrocity in the city's Casbah district. In *Sexy Magico*, the music illustrates a sequence on traffic control in Cameroon.

The act of striptease in the film progress to the ludicrous, climaxing with a tableau representing "African folklore" which consists of a prim white couple on safari who are possessed by the power of the jungle so that the woman is transformed into a wild savage. Her husband, meanwhile, is attacked by a slinky leopard woman, but survives when his wife shoots the beast. A trip to Cairo is an excuse for an exotic belly dancing routine. The film ends with three naked black women splashing water over each other in a river, this, for the director, an image representing the "mysterious earth; the course of time"...

The sheer surrealism of blatantly contrasting serious reportage on the decolonisation of Africa with highly staged and artificial strip routines is startling even by mondo standards and arguably set the scene for later Italian forays in infotainment such as the notorious *Striscia le Notizia* a news programme with dancing girls. The spirit of decadent Rome, where sex sells anything and everything, exemplified by Aichè Nanà in *Sexy Magico*, lives on...

SHOCKING ! INCREDIBLE!

see...
- London stripped of its veil of respectability
- The school for strippers
- Hippies talk of 'Free Love'
- The Mods and Rockers in their frank attitudes to life

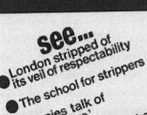

PRIMITIVE LONDON

EASTMANCOLOUR

the most **bizarre** motion picture you have ever seen!

PRIMITIVE LONDON

Directed by Arnold L Miller
(UK, 1965)

Despite that fact that *Mondo Cane*, and its successful imitations, was treated with sour contempt by the (self-appointed) Anglo-Saxon film intelligentsia, several British mondo films appeared in the mid-1960s, of which *Primitive London* is the most intriguing. The general artifice of the film is more palpable than with any other mondo documentary films, and that's saying something. But to give Miller and his cinematographer Stanley Long, both veterans of the sleaze circuit, credit where it's due the underlying theme of the film is the synthetic nature of postwar existence, and hence the fabricated nature of the film suits its theme. *Primitive London* is about the cynicism of modern western culture; yet, like a true mondo film, is itself extremely cynical in the way it expresses this philosophy.

Primitive London certainly looks like an Italian mondo film. Its gaudy Technicolor palette turns everything — blood, skin, cosmetics, chickens — into a psychedelic riot. The soundtrack is suitably weird, composed by the great experimental composer and arranger Basil Kirchin, a master of the soundscape of dystopian alien worlds (here, postwar inner London). Kirchin works a series of excellent abstract jazz modes into the seedy underworld of the city, a sordid, bastard offspring to the British Soho jazz scene then flourishing in the same locale. The mondo technique of cutting together seemingly unrelated phenomena is to some extent mastered, and the pompous voice-over by Canadian TV presenter David Gell carried off with aplomb. Mondo themes are writ large. A focus on unusual eating practices is relayed in a sequence on the grotesque factory farming of chickens (Long apparently "never ate chicken for a year" after the shoot. Film audiences forget that we can't smell the scenes," he noted). As with other mondo efforts 'real' people intervene from time to time, although here the effect is rather odd as they are often playing as 'actors' being 'real', if you see what I mean. For example, McDonald Hobley, a British TV personality, acts as an actor recording a voice-over for a consumer product, but is asked, by the client (writer and comedian Barry Cryer), to repeat the simple and idiotic phrase so many times that he loses his mind (and his tie).

But *Primitive London* is in many ways an incredibly shabby film. The staged sequences such as the advertising voice-over described above shatters any illusion of documentary, as does the inclusion of an unpleasant and unconvincing Jack the Ripper horror sequence (the pursued prostitute can clearly be seen running on the spot). This was inserted purely,

"The beat is off-beat!"

Strippers take a bath in *Primitive London*

offers an honest portrayal of the "cynical eroticism" of the modern world, but naturally wallows in this world to make a sensationalist moving picture. Fake tableaux of prostitute murders are visually arresting but leave a nasty taste in the mouth. The moralising as always is ludicrous, the narration describing the "sex lottery" of swingers as participating in the "death of love" and being the "true delinquents" (not mods and rockers!) while gleefully cramming the screen with as much female nudity, to the point of tedium, as is possible.

Despite the gaudy colours, a depressing grubby patina covers the entire film. The dressing rooms the 'non-stop' stripper rushes between have filthy walls, dingy lighting and smeared mirrors. In this world, everyone — pimps, club owners and exploitation film directors — is exploiting everyone else. Indeed, one of the grubby legacies of such films is that of the British tabloid press, recently held under close scrutiny for its salacious and often illegal pursuit of sensationalist news stories. The hypocrisy and ugliness of these practices, that have a particular metropolitan British bent, is to be found in films such as *Primitive London*.

The same Miller/Long team had earlier made *London in the Raw* (1964), a film remembered if at all for a particularly gruesome if revealing hair transplant sequence.

as Stanley Long later admitted, to secure an 'X' certificate. Unlike the tight structure of Jacopetti and Prosperi's mondo films, *Primitive London* lurches from scene to scene and then returns to scenarios to pad out the film. The complexity and exoticism of the location shoots for the Italian mondos is lacking and the cheapness of the quickie exploitation film looms large. The ageing director's mistrust and suspicion of youth cultures rears up again, here by portraying various mods, rockers and beatniks as buffoons, purveyors of the latest "peacock trend" (although the 'vox pop' interview with a self-styled beat poet is an interesting diversion from the hitherto purely post-synced world of mondo). The transience of pop music is represented by forgotten beat group the Zephyrs and by Billy J. Kramer being mobbed by hysterical girls while Terry Dene, the idol Kramer has supplanted looks wistfully on. Meanwhile girls shown adorning their bodies with tattoos are described as a "puzzle for psychiatry". Miller, with his portraits of strip clubs, prostitution and swinger parties

Que Viva Mexico

CHAPTER 4
"SENSATIONAL SHOCK SCENES"

Anti-narrative in Mondo

Mondo films visualise humanity's fears, phobias and subconscious desires as cut-up collages of raw mediated experience. According to critic Herman G Weinberg "film should be fluid, restless, visceral, dynamic" and in the stream of consciousness world of the mondo film such an assault on the audience's senses recalls many of the powerful features of the avant garde. Mondo films, like the work of the British author J G Ballard, alchemise the horrors of (post)modern culture and society from documentary evidence into cogent warnings of the present and the future. Ballard's book, *The Atrocity Exhibition*, namechecks the work of Jacopetti ("zooms for some new Jacopetti, the

"My version (of the fake newsreel)... would be a compilation so artfully faked as to convince the audience that it was real, while at the same time reminding them that it might be wholly contrived."
J G BALLARD

DON'T TURN
YOUR BACK ON
THIS FILM..

...IF YOU VALUE
YOUR MIND OR
YOUR LIFE.

TITICUT
FOLLIES

WINNER OF MANNHEIM
FILM FESTIVAL

newsreels" — for Ballard was best represented by the mondo film. Ballard's 'exhibition of atrocities' is a showcase with a "preoccupation with the theme of world cataclysm". If mondo films are accused of pessimism it is perhaps this aspect of the postmodern world — the destruction of all that is 'natural' — that is being articulated. It is the "psychotic imagination" of avant garde art that is captured by mondo films in terms of both form, and of content, where weird images flash past the viewer and the shock-art tropes of juxtaposition, expressionism fragmentation, distortion, blurring, freezing, free association startles and numbs. The films that are examined in more detail in this chapter have taken the grave form of the documentary film and blasted it into fragments of perversity, voyeurism, horror, shock and absurdity. In this sense, mondo films beautifully mimic art and the avant garde.

Yet this engagement takes a bizarrely contradictory form. On the one hand sequences in mondo films mock and chastise the excesses of the postwar avant garde. The places where burlesque visions and performance art merge are highlighted grotesquely, and the reactionary and conservative ideology of the mondo director and 'his' aesthetic is clear in repeated sequences where modern art in its profligate, difficult, concrete form

elegant declensions of serialised violence"), and the book's revolutionary experimental collage format can clearly (if strangely, given that mondo films are 'documentaries') be associated with mondo film aesthetics. *The Atrocity Exhibition* follows a fervently anti-linear, anti-narrative form. The text is punctuated by a series of shock headings that give way to startling and mesmerising provocations, which are at once poetry, reportage, fiction and social comment. In one edition of the book, Andrea Juno and V. Vale describe the work as a "flickering video collage in written form". Evidently this collage — "slow-motion is lampooned and mocked. Mondo directors thus view art experimentation as daft. Moreover, mondo films are polished and crafted: well shot and edited with consummate skill (prolific mondo editor Mario Morra, for example, went on to edit Giuseppe Tornatore's Oscar winning *Nuovo Cinema Paradiso*), and unlike art films, were often paid for by 'mainstream' film producers (Rizzoli, Titanus), benefiting from healthy commercial input. Mondo films were also popular, a crude commercial fact that negates them from most categories of avant garde art. Because mondo films, unlike many avant garde films, are not concerned with the subjective psyche of the director they remain absent from histories of the cinematic avant garde. Parker Tyler's account of 'underground film', for example, equates Frederick Wiseman's *Titicut Follies* (a candid-camera documentary), and Sjöman's *I Am Curious (Yellow)* (a fake documentary), as avant garde but no mondo films make the list. Tyler, however, identifies at the start of his book that to "taboo reality" is a crime.

"The film camera has for one of its most neglected functions that of invading and recording realism which have to some degree remained taboo — too private, too shocking, too immoral for photographic reproduction".

The "camera voyeur" is hailed as one of the principle functions of the cinematic art, "peephole excitement" being a significant presence. The mondo film, heretically coalescing pop culture and art, the extreme and the popular, acts this way. Again, while discussing *Titicut Follies*, Tyler observes that one of the qualities of the film for the observer is a "voyeur's vantage point" from which one can "leave... on impulse without fuss". This frank appraisal of the documentary art form

(*Titicut Follies* is a classic of 'direct cinema' as well as a work of the 'underground') suits the mondo film's aesthetic dimensions; the 'burlesque visions' of mondo are acute, painful and hypnotic. Tyler calls *Titicut Follies* a "psycho-nudie peepshow" — a better description of films such as *Mondo di Notte* and *Europa di Notte* would be hard to find. So on the other hand, mondo films, in their structure, form and narrative belie a richly experimental aesthetic. Aside from the noticeable collage effect of joining seemingly disparate events together in the edit process (*Il Pelo nel Mondo*), from the use of beautiful music to underscore scenes of ghastly despair (*Mondo di Notte 3*), to a freeform surreal conceptualisation (*Realtà romanzesca*), the mondo film itself is a work of modern art. Moreover, the mondo film's 'practices of looking' at the world and its events, the relentless desire to see the forbidden is a technique favoured by avant garde filmmakers as diverse as Brakhage, Franju and Jodorowsky.

It is intended that such propositions frame mondo films as works of underground cinema, film art, subversive art, taboo art, auteuristic expression. Hans Richter once stated that the

"In constructing *Mondo Cane*, Jacopetti utilised the avant garde arsenal of cut-up/ collage, alienation and shock in the brazenly unconvincing guise of the documentary film. *Mondo Cane* jumps from image to image in a purely subconscious and anti-linear way."
STUART SWEZEY/AMOK

Un Chien Andalou

and optical assault created by Buñuel at the opening of his surrealist classic, *Un Chien Andalou*, reverberates through many of the jolts spiralling out of mondo. The beauty of the images as filmed and edited, the "horrible truths" parading deliriously before the film audience, the cuts, slashes and piercings of the mondo film evoke the type of ritualistic sacrifice beloved of the surrealists' imagination (Georges Bataille). Mondo editing scrupulously follows the theories of Sergei Eisenstein, whose 'collision' technique, where sequences directly juxtaposed, evoked new images and ideas (there is another resonance with Eisenstein: his *Que Viva Mexico* — a poetic documentary film about Mexican ritual with vaguely pornographic undertones). In mondo, montage is used expressively (as opposed to narratively) with the specific purpose of producing an immediate 'panic' effect resulting in "that rare species: the artful documentary... surrealistic mostly through juxtaposition" (Parker Tyler).

The art world penchant for the work of the insane or the innocent (children) is a celebration of the purity of the individual untainted by contemporary lived experience. This too can be located within aspects of the mondo view of the world as Technicolor primitive-ritualistic spectacle (when filtered through the writing of occasional mondo scribe Alberto Moravia this seems again to be a reasonable association). I once took the liberty of aligning Jacopetti and Prosperi's mesmerising *Addio Zio Tom* with Jodorowsky's *El Topo* as both long-neglected films spiralled into surreal/stream of consciousness/freeform 1970s reality/unreality head aesthetics. *El Topo* has always been regarded as an art film and both this and *Addio Zio Tom* make extensive like-minded use

phenomenon of the avant garde had to be "international" and mondo films, perhaps more than any other film, exhibit this globalising tendency (albeit in a wildly perverted form). Unflinchingly filmed and presented, the mondo film assaults the viewer as an art film does — the same flash of horror, revulsion,

"The avant garde offers no solutions or programmatic statements, but a series of intricate challenges, hints, and coded messages, subverting both style and content."
AMOS VOGEL

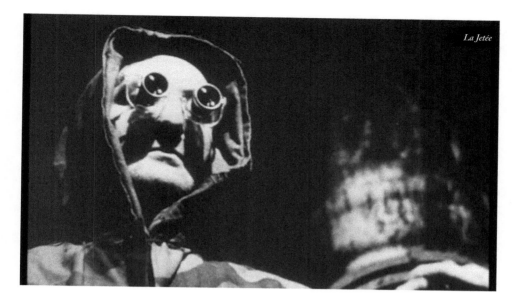
La Jetée

of dream-like sequences. Parker Tyler argues at the end of his book, *Underground Film*, that the "avant garde… has infiltrated commercial films". In mondo films, the ultimate absorbers of film style for effect, this notion came true.

In his essay, 'The Cinema of Poetry,' Pier Paolo Pasolini argues for film as a collapsing of reality (referent signs) and unreality (dreams). This was a troubling proposition for critics of cinema in the mid-1960s/early 1970s fixated as they were with 'true' realism but one within which the mondo film — a confusion of documentary reality and poetics that evokes the art film — seems to happily exist. For Pasolini, the filmmaker makes art out of enriching his or her memories and dreams with personal expression — a "language of poetry". Subjectivity is poetic for Pasolini and it is subjectivity that distinguishes the art film. Cinema-poetry comes from an intense and rich manipulation of cinematic codes (the contrary of placing a still camera observing an event — in other words *narrative*). Interestingly, mondo films bypass Pasolini's "free indirect subjective"

— where the filmmaker speaks through characters — by way of the bitter narration that carries the mondo anti-narrative (in *Mondo Cane*, Jacopetti speaks directly to the audience). Stan Brakhage identified the visionary rhetoric, the filmmaker as poet, where "the director bears a camera as economically, as flexible and as intimate as the pen". Meanwhile, Astruc's notion of the 'camera-stylo' — the camera wielded like a pen by the author/director, refers back to the mondo film's essay format. The essayist here acts as a total filmmaker, an auteur, and another crucial aspect of film as art.

Art film techniques

Extensive use of stop-motion, or the freeze-frame, emerged alongside the golden age of

"I dream of a theatre in which humour and poetry, panic and love would all be one."
FERNANDO ARRABAL

mondo as a viable film technique (previous to this the abstract quality was derided as too fake to be used — certainly in a documentary film). Art film employs still images (in the case of Chris Marker's *La Jetée* exclusively) but freezing the frame (repeating a frame) in mondo has a very different effect from this. Freeze-frame is used in mondo either to evoke reflection or make people look ridiculous. Often a freeze-frame ends a sequence (as in Truffaut's *400 Blows*). But uniquely mondo films, especially those of Jacopetti and Prosperi, direct the freeze-frame to begin sequences — a startlingly artificial device. Mondo films also make use of the trance flashback. In *Africa Addio* the trail of Mau Mau operatives is illustrated with misty and haunting images of the sites of the atrocities. The narration then becomes drenched in echo, the pictures are ghostly and hazy. Again, the artificiality and the poetry of Jacopetti's images contravenes the rules and laws of documentary film exposition. The assault on montage outlined by Amos Vogel and attributed to subversive art cinema is expressed in the mondo predilection for the intense manipulation of the film form. The classic editing structure, introducing a scenario through a long-shot and working into the object of attention is radically overturned in mondo. Scenes *begin* with extreme close-up or freeze-frame in a carefree dispensation with the aesthetics of objectivity. Scenes in mondo films are often not 'established' — the viewer needs to decode the 'meaning' of the context. Traditional devices for creating pleasing transitions between scenes are similarly eschewed — mondo films famously cut violently from one scene to the next — sometimes with logic other times not. In mondo what was once 'intrusive montage' becomes the reality of the shockumentary aesthetic. The poetry and lyrical (film about the director 'looking' — the contrary to documentary where the audience's look is the drive) qualities of mondo film represent beautifully the chaos and fracture of the contemporary world experience. The goal of Fernando Arrabal's 'panic' aesthetic is echoed in mondo: "Arrabal refuses to judge; he merely notes the position and shows that he finds it beyond his comprehension" (Esslin). Mondo deploys experimentally the language of cinema to map such psychogeographies. Vogel's description of the effect of experiments with montage echoes Jacopetti's thesis: "the assault on the old montage... an attempt... to increase the viewer's identification by forcing him into stronger mental and psychological response, thus jolting him from the comfortable safety of his own universe," as does Aristotle's theory of the catharsis — the purification of the emotions by art. The work of Proia, Vanzi and Blasetti, combinations of grand guignol and *commedia dell'arte*, celebrations of both the horror and the glory of life, are dedicated to the work of experimental film art.

"Life is an enormous novel," Ballard once remarked and it is arguably the mondo film that retells that story most lyrically, intensely and artistically.

"It may be a sign of richness in a work of art both that it attracts a conflict of critical judgements and also that it appeals strongly from several different aspects."
RALPH STEPHENSON & J R DEBRIX

IL PELO NEL MONDO (GO! GO! GO! WORLD)

Directed by Renato Marvi (Marco Vicario)
and Anthony M Dawson (Antonio Margheriti) (Italy, 1964)

Despite being described by Gualtiero Jacopetti as "a film I would not have been proud to have made", *Il Pelo nel Mondo* could rightly be held up as a fine example of a classic blueprint mondo, a documentary film gouged fresh and still warm from the *Mondo Cane* mould. The film was one of very many which followed quickly in the wake of the original and finest mondo works, and yet there are some spirited and dynamic aspects of the film that make it still one of the most watchable shockumentary feasts. The direction is sure and competent (Vicario has become known as a capable director of thriller and horror genre films). Vicario's vision for this film was aided by assistant director, and later western/sci-fi/horror director Antonio Margheriti, and both men maintained the Italian habit of adopting English language pseudonyms (Vicario chose the even more bewildering step of adopting an Italian pseudonym). Margheriti compiled library material for the film and shot some of the scenes with definite panache and occasionally one could be excused for detecting his eerily flamboyant style. But the film mostly bears all of the camp and vibrant marks of a Vicario production. The film's breathtaking pace meanwhile was largely down to some virtuoso editing by Mario Morra who would later play his own important role in the mondo story.

The film begins with a frenetic title sequence rendered in the style of the Italian *fumetto* (cartoon) later perfected by Osvaldo Cavandoli and most famously Bruno Bozzetto. The male cartoon character's zany frolics with an animated globe herald Bozzetto's popular creation, *Il Signor Rossi* (*Mr. Rossi* to kids brought up on doses of his adventures on British TV in the late 1970s). The film has a genuine cartoonish quality — fast, funny and stupid — which has been exaggerated in the English version of the film with its suitably lame, meaningless re-titling (the Italian

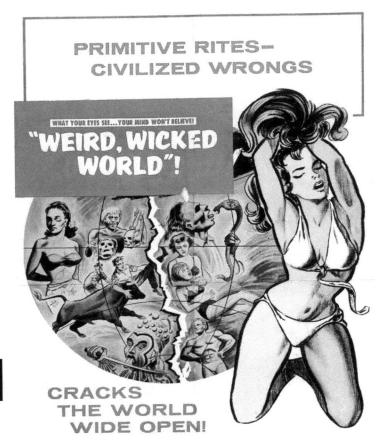

PRIMITIVE RITES-
CIVILIZED WRONGS

WHAT YOUR EYES SEE...YOUR MIND WON'T BELIEVE!

"WEIRD, WICKED
WORLD"!

CRACKS
THE WORLD
WIDE OPEN!

SCENES THAT WERE FORBIDDEN...HIDDEN! NOW CAPTURED BY THE CAMERA

NOT FOR THE TIMID, NOT FOR THE SQUEAMISH! CAN YOU TAKE IT?

WE DIDN'T MAKE THE WORLD — WE JUST PHOTOGRAPHED IT!

A MARCO VICARIO Presentation GO, GO, GO WORLD! Technicolor • Distributed by ABC FILMS Inc.

LP represents only about a third of the total score). The great mondo music tradition of trying to shadow the geographical visual locations with geographical audio cues is musically satisfying if sometimes ridiculous. There was so much material in the film and so much music that *Il Pelo nel Mondo* is one of the few mondo films to appear to have a surfeit of material (as opposed to the barrel-scraping exercises of the poorer examples of the genre). The suspect documentary claims of the earlier mondo

translation, *The Skin of the World*, as well as nicely maintaining the 'flesh' motif, foretells of mondo proclivities to come). As there are over fifty sequences in the film, the construction had to be tight and a mesmerising score by *Mondo Cane*/*Mondo Cane No.2* collaborator Nino Oliviero, aided by Bruno Nicolai, drives the film brilliantly (the accompanying soundtrack

films appears to have been dispensed with altogether in this film and a full panoply of techniques and effects is deployed by the directors to maintain the energy of the film's title sequence: a portrait on the Italian love of the car is demonstrated by way of the old film joke of thousands of people emerging from one small car; the depiction of English abattoir techniques is run backwards so that the slaughtered pigs are zipped-up. Blurred focus, violent zooms and hidden camera angles abound, a variation on the predictable mondo theme of striptease is offered when an Austrian act is speeded up in order to demonstrate that the modern man, "healthy, wealthy and dynamic," requires greater acceleration in his favoured nocturnal activity (naturally the comic speed slows right down at the end so that we can admire the girl's backside). There are sequences on the familiar terrains of Hawaii (the stupidity of American tourists), nightlife (lascivious portraits of sex clubs contrasted with moral guff on prostitution), animal use and abuse, religious and cult ritual, cod philosophising and so on.

So what makes this film special?

The trick *Il Pelo nel Mondo* manages to pull off, is in capturing the most entertaining aspects of the 'classic' mondo films and unshakably offering that material in an exciting, giddy manner. The film is finished with such a degree of energy and humour that it is impossible to be engaged by the activities on-screen — a 'skill' many of the later mondo films completely failed to register (even mondo historian David Flint was moved to admit the film a partial success — albeit despite its "dreadful narration"). There are two scenes in the film that for me stand out as exemplary mondo moments and these are worth recounting here as evidence of the film's verve. The first concerns the striptease, which even as early as 1964 had already become a tired act in the mondo theatre of the absurd. Vicario records a strip based around la belle époque, the 'beautiful age', between wars when European culture appeared to offer itself to the world a place of wonder. An

unpromising beginning, as the girl disrobes the scene takes a weird turn. We see a couple in the audience sat at a table laughing and smoking. The music switches tone from a light baroque bossa ("à la Mozart") to a sultry sax driven pulse as the stripper's face, eyes closed in mock ecstasy comes close to us, the viewer. As the naked flesh becomes revealed, an odd, fish-eye close-up of the man's face menacingly looms towards us too. After a few seconds the act concludes and the girl scuttles off to sparse applause; we are returned to normality. The odd thing about this scene is the switch from the objective record of an event (striptease) to a surreal representation of the inner emotion energising the act. I think Vicario (or did Margheriti lens this sequence?) was trying to spice up the scene but instead created a bizarre and hypnotic effect — a long-lasting one.

The second great moment in the film occurs at the end. We have just watched a searing condemnation of the Italian psyche and its car obsessions. Now we are informed that Italians look to the sky, to the future of air travel, to set themselves free. Glorious helicopter shots across Alpine vistas are supported by the ironic narration: "Earth looks clean at last — as they had always dreamed". These scenes could only be filmed in this way at the outset of global jet set living, the optimism and freedom offered by the skies untainted by what was to become. The film ends on a high — a real marvellous high.

I implied at the outset that *Il Pelo nel Mondo* could be held up as a classic textbook case-study of a mondo film. Although far from great, the film captures the energy of the best mondo aesthetics and Vicario, as his subsequent glossy thrillers proved, was more than just a shockumentary hack.

THE NIGHT LIFE OF EUROPE COMES TO TOWN
...in this great color spectacular!

"FABULOUS ... QUITE A SHOW"
—San Francisco Examiner

CRAZY HORSE SALOON

CABARET Place Pigalle

NOUVELLE EVE

EL CORRAL DE LA MORERIA

Join the after-dark-to-dawn cabaret whirl and thrill to some of the world's brightest entertainers!

EUROPEAN NIGHTS
EASTMANCOLOR

Carmen Sevilla • Domenico Modugno • The Platters • Channing Pollock • Henri Salvador
Coccinelle • Robert Lamouret • The Rastellis • Colin Hicks • Candid Comment—Henry Morgan
Presented by JOSEPH BURSTYN RELEASING

94

EUROPA DI NOTTE

Directed by Alessandro Blasetti
(Italy, 1959)

Watching this quaint, almost silly little film in the twenty-first century, it's hard to appreciate the significance of *Europa di Notte* to the mondo genre. The film was directed by Alessandro Blasetti, Italy's great inventor of the episode film, was assistant directed by Luigi Vanzi (who refined the first experiments with a mondo aesthetic) and was scripted by Gualtiero Jacopetti (who gave the mondo film it's 'voice' and finally created the quintessential examples of the genre). It is a film poised at the germinal of shockumentary film history. Blasetti's simple aim, to repurpose risqué nightclub entertainment as film entertainment, resulted in a mildly surprising melange of colourful sounds and images (as opposed to the brutal shock of later mondos). Blasetti concocted the key elements of early period mondo: the weird, the funny, and the sexy (films such as *Europa di Notte*, *Sexy al Neon*, *Mondo di Notte* are identified as 'mondo sexy' in Italian film lore). Although Jacopetti later repudiated the impact of the nightclub acts on his own film style as 'too fake', it's not difficult to note the elements of sexual titillation, voyeurism and the freakish in later more savage mondo films, elements in fact which have never left the genre. Above all, *Europa di Notte*, explores and revels in the burlesque, the circus aesthetic beloved of Italian film (especially Federico Fellini). Blasetti inter-cuts performance scenes with 'actuality' shots of different European locations. Strangely,

this works in opposition to later mondos and to Jacopetti's observations that these 'realties' were in fact infinitely richer, more intriguing and perverse than any of the contrived acts on show and on stage. In a similar way, shots of the audience are inserted, sometimes with corny 'real' dialogue, as a framing device for the acts. Throwaway perhaps, but looking at them now they rationalise and contextualise the intended impact of the burlesque acts on show (the leering middle-aged men, pulling out cameras and opera glasses for a better view of the female flesh are distained by their wives). We get behind-the-scenes glimpses of the strippers, fake and contrived, but an attempt, at the outset of the mondo genre, to get via the film 'into reality'. The narrator (I'm discussing the English language version) promises us at the beginning of the film, as the camera pans past a 3D model

Magician Channing Pollock in *Europa di Notte*

Europa di Notte

Bernard Delfont's Club Pigalle), yet each set up is so flat and over-lit that it's obviously fake. The audiences, realised in similarly subdued shots cut in-between the acts, reveal a bored and unexcited crowd. Only in the penultimate scene do the customers express any emotion when the British rocker Colin Hicks (brother of Tommy Steele and a frightening facsimile of his brother) 'lets rip'. The tame recreation of the real violence meted out at cinemas and clubs in the US and the UK at this time looks faintly ridiculous, a feeble parody of the sexual energy of rock that's as limp as Hick's contrived wildness.

That said, Blasetti occasionally teases the viewer with some proto-mondo cinematics. The visual record of the undistinguished circus act 'The Condoras' unfolds in slow-motion, deployed to give the stunt some tension. In the same way the camera suddenly swings to a POV shot of the trapeze artist, a giddy act of direction which at last brings the film to life. The underscore of weird avant-jazz lends the scene further intrigue. The climax of the film is an extended strip routine where three performers (a blonde, an 'oriental' and a "dark beauty") strip off with very little enthusiasm (the oriental woman wears a permanently pissed-off visage throughout). However, the stripper would be a frequent icon of the mid-period mondos to come.

Despite the tameness of *Europa di Notte* when viewed today, it is satisfying to witness many of the key elements of the mondo aesthetic put into place: sex, voyeurism, exoticism, sarcastic humour, crazy music. Vanzi and Jacopetti saw the future, and so next the cameras turned their corrupt gaze away from the stage on to the audience, and on to the world.

of Europe, the "greatest stars of European show biz — caught in the act!", and surprising though these acts may have been, it's hard not to feel a weird mix of pity tinged with lament. There then proceeds an array of essentially kitsch, 1950s eurotrash, augmented by Carlo Savina's fantastic swinging lounge beat: Belly dancers (Badia, "princess of the Orient"), clowns ('The Rastellis'), trapeze artists, singers and strippers. The film features several magicians: Mac Ronay performs non-magic in a buffoonish Tommy Cooper-esque manner while the more intriguing Channing Pollock perfects a superslick brand of trickery that is so creepy that it is not surprising that French horror master Georges Franju cast him in *Judex*. Brilliant Italian singer-songwriter, Domenico Modugno, receives what has since become the standard mondo mockery (his hymn to Neapolitan coffee is, according to narrator Henry Morgan, "exactly how it is espressoed in Naples"). All of the scenes are pastiches of real locations (i.e.

MONDO DI NOTTE 3 (ECCO)

Directed by Gianni Proia
(Italy, 1963)

The languid voice of English actor George Sanders, grave and mordant, accompanied by the sound of an eerie wind, speaks over a black screen, opening this 'classic' period mondo film in absurdist style:

"The globe has spun around many times before the probing eye of the motion picture camera; so may times in fact, that you may wonder if there is anything left to discover. But to the persistently curious, the world continually reveals new secrets and sights. As Shakespeare put it: 'there are more things in heaven and earth and between sunset and dawn than are dreamt of in your philosophy.' Therefore: 'ecco', which means look, witness, observe and behold! We show you our world beyond your most outrageous fantasies."

Proia had cut his teeth on previous *Mondo di Notte* efforts and was therefore well placed to portray the world through the shockumentary filter. This film contains numerous burlesque scenarios that pay homage to the director's formative cinematic experiences (the supposed last performance of the Grand Guignol in Paris; a pulsating bongo-driven psychedelic striptease; the fraternity of "Touch Buttocks" where the female backside is venerated; lesbian clubs; the "housewives burlesque" of Reno, Nevada, where male strippers provide titillation for a change). The gay opening titles, portraits of Romans going about their daily business, decorated by a song in the style of the Italian *canzoncini* (children's songs) belies the taste of shocking images to come (although the use of freeze-frames to end each character's portrait provokes some viewer unease). The right and proper elements of the shockumentary tradition then parade before us: a grim portrait of Berlin divided by the wall — "a city still expiating guilt as frightful as its ruins" — gives way to the activities of an occultist duelling society by way of "a song guiding us to the secrets of the German soul". Over tracking portraits of the young Berliners singing and drinking, Sander's describes "a people that gave the world Goethe, Beethoven, Einstein and Mozart... a nation that made lampshades of human skin!" The masked duellists must slash each others' faces. This is bitter, twisted stuff — ideally exemplifying the mondo tendency for smug moralising — a

A THOUSAND THRILLS CRAMMED INTO ONE HUNDRED MINUTES!

An Incredible Orgy of SIGHTS and SOUNDS!

BIZZARRE DARKNESS... SIGHTS NEVER BEFORE PUT IN FILM

A MASTERPIECE IN FILM MAKING

ASK YOUR FRIENDS, THEY CAN'T STOP TALKING ABOUT IT!

VIOLENT BEYOND BELIEF... YET BEAUTIFUL BEYOND COMPREHENSION

ECCO
GEORGE SANDERS in TECHNICOLOR ROMA and WIDE SCREEN   A OMEGA-ROMA RELEASE   Music by RIZ ORTOLANI

ANTI-NARRATIVE IN MONDO

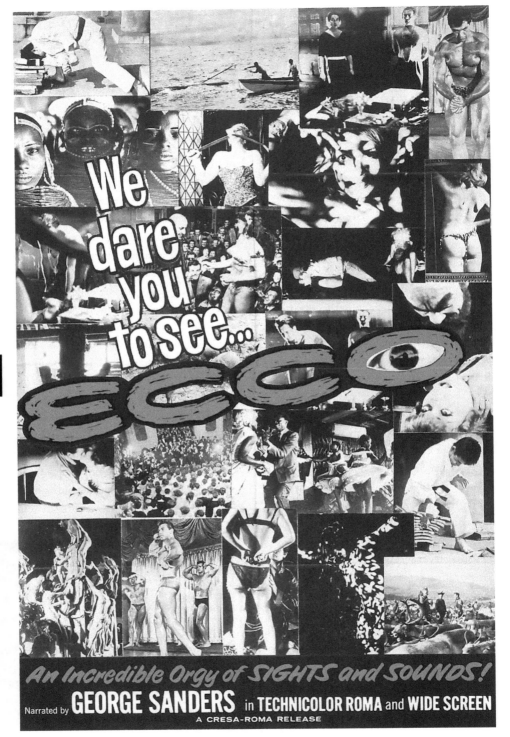

We dare you to see...

ECCO

An Incredible Orgy of SIGHTS and SOUNDS!

Narrated by **GEORGE SANDERS** in **TECHNICOLOR ROMA** and **WIDE SCREEN**

A CRESA-ROMA RELEASE

SWEET & SAVAGE

brilliant start to the film. Proia demonstrates clearly throughout this film the ideology of the binary opposite. And so, like in *Mondo Cane*, the competing trends of modern society, whether it is the rich French debutantes at a "fairy tale" dance juxtaposed with their beggar counterparts whose "crude violence, cruel provocative humanity" is glimpsed, or racial reconfiguration in Nairobi where black women dance in 'primitive' style for tourists and in a 'jazz style' for themselves. Another mondo trait of the empathetic cut is also displayed. An insane circus act, where trapeze artists ride a motorcycle up a high-wire to a church tower merges with the mountainous retreat of celibate hermit monks — "divine fishermen" where, accompanying shots of skulls, we are informed that "no priest comes down".

Shock and disgust appear in the tale of the Portuguese whalers, still hunting with harpoons, whose ghostly nocturnal activities ("bloody, uncertain and fierce; a savage corrida of the sea whose arena is the infinite and whose only spectator is God") proceed to the haunting sound of the Fado song. Probably the most famous scene in the film is the depiction of French illusionist, Evon Evar, the "apostle of the will", whose 'act' involves the careful insertion of rapier blades into and through parts of his body, neck and face. It is paramount that Evar avoids the jugular vein when spearing his neck with a blade. The blades are removed by audience members. A small trickle of blood emerges. The repellent visual qualities of this scene were used to sell the picture, most notably in the US where it was repackaged by the notorious Bob Cresse/R L Frost partnership; the antics of Evar certainly highlight the burlesque/performance aspect of mondo films of this period.

The aesthetics of horror also play in the movie. A staged but atmospheric sequence on witchcraft at Dunsmore Castle in the English countryside introduced with a quote from French satirist Voltaire: "there are no more witches since we stopped burning them. He was wrong." The aesthetics of the horror film are played out as the creepy ghoulish music — wailing voices and layers of organ, percussion (gongs, woodblock) — propels the act of ritual bloody sacrifice, a woman being covered in chicken blood before being defiled. Curiously the device of filming the participants through a grilled window as "they were afraid to allow our cameras inside their church" is replaced by full-screen clarity for the latter scenario. The transfer from a sexualised naked bloody young woman to the towering Christ of Rio's Corcovado, offers another of the films shock edits.

The Italian mondo obsession with Scandinavian culture and society, especially that of "cold, sombre, prosperous" Sweden, is visualised by an account of Swedish 'Teddy Boys' whose violent terror campaigns incorporating reckless driving and the destruction of a funfair end with a couple making love on the roof of a car encircled, Wild West style, by other gang members. A group of guardians look on in shocked disgust. The girl's face is utterly blank, a "frightening kind of despair".

Riz Ortolani turns in another brilliant soundtrack capturing the psychological loneliness of hermits to the pummelling beat of the Rio Carnival. The above sequence on Evan Ever is made all the more disturbing by the inclusion of Ortolani's experimental, electronic soundscape; a clear demonstration that the composer's virtuosity can incorporate

Prize-winning bottom in *Mondo di Notte 3 (Ecco)*

the work of electro sound giants such as Giampiero Boneschi, Pierre Henry, Alain Gourager and Michel Colombier.

No classic example of the mondo genre would be complete without the punctuation of moral certitude, and in *Mondo di Notte*, two sequences offer a gloomy vision of man's future. The first deals with the development of artificial insemination at the world famous fertility clinic in Exeter, United Kingdom. Aspects of this operation are emphasised and elements of this practice, that must be laboratorised, are played up. The female donor for the process even has her eyes crudely scratched out on the film as if she should be ashamed of the ritual, coded as an unnatural act of the desperate.

The final denouement represents another case of 'deluded motherhood'. Drawing on ancient beliefs, a woman must climb the many steps of a Roman church in order to be blessed with children by a jewel-encrusted statue of Christ. As the woman in this film makes her painful ascent she is watched by a cameraman who intrusively snatches images of her pain. No clearer metaphor need be offered about the motives driving mondo filmmakers in their quest for the sensational, the desperate and the sad. Shakespeare is quoted again: "for there are more things in heaven and earth and between sunset and dawn than are dreamt of in your philosophy"

The film ends to the climax of the sweeping choral score on a still frame of the woman's face; another fixed and manufactured moment of human pain.

REALTÀ ROMANZESCA
(REALITIES AROUND THE WORLD)

Directed by Gianni Proia
(Italy, 1967)

Realtà Romanzesca is easily one of the oddest contributions to the mondo film canon. At first viewing, the film looks simple enough: a compilation of eleven staged re-enactments of 'light' news stories from around the world. The teletype machine, symbol of the global transfer of news communication, which brackets the film signifies the newsworthiness of the stories and has been included to lend the film a patina of journalistic credibility. A still of a newspaper headline ends each scene, but these look fake. The sequences unfold in a comic strip style. Hence the title: 'true stories' (as usual the English translation — *Realties around the World* — loses the nuanced irony of the original Italian). The common mondo elements are all staunchly in place. Stereotypes appear in the form of the French, who are always leering at young girls and/or crashing their cars; and indistinct Japanese and miserable Germanic characters. Musical signifiers are employed to exaggerate these stereotypes while shock elements are injected to revive audience interest. Indeed, Proia had already underscored his mondo credentials by contributing the classic mondo *Mondo di Notte* (*Ecco* — see review). Yet as *Realtà romanzesca* unfolds we discover that Proia has deployed the sequential montage of the film to create a freeform cinema experiment with powerful expressionistic tendencies. Expressionism should launch "an almost physical attack on the observer" according to

RS Furness, and mondo films, especially the work of Proia in this field, certainly offer such thrills. Far from being standard presentations of weird and wonderful 'real' events, the film offers a pungent display of generic qualities (fiction, documentary and travelogue) augmented with occasional philosophical diatribe and juvenile poetic sensibilities. The film recreates and re-presents the stories to us in colourful form (Proia even thanks Teletype at the end for "making these stories up") and the scenes in the film are unapologetically staged. Proia used real thespians to act out the roles but at times the acting is histrionic, as if the director strove to convey realism through amateurism. This dubious quality merely adds humour to the project. The opening virtuoso sequence of the converging of characters (a secondhand furniture dealer, a motorcyclist, a truck driver, a car full of Japanese businessmen, a commuter bus) towards a fatality in a southern French town, although ludicrous, is well staged, tense and captivating: "*Ce'st la fin de la Monde!*" cries an old man surveying the carnage. The film is expressionistic in the sense that it assaults the viewer with poetic abstractions of the 'true' event, none more so than in the surreal tale of a jaded reporter who deploys the wonders of newly developing international travel to conduct a long-range affair. "I needed a vacation from war, famine, pestilence, sudden death," he recounts, wearily and bizarrely. The sequence uses the time-play made possible by judicious film editing to evoke the possibilities of love conducted at a distance and via transatlantic phone calls. The lovers meet in one location before jetting off again to another (New York, San Francisco, Honolulu, Hong Kong). These trips are used as metaphors for the mind expansion offered by drugs as the couple's participation at an LSD party vividly illustrates. Suddenly, the scene switches to philosophical musings on the existential state. "You can defy the clock and the sun… but you can't control fate," the man despairs launching the scene into another dimension. Driving to a final rendezvous in Paris the couple crash into each other and are killed. The meeting, helped by Ortolani's music, is delivered in the giallo style. The psychedelic overtones to this strange sequence are highlighted by the use of fragmented shots of the sky and clouds (to symbolise infinity), 'unrealistic colours' (another expressionist trope), and a posterisation filter applied to the final car crash, making it a Warhol-like disaster scenario amplified for screaming shock. In these scenes Proia employs colour deftly as opposed to conventional form and metaphor to express emotion.

However, more conventional mondo sequences are present: a San Franciscan experiment in cryonics comes complete with a space-age musical abstraction of the celeste; there is computerised dating in Tokyo. Meanwhile the 'clan of the perfect wave' exhibits the usual mondo suspicion of youth culture. A surfer riffs on the endless quest for thrills, blonde girls are imaged, and a flute/bongo primitive jazz melody supplies a bohemian atmosphere. Yet almost all of these sequences bear traces of the avant garde, whether through futuristic musical arrangements, sometimes inept shock tactics, and rough montage. Throughout the film the still image is used to disrupt the illusion of 'reality': at the end of the patently daft tale of the truck driver and Tony Soprano look-a-like Francesco Scarab Otto and his unfaithful wife (the audience is left to imagine the fate of the adulterer as Scarabotto's discovery of him in bed with is wife leaps into monochrome stop-frame action — much like a photo-roman); the sexual fantasies of a Japanese loner are rendered through pin-up stills; an unsuccessful attempt by an Italian woman to wed her ailing fiancé before he dies ends with frozen portraits of her grief — the emotion of the moment of death imaged via freeze-frame. "A freeze-frame permits a gaze that is detached from the necessity for response or reaction," noted Thomas Sutcliffe, a near perfect account of such mondo voyeuristic tendency. The freeze-frames in *Realtà romanzesca* portray the imagination of remembered events — they are supposed

Realtà romanzesca

to convey the spirit of newspaper (photo) journalism to the reading of the stories told. The crude and primitive way in which these stills are rendered is again expressionistic rather than realistic. Poetic narrative rears its head in another odd sequence about a female suicide ("*Nulla* — nothing," she cries at numerous intervals). Shots of the woman leaving her apartment in a negligee before racing off in her sports car recall Claude LeLouch's stylised romance classic, *Un Homme et une Femme*. As she is about to leap from a bridge a man grabs her, pulling her towards him. Their eyes meet and she has a change of heart about suicide. "Null La La!" is her punch line to the scene, and the bombastic ballad, *Ha La Vita*, resounds around the scenario.

Composer Riz Ortolani has once again excelled in producing a brilliant and innovative score for what is a largely uneven film. The music ranges from bossa nova to jazz, and the composer's arranging skills (particularly for orchestra) are exemplified often and with good effect. The final sequence, "the making of a folk hero," pulls out all the stops in this regard. To a swinging Fellini-esque march a young mini-skirted woman strides through Naples, accompanied by the usual taunts, glances and wolf-whistles. A bearded man sidles up close to her and proceeds to follow her into the caged lift of an apartment block. Once inside the man refuses to let the women free until she has stripped naked. As she does this a crowd of onlookers builds (they can see through the iron shutters of the lift), yelping and whooping with delight at the free and public sexual degradation. The music increases the drama and tension of the scene as the man urges the girl on, goggle-eyed. The sexual politics of the mondo film are highlighted again in this climactic scene — the notion that a man becomes a 'folk hero' by forcing a woman to strip in public could only have been borne in an Italian, especially mondo, imagination.

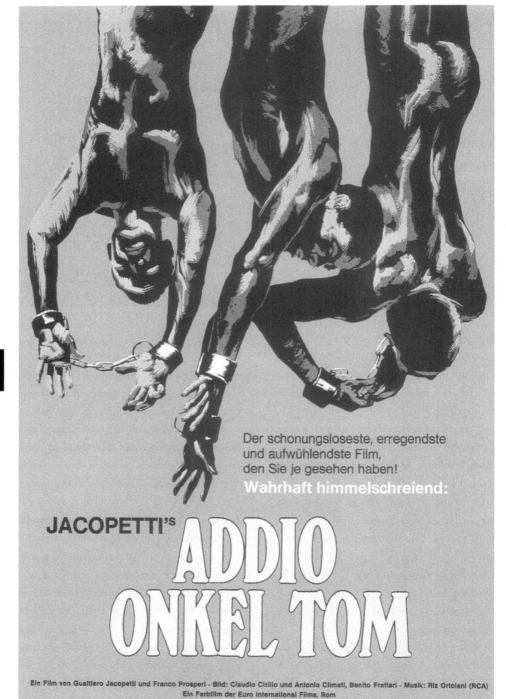

Der schonungsloseste, erregendste
und aufwühlendste Film,
den Sie je gesehen haben!
Wahrhaft himmelschreiend:

JACOPETTI's ADDIO ONKEL TOM

Ein Film von Gualtiero Jacopetti und Franco Prosperi · Bild: Claudio Cirillo und Antonio Climati, Benito Frattari · Musik: Riz Ortolani (RCA)
Ein Farbfilm der Euro International Films, Rom

Alemannia / *arabella* -Filmverleih

ADDIO ZIO TOM

Directed by Gualtiero Jacopetti and Franco Prosperi
(Italy, 1971)

Jacopetti and Prosperi's *Addio Zio Tom*, arguably the supreme mondo film, is one of the most staggering contributions to the history of cinematic art. It is a film conceived in the same epic proportions as *Africa Addio* (perhaps the purest distillation of mondo filmmaking aesthetics/ethics), and attacks the history of a continent as vast and complex. Like *Africa Addio* the film has attracted waves of controversy which, if not as politically and socially deep, were profound in the shocks the film delivered to the institutions of cinema and anyone intrigued by film narratives that defy belief. Jacopetti and Prosperi retreated, stung emotionally by the vitriol *Africa Addio* provoked and physically drained by travelling across the world's vastest continent for four years, from the documentary form and entered the world of the historical reconstruction film. This approach to historical reinvention was pioneered most effectively by British director Peter Watkins. Jacopetti and Prosperi made similar use of nonprofessional actors, used crew as makeshift actors and liked to close in uncomfortably on actors' faces. However, the Italians created a twisted and hallucinogenic variant of Watkins' intricate social critiques. Somewhat ironically, Watkins was hounded for the shock elements in his film *The War Game* and soon after left his homeland to work and live abroad). The British *Monthly Film Bulletin* dismissed *Zio Tom* describing the film unfavourably as an "exposé journalism parody" of Watkins' work. Respected American critic, Pauline Kael, in the *New Yorker* magazine, also dismissed the film, famously describing Jacopetti and Prosperi as "perhaps the most devious and irresponsible filmmakers who have ever lived". Yet the very aspects of the film that offended in the past are those which now excite and mesmerise: the grand, sweeping helicopter shots of the opening titles, invading the cotton-pickers below; the Bruegel-like gargoyle features of the lynchpin characters; the guileless depictions of the sexual perversions and slow-motion violence of brutal slavery; the lurid tropes of psychedelic

JACOPETTI's
explosiver Schocker:

ADDIO ONKEL TOM

Jemens / arabella -Filmverleih

1970s cinematic; the reflexive approach to the filmmaking process (used to praise the likes of Watkins' *Culloden* but to condemn *Zio Tom*) and the stream of consciousness adaptations of literary modes from Harriet Beecher Stowe via Fanny Kemble to Malcolm X (the film's title, and some of its impetus is borrowed from J C Furnas' 1956 study *Goodbye to Uncle Tom*). Jacopetti and Prosperi are on record as acknowledging the 'failures' of the film, lamenting that they did not, at the time, include more 'contextual' information (Jacopetti's recently issued 'director's cut' of the film attempts to amend this). But arguably this is unnecessary self-flagellation. *Zio Tom* is certainly a difficult, demanding and disturbing film portrait of an embarrassing and shocking period in American history; the film mocks the frayed concepts of American freedom and democracy and maybe it is for this reason that the film has been hated for so long. Truly everything about the film

is exaggerated, amplified and heightened — but rightly so; this was a disgusting and shameful part of history that needed to be 'felt' to be understood. At first glance the affiliations with radical black thought (Martin Luther King, Black Panther leaders such as Stokely Carmichael and the imagined slave testimonies of Leroy Jones and Nat Turner) seem odd and incongruous. Yet these accounts were delivered in a language of violence (and in William Styron's case, Pulitzer Prize-winning *Confessions of Nat Turner*, formally a stream of consciousness narrative) and it is this same gut reaction that Jacopetti and Prosperi urge audiences to feel, really feel. *Zio Tom* deliberately pushed the language of cinema to the limits of endurance, to shake the audience into some form of disturbed awareness. As a social comment it may be flawed, but as a lived experience there are few like it in film history. The reflexivity of the film is obvious in the way that scenes swing from the past to the present day and back again via the imagined here and now. Parallels are drawn between the treatments of black African slaves in the seventeenth century and treatment of Afro-Americans in the late 1960s/early 1970s. Events are linked and determined by each other. The memorable exchange between a 'contented' slave and the filmmakers (used for the Italian trailer for the film) illustrates this point precisely: a historical pathology paving way for the contradictions and difficulties of the historical present. As the 'crew' physically recoil from what this 'slave' is articulating they protest: "apologist… Uncle Tom!"

The considerations presented here on *Zio Tom* will be confined mostly to the original 1970s version of the film, devoid of the historical, documentary footage recently, as noted, reinstated. Important and interesting though this new edit is (with around thirteen minutes of 'real' documentary footage added and numerous cameos excised from the original cut) I want to consider the film as it was presented to audiences originally; if the film needs to be defended or reassessed then let us begin with the film viewed in those times past.

Jacopetti and Prosperi's cinematic language, perfected and honed since *Mondo Cane*, offers the hideous pictures of world events past and present to us in a style that is unflinching, decadent and ambiguous. And so the opening shots of *Zio Tom*, a soft-focused portrait of the grand colonial mansions of the American South and their inhabitants are designed, like those of the colonial powers of white South Africa in *Africa Addio*, to evoke images of a bad dream: ghostly, ethereal, surreal. Are they happy images or gross and sickly images? The audience must respond and

decide because the filmmakers here will not 'tell' you. Jacopetti said of this scene: "I believed it was enforcing the idea of the absurdity, the 'virtuality' — one would say today — of the situation" — a message one could extend to the entire film. The first formal scenes introduce Jacopetti and Prosperi as cinejournalists ("travelling photographers" as they identify themselves on the side of a wagon) conducting an enquiry into the slave trade of the south, to a dinner audience of real historical characters (John Randolph, John Pithiou). This scene is shot via point of view camera work and we hear the voices of the crew interacting with the characters. These are the scenes that provoked disquiet in original reviews of the film, Jacopetti and Prosperi's mischievous black humour seemingly unappreciated. Scenes based on the shipment of slaves show the stinking brutality of this practice in all its gory details, complete with outbreaks of runny diarrhoea and dysentery, and forced feeding where blood

flows out of the mouths of slaves together with a sickening combination of broken, rotten teeth and a disgusting porridge substance. The awfulness of the experience is contrasted with one of Riz Ortolani's trademark sweeping scores, this time a reworking of his Flying Clipper/Mediterranean Holiday score, the evocation of high adventure and sea-bound freedom contrasting violently with the sub-animal cramped existence of the slaves. When the 'cargo' arrives at Louisiana to be 'processed' more horrors occur when slaves are caged (images for the promotion of the film originate from these shots), are fumigated and hung upside down to cure epilepsy (there are some excellent demonstrations of Climati's camerawork here), before being fed cornmeal. In a suddenly absurd development, the white slaver protests to the camera "this is not an Italian restaurant!" There are more examples of Jacopetti and Prosperi's trademark counterpoint methods where a violent sequence recording the sexual abuse of black slaves by poor white plantation workers (known as "The Crackers") is scored with pomp rock music trimmings: a highly surreal moment. Another Jacopetti and Prosperi trademark is that of the 'ugly' character, and there are many examples in Zio Tom (almost always white — did the objections in the 1970s betray some racism of their own?). One of the most memorable is a plantation worker looking on with scorn at the public castration of a black 'rapist'. The screams of the victim blend with the worker's gaping, mocking, hideous laugh as her mouth devours the entire screen. In her classic anti-slavery journal, English actress Fanny Kemble depicted the sordidness of the southern white slavers; Zio Tom simply visualises this cinematically. By now it is noticeable that the cinematography in Zio Tom is superb: shot by Antonio Climati, with his trademark wide-angled close-ups and long tracking shots (and combinations of the two) this time augmented by the work of Claudio Cirillo who beautifully, if controversially, recreated these landscapes of this history of death and murder in the Haitian nightmare paradise of dictator François 'Papa Doc' Duvalier.

The by now common jarring edit takes place when a brief refuge in a modern-day New Orleans funeral is interrupted with a solemn bell tolling as an introduction to a critique of how the Protestant church of the time peddled racist ideology: "slavery is a divine institution ordered and sanctioned by God." As ever, the cuts determine and shape the viewer's shock reflexes.

The documentary reflexivity of the film, another commonly derided aspect, occur in moments when the camera crew interact with the on-screen characters (and to a lesser degree to those who recognise the key crew members Jacopetti, Prosperi and location manager Giampaolo Lomi playing characters): the Georgian mansion where the mammy of the house tells the crew, as they track past her, to "shush!"; the slave market at New Orleans where one of the administrators borrows a ball-point pen from behind the camera. The foetid stench of racism permeates the entire film no more so than the section on white sexual slavery and perversion — jaded white plantation owners ritually abuse young black girls — and that of the various 'scientific' justifications of racial theory — i.e. Professor Cartwright who has 'studied' black physiogimy and concluded that black cranial capacity, sweat, hair and eyes all point to "an inferior race". The 'perverse politics' of the mondo film play out in the slave markets where black bodies of all persuasion are

New Orleans slave market in *Addio Zio Tom*

marketed for the sexual appetites of white rulers: a large, sweaty man called Buzz, oils naked female slaves before they are auctioned; a dwarf called 'The General' parades "virgin whores" for the camera in an exotically photographed pornographic/voyeuristic segment that raises the audiences confused stimulated/repulsed emotional responses; and a stereotypically camp homosexual responsible for the 'sexual freaks' (one statuesque black man has "three balls"). At a wax museum, Madame La Laurie sexually exploits blacks, male and female, to satisfy her Sadeian impulses. Then an underage girl prostitute begins to seduce the filmmaker/cameraman in a wilfully uncomfortable alienation scenario: the viewer appears to get into bed with the girl. Uncomfortable viewing — and it should be. The sexual mistreatment of blacks reaches is zenith at the stud farm of Mr Bighorn who 'breeds' slaves like dogs (he refers to the women as bitches/wenches and the men as studs). The violent animalistic rape of a new

'virgin' girl heralds the climax of the film and instils a vengeful fury sated by the subsequent horrific massacres of Nat Turner's imagination, transposed to the present day. In the context of the time the 'black power'-style revenge for all of this misery, abuse, violence and death is designed to act as a supportive gesture towards civil rights movements and their antecedents (this seems to have also been ignored in reviews of the day). This violent, surreal and anti-narrative finale is probably the best moment in the film and would be unrepeatable now (although echoes of the film style are located in Jodorowsky's trippy Zen western *El Topo* made around the same time) infused as they are with horror, psychedelia, testimony and fear. The slow-motion Peckinpah-style violence of the scenes echoes the blood splattered 'human' hunting trip depicted earlier in reverse; this time the blacks are the hunters. Here, violence is stylised and deployed by Jacopetti and Prosperi as an antidote to or reaction against the 'real'

Louisiana processing centre in *Addio Zio Tom*

JACOPETTI'S
explosiver Schocker:
ADDIO ONKEL TOM

violence of documentary news reportage and mainstream cinema traditions, perfectly in accordance with Peckinpah's own philosophy: "to negate violence it must be shown for what it is: a horrifying brutalizing, destructive, ingrained part of humanity". You may be sickened by these images and words and sounds but they are located within a cruel reality and therefore must be (in)digested openly and honestly. As well as the slow-motion moments the Miami sequence includes a kaleidoscope of other cinematic effects: shock cuts, contrasts between temporal 'reality' and slow-motion 'fantasy', soft focus, voice-over effects, daylight horror/gore etc. Part of the sequence where two black militants/slaves, updated from the Nat Turner testimony, have axed a family to death, and then proceed to ransack their apartment, recall Antonioni's beautiful, poetic, slow-motion explosions of consumer durables in *Zabriskie Point*. The whites in this scene are made grossly evil by shooting them as idealised, advertising language images. The most haunting scene (which has been reinstated in the director's cut) features some shots of a space launch at Cape Canaveral in Florida. As we watch shots of rockets launching the narrator warns whites of "running away from the past" a bitter and accusatory condemnation of technological capitalist 'advancement' being used as attempt to deny and repress the grim reality of historical materialism and a warning to the future.

Jacopetti and Prosperi's parting shot of the film, that "This film is a documentary. The events occurred in history and the characters really existed" only muddies the waters. It seems you will find *Zio Tom* compulsive, fascinating, awful viewing or stomach churning exploitation. Whether this is in reference to the original or to the director's cuts is immaterial; you either get the malevolent terrifying beauty of *Zio Tom* and its ugly message or you don't.

AUSTRALIA AFTER DARK

Directed by John D. Lamond
(Australia, 1975)

It is fitting that Australia has its own, not entirely disgraceful, contribution to the field of the mondo film. The country after all features prominently in Jacopetti, Prosperi and Cavrara's *Mondo Cane*, both in its ancient and modern conceptions. Dubious talents of the female lifesavers of Bondi Beach are paraded halfway through the film, indicative supposedly of an island paradise of athletic blonde 'Sheilas' and ruggedly handsome 'Bruces'. The somewhat sad finale to the film, documenting the Cargo Cults of Port Moresby, tries to suggest that in the hypermodern can be found the remnants of primordial beliefs, ideologies that can be weirdly transposed into the ever-advancing technologies of futurism.

The director John D. Lamond continues this ancient/modern or primitive/enlightened dichotomy in his quirky look at contemporary Australian mores and customs. Australia is on the one hand (according to the narration) a "land hostile to men" and on the other a sexy modern playground. Native cultures were swept aside by white men who were, according to Dennis Gascoigne's script, "hard-drinking descendants of convicts." Over shots of an ambulance racing to deal with a suicide at the Sydney Harbour Bridge, the narrator, Hayes Gordon, warns us that what we are about to see is "not all beautiful… but it is all true". This prologue is followed by some psychedelic titles where a fully naked woman gyrates beneath a strobing flashlight. Thus we can settle back and enjoy the film safe in the knowledge that all the required elements of mondo — the pretence of documentary fact; sensationalism; titillation — are firmly in place.

Australia After Dark was Lamond's first feature as director. Lacking the funds to create other genre films, such as horror, for what he described as the "Melbourne drive-ins", he realised that the mondo documentary offered a cheap and potentially lucrative alternative. Lamond channelled a sensationalist Melbourne newspaper ironically called *Truth* and *Mondo Cane* successfully, imitating the cycle of 'titillation, humour, pathos, oddity' he

At Last! the Australia you've always wanted to see but... have never DARED!

AUSTRALIA AFTER DARK

course less refined than their French counterparts; instead of orchestrating them gracefully against an avant garde symphony, Penberthy makes them roll around together in a sticky, acrylic mess. Another *Mondo Cane* trope is 'weird food' and Lamond supplies us with snake dishes and witchetty grubs, which are fried alive. Melbourne, like Rome, has its own museum of the macabre in the shape of the Jail museum where death mask of murderers, rapists, and occasionally their executioners, can be viewed. Oz witchcraft is also on display. The figure of Eddie Pielke, a genuine white witch, is slightly undercut by an entirely staged satanic ritual featuring throbbing organ music, a naked woman and a dripping phallic candle.

A section on 'perversions' focuses on Madame Lash and her club for fetishists. Lamond filmed an orgy at her club, admitting later it was fabricated and that his crew had built an inverted cross for penitents to be tied to. Any eroticism is quickly dispelled by the shot of a man wearing only a motorcycle helmet and extremely tight black underpants. Other sexploitation tricks include nude and mud bathing (à la *Mondo Cane*) which the director tries to justify by calling it a re-enactment of a "folk memory". There is also a gay wedding, a brothel, and the shooting of porn movies.

Lamond has certainly fully absorbed the mondo director's disingenuousness. An extended montage of female bottoms is justified as a fetishist "national characteristic".

himself ascribed to Jacopetti and Prosperi's oeuvre. This meant moving between the real tragedy of the Native Australian descent into homelessness and alcoholism to the outlandish absurdity of self-styled 'cosmic entertainer' Count Copernicus, a cabaret act of dubious taste. The poverty of Aboriginal alcoholism is contrasted with the longest bar in the world, and what looks like the fattest beer drinker in the world, consuming a yard of ale, played purely for comic effect by adopting the stereotype of the permanently pissed Aussie white male. The film also included the requisite dramatic ballad, in this case the song Turn Back The Times written by Eddie Pielke (see below) and sung by Leonie Goodwin, a little known session singer, who was once part of the short-lived Australian soft-rock group White Wine.

Sex and nudity are naturally to the fore. There is a nod to Yves Klein in the shape of Wes Penberthy who is filmed in his Tom Boy Studios smearing his female models with paint before plastering them over his enormous canvases. Australian artists are of

I suppose it could be true... A more lyrical moment occurs at the end when Gina Allen, a naked scuba diver, glides through the ultramarine ocean bed, or the "mother sea which gave us life", accompanied by Johnny Pearson's Sleepy Shore, previously the theme for the TV series *Owen, M.D.* Lamond also tried to give the film a 'European' feel by using French and Italian library music extensively on the soundtrack and especially the title sequence which is straight out of one of Luigi Scattini's mondo classics.

Lamond took the sleaze credentials acquired in the dark arts of mondo (and the funds from the success of the film) and applied them successfully to a subsequent sex documentary, *The ABC of Love and Sex: Australia Style* (1978), and *Felicity* (1979), one of many dodgy schoolgirl erotic films of the

era. His work was celebrated in Mark Hartley's excellent documentary on 'Ozploitation' cinema, *Not Quite Hollywood* (2009).

Despite being (somewhat predictably) described by the *MFB* as "dull and tasteless", *Australia After Dark* is actually a pleasing, entertaining and novel contribution to the mondo genre. It lacks the cynicism, morbidity and ugliness of many other mid-1970 efforts. For non-Australians, the film manages to avoid many of the clichéd stereotypes coming out of the country and offers instead a few subversive characters. In Michael Powell's 1966 film *They're a Weird Mob*, an Italian, played by Walter Chiari, stumbles around Australia trying to comprehend the country's way of life. John Lamond has given us a glimpse into the strange world, half familiar and half utterly bewildering, that Chiari saw.

Africa Addio – Massacre of Arabs in Zanzibar

CHAPTER 5
"EVERY INCREDIBLE SCENE IS REAL"

The Frame of Mondo

The concept and practice of framing in any documentary film means the construction of specific codes, practices and meanings in an attempt at telling a story in a particular manner. According to documentary filmmaker and theorist Michael Rabiger: "the message… for documentary [film] makers is that framing is arranged — as far as is legitimate — according to an interpretation of the subject's meaning; composition helps define the subtext." In documentary and ethnographic film, codes are used to convey strong meaning about the subject(s) whether these are Bill Nichols' 'documentary modes of representation' (expositional; observational; interactive; reflexive; performative) or Michael Renov's 'poetic tendencies' (to record; to persuade or promote; to analyse or interrogate; to express).

The film camera exists as a substitute for human movement, hand-held cameras in the cinéma vérité movement emphasised this. Such techniques, taken up by Antonio Climati and Benito Frattari and then others, in mondo films were driven to extremes; a direct and thrilling, if controversial, perversion of the attributes normally found in documentary/ethnographic filmmaking modes. In his book, *Ethnographic Film*, Karl G Heider posits what he calls "attribute dimensions" against which a film's 'ethnographic status' can be verified. Those forbidden, and those which mondo film flagrantly celebrate, are fragmentation; inappropriate use of music; the denial of the presence of the filmmaker; images and acts shown out of context; people depicted as "only faceless masses"; distortion of temporal aspects. Critical to the manner in which mondo films transgress these 'rules' is the way that they are framed and shot, the ways in which the subjects of mondo documentary are recorded and presented to audiences.

Filmmakers are limited and bound by the cinema screen and its sharply defined 'frame'. Attempts at overcoming this have included the introduction of larger format film stocks, and processes such as Cinerama, CinemaScope and TechniScope. The latter of these processes was used most effectively by mondo directors particularly and spectacularly in Jacopetti and Prosperi's *Africa Addio*, an exemplar of mondo framing devices, where not only did the 'scope' of the subject (a feature film survey of the upheavals of large sections of a vast continent) warrant such framing, but immersion of the spectator into this often frightening and shocking 'reality' demanded that the screen and the frame be suitably immense. In his book on *Africa Addio*, John Cohen defines this as a 'new' approach to the documentary film where film "presents reality 'as big as life'".

Climati's approach to capturing moments of such realities regularly bordered on the insane. Consider the attempts made during *Africa Addio* by Jacopetti, Nievo and Climati to record a military mutiny and racist mass killing

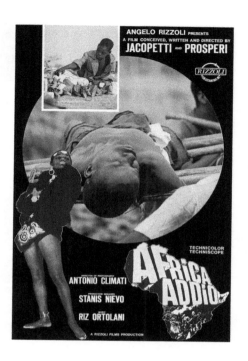

of Arabs by black Africans in Dar es Salaam. As it is seen in the film, and recorded in the book of the film, the drive to capture good pictures of such African horrors almost resulted in death:

"The camera has barely a second to photograph the scene, for as the soldiers spot the car they wave it off. Jacopetti, who is driving, backs out slowly to give Climati as much time to film as possible. But the slowness enrages one soldier who rushes up to the car, raises his rifle over his head, and smashes it down butt-first into the windscreen... The glass shatters and fragments spray across Jacopetti's face, cutting a vein behind his ear..."

"The scenes are so terrifying and horrific that at times one has to look away from the screen." DOMENICA DEL CORRIERE REVIEW OF *AFRICA ADDIO*

Africa Addio – Arrest of Jacopetti, Nievo and Climati in Zanzibar

He stops the car, but Climati keeps his camera rolling. Two soldiers jerk the door open and haul Jacopetti out. Climati, ensconced in the back seat, relentlessly films the whole sequence — Jacopetti being pulled away, the side of his head streaming with blood, turning his face back to the car to shout more instructions".

"Climati kept filming until they reached into the car and grabbed him too," recalled Jacopetti of this bizarre event, an excellent portrait of the madness required to create the stunning pictures exhibited throughout the film. The dangers of capturing these moments on film in this manner came vividly to life when a report in the Italian journal *L'Espresso* accused the Italian crew of colluding with mercenaries (trying to recapture the Congo town Boende from rebel groups) in order to get 'better pictures':

"... *the South African mercenary Ben Louw...*

put his finger on the trigger of his machine gun and then, instead of shooting, turned round towards the first truck less than ten metres behind him, saw Climati the cameraman, who was looking through his camera, eye to the aperture, hands on the focus finder; saw Nievo and Jacopetti at Climati's side... leaning on the tripod to keep it as steady as possible; and asked him if they were 'ready'. But they weren't. The rebels had appeared suddenly far down the road, and they were much too far away to be photographed without changing the lens. And there was no time to lose because Louw was in a hurry. Louw turned around for the second time, then a third, cursing and saying that he was going to shoot anyway; but at that moment Climati signalled with his hand for Louw to go ahead. The Arriflex rolled together with the machine gun mechanism... the rebels fell onto the road."

Although this account, by the journalist and former protégée of Jacopetti, Carlo

Africa Addio

Gregoretti (*L'Espresso*, December 20, 1964), was later refuted by Jacopetti (and disproved after a bitter Italian court case), a vivid portrait remains of the camera acting like a gun and of the obsessive, aggressive nature of this type of cinematography. Jacopetti once described Climati as a "human dolly", being "able to do on his own what normally you would need many machines and many people to achieve", a weird embodiment of Jean Rouch's 'direct-cinema cameraman' those that "know how to walk with their cameras... becoming the living cameras, the 'cine-eye' of Vertov", and his fluid, restless camera work is certainly one of the principle, irrefutable features of the mondo aesthetic (*Zio Tom* production manager Giampaolo Lomi also once spoke to me of his amazement at Climati's dedication to obtaining startling film images).

The anamorphic stretching distortion of the TechniScope mondo film tries to compensate for the limits of the film screen/frame, instead immersing the audience right into the action. This works in the landscape shots of *Africa Addio, Zio Tom* etc. but also paradoxically in the extreme close-ups where faces loom large, occasionally beautiful, and sometimes hideous into our mental or even physical space. Climati's work encompasses both of these attributes; the panorama of a helicopter shot of a landscape and the violent thrusting of human facial landscapes working as one.

"Good close-ups are lyrical," Béla Bálasz once observed, "reflected expressions of our own subconscious feeling" and in the mondo film it is this notion of the "[camera] eye as the gateway to the strange dimensions of the soul" that is sought after vigorously. Bálasz's notion of the "silent soliloquy" where film faces reveal the depths of human emotion often without speaking literally can be amply found in the cinematography of mondo. Italian cinema understands this completely anyway as Clint Eastwood observed from working with Leone: "Leone believed… as a lot of Italian director's do, that the face means everything."

Composition of shots becomes paramount and the shape of the widescreen image dictates the pictorial use of space, that which, according to Ralph Stevenson and J R Debrix, creates "an architecture, an equilibrium, a meaning". Yet also critical to the frame of mondo is the relationship between the composition and movement within these compositions. And one of the most notable attributes of this in the mondo film is the use of the zoom. Climati is a master of this too and his technique has been widely copied in subsequent (especially Italian) mondo films. The zoom in mondo films is a framing device used for visual punctuation, a trait that often irritated reviewers (especially British) of mondo films weaned on the solemn neo-realism/ vérité approach to documentary filmmaking (Italian film generally exhibits a more relaxed attitude to such alienation effects: De Sica and Bertolucci being just two directors happy to deploy the zoom to simulate violent emotion). Climati also makes use in his work with Jacopetti of the 'reverse' zoom, a device that moves from the specific to the general in a dizzying physical manner. This enhances sequences of extreme violence such as the animal harvests in *Africa Addio* where the camera follows the trajectory of the high-powered bullet towards the unknowing animal victim, and the blank, sullen stares of Mau Mau detainees. A relation of the zoom

is the zip-pan (or swish pan or whip shot), a very fast turn that is used in mondo as a device to blur sensations and switch between scenarios. Then oblique framing occurs when Climati swirls around subjects (the suspended slaves and dream sequences of *Zio Tom*), or shoots from below or within figures (the simulated Zulu rituals *Africa Addio*).

The violence of the camera perspective, what Carol J Clover, discussing the horror film, defines as an "assaultative gaze", the effect the camera has of violating and attacking the subject, either imaginatively (as in fantasy of horror) or in 'reality' (accusations levelled at *Africa Addio*) is a powerful concept. In recalling that the Italian title for the British voyeur-thriller *Peeping Tom* is *L'Occhio Uccide* ('the eye that kills') and Clover connects this form of cine-voyeurism, a strong feature of Italian horror in particular (see the threateningly subjective camerawork in Andrea Bianchi's *Nude per L'Assassino* for example) with mondo methodology. In making *L'Occhio Selvaggio* (*The Wild Eye*), Paolo Cavara was exploring precisely this troublesome aspect of the intrusive world of the mondo cameraman, his apparatus, what he shows us and what we see (in our own minds).

This terror mode, arguably the definitive, long-lasting effect of mondo cinema reached its apogee in Climati's own mid-period mondo creation *Ultime Gride dalla Savana* (Climati later recreated certain aspects of his craft in *Natura Contro* but these images were a pale imitation of his greatest work). By describing the film as a "beautifully filmed hymn to death", the reviewer offers a fitting tribute to the cinematographic framing and composition of the mondo film and its prime exponent.

Africa Addio – Hippopotamus hunt

AFRICA ADDIO

Directed by Gualtiero Jacopetti and Franco Prosperi
(Italy, 1965)

Charles Kilgore once described Jacopetti and Prosperi's *Africa Addio* as "the *Moby Dick* of mondo movies" and it is not hard, given the film's grandiose ambition (the crew covered more than 130,000 miles across one of the world's largest continents), its length (over 139 minutes), and the personal cost (three years), to see why. The bold moral ambiguity of the film has ensured that its reception has been, since release, difficult. *Africa Addio* tends to invite polarisation: the Italian Socialist newspaper *Avanti* argued the film was "photographed through a distorted lens… an orgy of sadism and fascist racism," while the Conservative *Il Tempo* found the film "a remarkable piece of reportage… excellently shot and conceived". At a screen talk in 2003 with Jacopetti the audience seemed divided as to whether the film showed great courage in critiquing many aspects of African independence or was biased, selective and distorted. Most importantly, Jacopetti and Prosperi refused to participate in what John Cohen describes as the two "conspiracies concerning Africa": the first is that Africans are incapable of governing themselves and are making a mess of everything; the second is a refusal to acknowledge the turmoil and confusion in Africa (then and arguably still now) for fear of 'offending' the emerging African independence movements. According to Cohen, Jacopetti and Prosperi "participated in neither of these conspiracies". And what

"After a century of colonization let us not forget that it is partially a deformed image of our own selves that… reflects back at us."
BARBET SCHROEDER

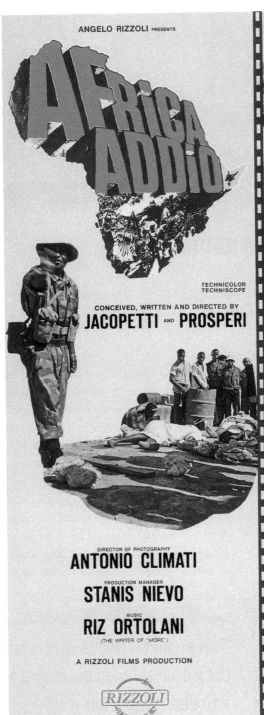

Africa Addio does, very powerfully, is to portray this turmoil, and other aspects of this vital historical phase, in a film that is somehow a 'beautiful' image of the "agony" of a continent in violent transition.

The ferocious hatred aimed at the film when it was released was notable, both in reviews by the 'liberal' west and in the revolutionary critiques of Third Cinema, where postcolonial theorists such as Octavio Getino and Fernando Solanas harshly denounced the project ("the more exploited a man is... the more he resists, the more he is viewed as a beast. This can be seen in *Africa Addio* by the fascist Jacopetti; the African savages, killer animals, wallow in abject anarchy once they escaped from their white protection. Fantasy has been replaced by phantoms, and man is turned into an extra who dies so Jacopetti can comfortably filmed his execution," they wrote in *Towards a Third Cinema*). As recently as 1994 Kenneth M. Cameron in *Africa on Film* labelled the film a "low" and "sensational" nonfiction film (as opposed to a "high" and "environmental" one). Despite this, *Africa Addio* remains Jacopetti and Prosperi's best film, the pinnacle of mondo filmmaking and one of the most powerful cinematic documents ever made.

Africa Addio was set against a backdrop of literary and film portraits of the 'dark continent' mostly imbued with nineteenth century colonialist beliefs. These were the ideologies perpetuated by the myths of colonisation, the heroic adventures of Stanley, Churchill et al. These are the myths that Jacopetti and Prosperi, spurred into action by a letter from an English friend Carolyn Thompson (alerting Jacopetti to the brutal change taking place in Africa) desperately wanted to explore and portray. In

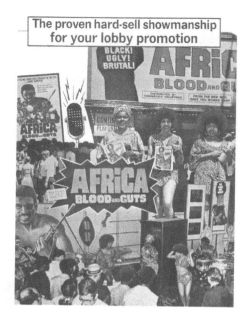

fellow Italian Alberto Moravia's accounts of travels in Africa, *Which Tribe do You Belong To?*, the ancient myths of Africa fade and die (or at least transmogrify) before the writer's eyes. In articulating the violent changes being thrust upon Africa — "we have moved away from the old colonialism with its decaying bungalows, its Victorian hotels, its slave-owners' bars, its dusty shops, and indeed its Conrad-like picturesqueness" — Moravia was echoing the images and sounds of *Africa Addio*. If *Africa Addio* owes anything to these colonial assumptions it is more like the assessment of the colonial myths as elucidated by Sven Lindqvist, whose brilliant account of the psychotic violence

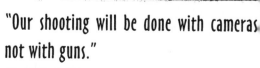

"Our shooting will be done with cameras not with guns."
ARMAND DENIS

Africa Addio

of the British imperial project, *Exterminate All the Brutes* argues a similarly bleak pathology of the colonisation of Africa. For Lindqvist the work of Conrad reveals a grim portrait of the true evils of empire and *Africa Addio*, in its savage critique, offers the same ugly truism; it forces us, the audience, to reflect and be shamed by our disgusting history. The film was not even released in France (despite an expensive translation job and a lush, full colour article in *Paris Match*), due to political pressure imposed onto the producer Angelo Rizzoli by the De Gaulle government concerned with France's own 'colonial' problems in Algeria. Most damagingly the accusations levelled at Jacopetti and Prosperi of "voluntary homicide" (in response to the Carlo Gregoretti claims in *L'Espresso*) although later thrown out of court, along with the subsequent political wranglings over the content and production of the film, restricted its proper reception. The

reputation of *Africa Addio* therefore has always preceded any sensible or careful analysis of the film's content.

Jacopetti and Prosperi from the outset were keen to capture and expose the fragmentation of myths of colonial and postcolonial Africa. Indeed this is expressed in the film's opening vista of a handing over ceremony in Kenya. As the standards of the coloniser and the colonised are exchanged the camera suddenly zooms in and freeze-frames on the two hands — one black, one white — the moment accentuated by the dramatic, violent stabs of the score. It is a jolting moment of ritual, exchange and hostility. The opening text of the film then outlines the philosophy behind the realisation of the film beautifully:

"The Africa of the great explorers, the huge land of hunting and adventure, adored by entire generations of children has disappeared forever. To that age-old Africa, swept away and destroyed by the tremendous speed of progress, we have said farewell. The devastation, the slaughter, the massacres which we assisted belong to a new Africa — one which if it emerges from its ruins to be more modern, more rational, more functional, more conscious — will be unrecognisable. On the other hand the world is racing towards better times. The new America rose from the ashes of a few white men, all the redskins and the bones of million of buffalo. The new carved up Africa will rise again upon the tombs of a few white men, millions of black men and upon those immense graveyards that were once its game reserves. The endeavour is so modern and recent that there is no room to discuss it at the moral level. The purpose of this film is only to bid farewell to the old Africa that is dying and entrust to history the documentation of its agony."

This philosophy is further exemplified by the subsequent scenes giving Africa 'back to the Africans'. The idea of Africa entering the modern world is demonstrated by the adoption of new technologies (microphones for electioneering) and new 'democratic' leaders. The peoples that sit transfixed by these new leaders are represented as 'peasants' — still backward and awaiting enlightenment. "Europe is leaving in a hurry and on tiptoe… just at the moment when Africa needs it the most… even if it has given far more than it has taken," accuses the narration, thus articulating Jacopetti's wry take on the momentous events unfolding before the camera lens. This next section of the film deals in contrasts to represent this changeover in its rapidity: in Kenya the chaotic, wild street celebrations of the new black independence is contrasted with the almost silent solemnity of white church services; the new black army "marches in" aggressively while the English colonial regiments "parade out" (with accompanying pompous military music). At a reception garden party the 'symbiosis' of the old whites and the new blacks is visually illustrated with shots of two women both sporting enormous buckteeth. Later in the film the contrast is highlighted between South Africa, "sanctuary of the whites" (shot in the sickly style of a shampoo commercial) with Zulu tribes (the camera here shooting low and thrusting from behind emphasising the 'primitive' rhythms of black cultures). By cleverly manipulating the techniques offered by the film art — framing, musical score, and narration — political, albeit sensational demarcations are made. At the finale of the film the black poverty of 'apartheid', workers in the gold and diamond mines, is contrasted with the wealth the white population makes from the international trading of these materials.

123

JACOPETTI AND PROSPERI
AFRICA ADDIO

Pile of amputated Tutsi hands in *Africa Addio*

The film throughout is terrifyingly beautiful and the use of Technicolor and the widescreen process TechniScope are stunning. Rarely has a film about a certain location of the world been so luxuriously visualised using the film camera. In contrast to the common vérité belief of the epoch that documentary needs to be rendered in monochrome, the colour process here greatly heightens the impact of the scenes, and is also exploited in the press material, graphics and posters associated with the film (the *MFB*, however, claimed the beauty of the shots compromised its "impartiality"). This 'creativity' may be a troubling aspect for documentary purists but is arguably the reason why the film is so fascinating when assessed today. The camerawork of Antonio Climati is superb throughout, even when he is stuck within helicopters, filming from the air, or shooting from fast moving cars. The shots are exquisitely composed and worthy in themselves of the Donatello David (the Italian version of an Oscar) the film eventually received. Inventive compositions, include Vaseline-lensed portraits of the events resulting from the white exodus from East Africa (farms and land being sold to black Africans) and the recollections of Mau Mau atrocities (the sites of 'terrorist' massacres of whites are eerily imaged), extensive use of zooms, intrusive close-ups and glossily picturesque location shots. A particularly vivid example of this is the footage of a young zebra being rescued by the Wildlife Society along the Zambezi river, which ends with the unfortunate animal being air-lifted out by helicopter against a vibrant orange sunset — one of the most iconic images of the film. Moravia's observation that "In Africa the aeroplane is more revealing than the car", was put to effective cinematic use. Many of the aircraft shots assist in either the panorama of the landscape (Cape Town) or the horror of decolonisation (Zanzibar) — and sometimes both. The film is again edited brilliantly using the familiar devices of the shock cut (the depiction of the East African 'animal harvests', "operation cropping" where exotic images of the imagined old Africa violently explode with the carnage and bloodshed of elephants, hippos and gazelle being shot to pieces). The commentary arguing "the truth is that in all of Africa there is only one truly ferocious animal: man" hints at an ecological argument being presented by the filmmakers, known for their interest in

124

Africa Addio

conservation. In addition, the score, composed by Riz Ortolani, is still acknowledged as one of his best. As well as the use of his trademark lush orchestrations which add emotion to events, and his ability to connote filmic genre traits (Wild West, comedy) his mesmerising symphony of terror for the Acholi animal slaughter scenes, where each blade and bullet moves synchronously with the music was a unique, virtuoso piece of film scoring.

Two sequences in particular strengthen the notion that not only was *Africa Addio* in fact an accurate portrait of the times but that it was prescient in its warnings of both the corruption taking place within the new African leaderships and the interference of outside powers (the politics of the Cold War) in such socio-political vacuums. The first represents the slaughter of the Watutsi tribe by the Hutu in Rwanda, a tribal yet colonially affected act of reprisal and revenge. Various gory scenes illustrate this tragic picture: a pile of fifty-two severed Watutsi hands found in a hidden forest location; the Kagera river overflowing with rotting corpses. These are eventually burnt on a hilltop bonfire in a perversely picturesque silhouette image shot.

The second concerns the events in the former Belgium Congo in November 1964 where the town of Boende had been looted and captured by communist-backed Simba rebel groups. The new leadership of Moise Tshombe employed mercenaries (*Les Affreux* — the horrors) to help recapture the town and Jacopetti was there to film it. The tragic circularity of such killings is described in the film thus:

"Africa has no fallen soldiers on either side — it only has corpses. It's an absurd and tragic dance that's been going on for five years now. Whites against blacks, and blacks against whites. They take turns killing and dying, like a cruel children's game. No one wins and no one loses, once and for all. No condition is definitive except for white and black deaths that together infect the ruins and dissolve, amidst the buzz of flies, into absolute biological equality."

This demonstrates that such aspects of African history repeat themselves with tragic monotony. "*Africa Addio* still exists, it is still relevant today. This comforts me immensely," Jacopetti stated in later years. His intuition of the future, the "picture of this agony", is now there for all to see.

There are, however, lighter, more

Africa Addio

traditionally 'mondo' aspects to the film. A sequence on foxhunting in Kenya, where the British imperialists, because there are no foxes in Kenya, hunt instead a black houseboy dragging dead meat (we see women applying lipstick as the opening of the scene) is reminiscent of earlier Jacopetti/Prosperi stylistics. There is even an amusing scene critiquing the new mass media image of Africa being sold to the world. A pulsating Zulu tribal dance is revealed, as the camera pulls out, to be the invention of an English film crew attempting to simulate the 'old Africa' before it disappears. The 'new Africa' is revealed through shots depicting the dancers changing from their 'traditional costume' into modern fashions before they drive off in fast cars and on motorcycles. The African girls are peeped at through the gaps in a thatched tent as the commentary observes:

"The African female has discovered she is a woman and is beginning to behave as such. She wants to be modern because she feels that the past is against her. When she was naked, she had two mammary glands. Now that she is clothed she has two breasts. She does not want to display herself. She wants to be looked at to make you guess what's under her alluring clothes. She covers her intimacy not out of modesty but to be flirtatious. She undresses to surrender, and dresses to attack. Naked, she was prey, like a black female. Clothed she is a tyrant like a white woman. Africa covers itself consciously and all wrapped up in the veils of its consciousness, Africa disappears."

The female body is used as a metaphor, a symbol of 'pure Africa' for the changing continent. This is not to say that the (vaguely sexist) caricature of these representations was not attributed to white populations too. Examples of Moravia's construct of the colonialist Protestant "homo Victorianus" are amply displayed (the authorities holding the Mau Mau trials, Sir Richard Turnbull, the last governor of "the last outpost of empire" Tanganyika) where the English are mocked as arrogant, upper-crust eccentrics, unconcerned with the effects of their imperialist actions and speaking with daft, clipped accents. In constructing the film Jacopetti and Prosperi transgressed the practical rules of sensitive, ethical documentary filmmaking. Frequently

Africa Addio

they resorted to bribes, manipulation and deception to secure their footage and the suspicion with which documentary subjects regard cinejournalists had to be faced up to (Moravia, again in *Which Tribe...?* observed this tendency: his photographing of a group of women from Chad was criticised by young nationalists witnessing the event as "neo-colonialist").

At the end of the film, after a typical Jacopettian comparison between the history of penguins isolated on a lost continent, and the history of the white colonialist invaders of that continent, Jacopetti and Prosperi offered the following conclusion:

"This film, born without prejudice does not attempt and has never attempted to create new ones. It has only tried to document the reality of how blood spilled anywhere represents a loss of wealth for the entire world."

Sadly it seems that the world of cinema and the broader geo-political strata has paid scant regard to the concerns raised in *Africa Addio*, and this is the ultimate 'failure' of what is in reality an unforgettable documentary film experience.

The unfortunate postscript to *Africa Addio* is that the film was re-released in 1971 by the American Jerry Gross organisation. This version, a hideously truncated and hypersensationalist version, was re-titled *Africa Blood and Guts* with the tag-line "every scene looks you in the eye, and spits". The promotional devices alone for the selling of the film, incorporating black American actors dressed as Zulus, were laughably offensive — an extreme reading of the already shameless exploitation textbook. A myth has also developed that in this version it was the historical or contextual material that was excised. Rather, a random collection of scenes (the Mau Mau trials for example) have been removed from the film solely to make it 'sellable' to the limited attention spans of US audiences, both theatrically and subsequently on domestic video release. The magnificence of the original film image was lost in this cheap, risible 'translation'. One needs only to view the trailer, with its preposterous growling voice-over, to understand the contempt (Jacopetti described it as a "betrayal") with which all those involved in the production of the film view the exercise.

CHAPTER 6
"A SLOW-MOTION HYMN TO KILLING"

Animals in Mondo Film

Film critic, Mark Kermode, once remarked that in cinema there were still two unacceptable issues: child abuse and "animal cruelty". Whilst the mondo film has never been charged directly with the promotion of abuses against children, accusations of abuse of animals have been plentiful. Animals feature strongly in mondo films, either drawing 'anthropological' links between the human and non-human animal worlds or as metaphors for suffering and misery in the twentieth century milieu. The agony of animals engenders a peculiar kind of tragedy and evokes the next best thing to the emotional power of witnessing/experiencing human death in film. Clearly the act of visualising animal suffering, particularly in the UK, is problematic and has been so for some time. The 1937 Cinematograph Films (Animals) Act, which "Prohibits exhibition or supply of a film if animals are harmed in the filmmaking process by: the cruel infliction of pain or terror; the cruel goading of any animals to fury" developed from the first annual BBFC report of 1914 (of which 'cruelty to animals' was one of twenty-two grounds for cuts or rejection). Three years later on BBFC president T P O'Connor's list of guidelines for cutting films (known as 'O'Connor's 43'), included "Cruelty to animals" as forbidden and this appears to be one of the few devices from the list still addressed with any seriousness. In 1919 more specific clauses containing animals were added to ban the appearance of cock-fighting and "images of animals gnawing men and children". How apt…

A Dog's Life?

One of the films containing animal cruelty to be first censored by the BBFC was the 1930 African adventure yarn, *Trader Horn*, directed by W S Van Dyke. It contained footage of animals being killed and animal fights, and as such has been identified as one of the first ever 'mondo' films. In a review of Jonathan Burt's *Animals in Film*, K H Brown notes the importance of the book but laments the omittance of any material on the Italian mondo film in this particular discussion; certainly the links that Burt makes between film and politics, censorship and control, a key aspect of his thesis, are amply presented by the mondo film (there may also be prescience of the mondo film found in the work of Luca Comerio, who, according to Burt, made travelogues from around the world containing many animal killing scenes). The central metaphor of *Mondo Cane* (a Tuscan expression of good-natured bewilderment, commonly translated as 'it's a dog's life'), and thus the mondo genre, is that of animals, in particular the dog. Indeed the film opens with a sequence of a dog being dragged reluctantly towards a compound and proceeds with numerous animal related scenes. In one of the film's most noted 'shock cuts' a juxtaposition is made

between the breasts of a young American 'bikini babe' and that of a New Guinea native suckling a piglet (whose mother has died). The contrast between the adoration heaped upon pets by Americans at the famous Pasadena Pet Cemetery with that of the inhabitants of the Hong Kong island of Formosa, where dogs are not-controversially eaten is shown. In a New York restaurant insects are consumed à la carte, a scene included to depict the lengths that sophisticated urbanites will go to appear cultured and daring. As well as these skilfully executed juxtapositions there are many scenes of violence against animals in the film, from tribal feasts where wild boar are bludgeoned

"Violence is a form of objectivity. Violence exists in the world so why not show it?" FRANCO PROSPERI

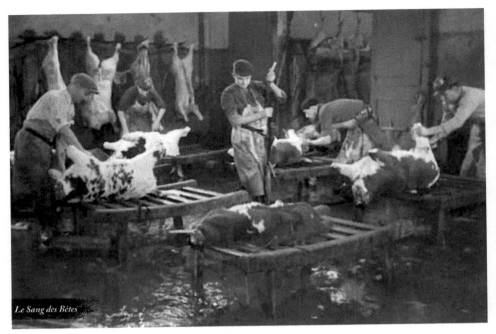
Le Sang des Bêtes

and roasted, to Ghurkha military ceremonies where cattle are beheaded with one stroke of a sword for neo-colonial (in this instance British) entertainment (a smiliar scene appears in nightmarish form in both *Apocalypse Now* and the documentary of its making, *Hearts of Darkness: A Filmmaker's Apocalypse*). Another key element, which would find resonance in subsequent mondos, was the usage of a sentimental musical theme attached to images of cruelty towards animals. This technique originated in *Mondo Cane*, where chicks are

dyed and blow-dried before being placed inside chocolate Easter eggs, and continued in a distressing account of the destruction of Bikini atoll by nuclear contamination where sea turtles die in the baking sun as they lose all sense of orientation. Ortolani and Oliviero's now very famous theme from *Mondo Cane* plays over such scenes both with dramatic irony and deliberate emotional manipulation. Critic Raymond Durgnat has aligned the work of Jacopetti to that of Georges Franju in casting both directors as makers of "pessimistic documentaries involving cruelty to animals". Franju's use of a sentimental French Ballad (La Mer) in his precise abattoir drama, *Le Sang des Bêtes*, is echoed in the tactics of *Mondo Cane* and beyond. Burt's notion of a "slaughterhouse aesthetic" where "material documenting the torture and murder of animals seems to provide a stop-gap for the hungry sadistic eye" is here exploited most effectively.

"Do movie patrons want the guts of reality in their documentaries? Here they get them: literally, and with the trimmings too."
PARKER TYLER

Zebra rescue in *Africa Addio*

The subsequent development of the mondo film saw the subgenre develop a number of specific filmic modes in relation to the depiction of animals; codes which, moreover, may occur all at once in any film. The modes are thus keywords for mondo because the way in which these codes exploit animals continues to be problematic for critics and historians alike.

Ritual

Mondo films commonly employ representations of ritual activity in the development of shock cinema effects (see also chapter seven). *Mondo Freudo* contains scenes of a New York (Puerto Rican) black mass where "the blood of a chicken and a hog's head represents death". Snakes and chickens are sacrificed in another R L Frost effort, *Mondo Bizarro*. Mid-period mondo films such as Scattini's *Angeli Bianchi, Angeli Neri* (*Witchcraft '70*) depicts animal kill 'voodoo' rituals in Miami through a "secret, hidden" camera. This was later reprised in Harvey Keith's *Mondo New York* when the

film's protagonist wanders into a bloody cock-fight run by Puerto Ricans.

Politics

The use of animal tragedy as a metaphor for human ills runs strongly throughout the mondo genre. In Jacopetti and Prosperi's later films, such as *Africa Addio* and *Addio Zio Tom*, the treatment of blacks (Africans and African-Americans respectively) is likened to that of animals. A scene in *Africa Addio* shows whites in Kenya hunting a black boy instead of a fox. In *Addio Zio Tom*, a black slave boy appears in a playful garden scene tethered around the neck like a dog by his young white mistress.

Danger

Mondo films, like the adventure films that preceded them and the wildlife programmes that have replaced them, were not averse to representing animals as dangerous, deadly creatures. In *Brutes and Savages*, an African tribesman is attacked and eaten by a crocodile in a patently fabricated sequence. The later

Ultime Grida Dalla Savana – man eaten by lions in Angola

period mondo, *Faces of Death*, includes a fake sequence of an American ranger being eaten by a crocodile. In one of the most controversial mondo films, *Ultime grida dalla savana*, a scene is shown of a man being eaten by a lion in an Angolan national park. The incident, supposedly based on a real occurrence is presented as amateur super-8 footage and although it has been dismissed as fake by Kerekes and Slater it remains a powerful filmic experience and was required viewing for a generation of young Italian thrill seekers. The most common re-titling of the film as *Savage Man… Savage Beast* demonstrates how the film was perceived to violently collapse the human and non-human animal worlds.

Violence

Some of the first scenes shot for *Africa Addio*, were records of the effect of post-colonialism on the African wildlife — "the animal harvests". Scenes of tribal hunting, though brutal to western audiences, are contrasted, as usual, with the barbarity of white 'tourist' hunting (in this case an elephant hunting service described as the "fifteen minute safari"). The killing of antelope, hippopotamus and elephant is choreographed to the romantic musical score by Riz Ortolani creating a 'symphony of violence'. Ortolani tellingly based his synchronisation on observing the anthropomorphic work of the Walt Disney studio productions.

Horror

Mondo films became increasingly violent in the 1970s and 1980s and frequently incorporated extreme footage of real animal cruelty and violence as a cynical thrill-seeking device. Key examples of this are the above mentioned *Brutes and Savages* where goats are sacrificed on the Sudan/Ugandan border, a

turtle is sacrificed as part of a Bolivian wedding ceremony ("to our eyes an atrocity" intones the narrator) and a Bolivian llama is ritually killed (its still-beating heart is ripped out to an incongruous disco beat) together with some 'animal on animal violence' as alligators attack and kill snakes and jaguars. The notorious *Faces of Death* franchise contained amongst other animal horrors pit-bull dogfights in Mexico, piranhas in the Amazon, a tribe of monkey-killing savages, (kosher) slaughterhouse scenes, seal clubbing and a ridiculous segment where, after being beaten to death at a dining table, a monkey's brains are eaten as a delicacy (these scenes are reprised from *Sadismo* which also features a bear being "skinned alive"). According to Kerekes and Slater these films are clearly employing "animal slaughter as a supplementary shock factor" an approach we shall see reached its nadir in the post-mondo world.

Comic

It has been already noted that mondo films are commonly structured around violent contrasts and one of these is the juxtaposition of 'dark' and 'light' cinematic moments. Thus humour plays a role in the delivery of shock cinema to audiences. As a protest against the censorship *Mondo Cane* received in Britain (it was refused a certificate by the BBFC) Jacopetti opened the follow up, *Mondo Cane No.2*, with a parody of the dog pound shot that begins his first film. This time it is revealed that the dogs have had their vocal cord cut. The narration duly invites the British censors to cut this sequence out in the same way that the surgeons have cut out the dog's barks. In Climati and Morra's *Savana Violenta*, the use of monkeys in tribal hunting is presented as comical: the monkeys jump on the backs of the hunted boar to slow them down and the sequence is speeded up to make it even more 'comical'. In *Africa*

13

Addio, the score is written and synchronised to mimic the perceived characteristics of the animal being shown (bumbling, slow hippos; stilted birds etc.). This aspect of the mondo film was acknowledged in the spoof-mondo, *Mr Mike's Mondo Video*, in a sequence where cats are thrown into a swimming pool in order to learn how to swim.

Animal Holocaust: the post-mondo film

Jonathan Burt identifies the way in which meanings are 'collapsed' in the representation of animals in film. In mondo this manifests itself as meaning created from the fusing of animal and human characteristics, from a critique of the way in which humans treat other animals and from animal violence used as a shock-horror tactic. The unusual way in which animal films develop the idea of the pornographic "eco-porn" is most powerfully developed in the post-mondo films, such as the notorious mondo critique and 'video nasty', *Cannibal Holocaust*. In this film real animal killing, along a journey into exploitation and depravity, merges with simulated human killing to create the ultimate shock effect — a cinema of pain and of disgust. If, as Burt argues, it is the particular combination of the natural and the visual which is troubling in terms of violence on-screen, then most extreme mondo films and the post-mondo film articulate this very well. In the post-mondo the ritualised violence of the mondo film is heightened, recalling the extreme performance of artists such as the Vienna 'Action' artists where naked flesh, dead animals, blood and gore were merged into a Freudian 'theatre of cruelty'. The attraction of such 'cannibal films' where animals are openly killed as part of the *mise en scène* (other key examples include Umberto Lenzi's *Cannibal Ferox*, Antonio Margheriti's *Cannibal Apocalypse*, Sergio Martino's *Mountain of the Cannibal God*) was the combination of sex and violence pursued to vicious extremes. The frequent bouts of sex in these films is presented as 'animalistic' continuing the trend since Muybridge of coalescing the eroticised, objectified body of women with that of the 'animal'. The boundaries of representation and reality are

Cannibal Holocaust

transgressed in such films and any 'critical' message (in *Cannibal Holocaust* that being the rape of the natural world by the unnatural; the exploitation of 'primitive' cultures for western entertainment) is confused with the violent 'zoophilic' acts themselves as voyeuristic outrage. Further exploration of human/animal trauma as ritualised entertainment occur in *Des Morts* author Thierry Zeno's *Vase de Noces* (aka *Wedding Trough/The Pig-fucking Movie*), which exists within the realms of avant garde rather than exploitation. Franco Prosperi contributed *Wild Beasts* as an ecological horror film, featuring abuse of real animals set to a 1980s funk beat, to this particular aspect of mondo.

John Pym, writing in the *MFB*, once noted that the "Italian documentary tradition indulges in a gloating delight in the slaughter of small creatures" an indication that the real motivation behind such cinematic scenes is purely sadistic. Thus, the post-mondo film cleverly (some would say cynically) combines elements of the mondo aesthetic: the documentary 'shock cut'; a fascination

with the anthropological with elements of the visceral horror movie to create a consistently troubling cinematic subgenre and one which is still problematic for censors today.

The mondo and post-mondo film utilises the cinematographic arts to present shocking and disturbing images as violent entertainment. In doing this, animal usage and abusage are key factors in challenging the acceptability of what can be shown in film. The mondo aesthetic is alive in the cinema of Godfrey Reggio and the cable and satellite network television shows devoted to the grotesque, violent and voyeuristic. Ron Fricke's *Baraka* — a new-age mondo film — even contains a sequence depicting the industrialization of animal manufacture as thousands of chicks have their beaks burnt off in a factory that bears a direct relation to *Mondo Cane*. Its wordless, challenging narrative on the distress and violence met out to the animal world thus echoes the 'dog's life' of earlier mondo, a life that seems to have little value outside of 'spectacular' mass media thrills and spills.

ULTIME GRIDA DALLA SAVANA
(SAVAGE MAN... SAVAGE BEAST)

Directed by Antonio Climati and Mario Morra
(Italy 1974)

And the animal kills another animal for food
And the animal kills man for food
And man kills the animal for food
And man kills man

So begins this remarkable, pseudo-philosophical mondo examination of hunting fixated on the cyclical, the (inter)relationship between the hunter and the hunted. *Ultime grida dalla savana* was a hugely influential documentary film although few people appreciate this now, its reputation as a "thinly disguised sensational exploiter" going before it. The notoriety of the film in the UK was heightened when the RSPCA raised concerns over the animal violence featured in it, as they did later with Climati's *Natura Contro*, where a "sight of real animal cruelty (a monkey hit with a blowdart)" had to be cut out. The macho condemnation of attempts at wildlife preservation, described at one point as "a pathetic and desperate undertaking", ensured the film a guarded reception in any place promoting itself to be a nation of 'animal lovers'. In contrast the film has always been popular in Asia (being the second most popular film in Hong Kong in 1976, after *Jaws*) and left an indelible impression on a whole generation of Italian youths as some

sort of cinematic rite of passage. As well as providing a partial critique of the process of presenting wildlife on the cinema screen (see below) the film provided a vital link between the 'classic' shockumentaries of the early-mid-1960s and the much crueller mondos of the mid-1970s and beyond. The key aspect of this, naturally, was the presence of Jacopetti and Prosperi's principal cinematographer Antonio Climati, who orchestrated the photography in the film (*Addio Zio Tom* organisational manager Giampaolo Lomi also assisted with the production). Climati's co-director was Mario Morra, a legendary, proficient editor of Italian genre films from the 1960s, a roll-call of which acts as an ideal litany of this 'golden age' (Morra edited Pontecorvo's *La Battaglia di Algeri* (*The Battle of Algiers*) and *Queimada* (*Burn!*), mondo narrator Enrico Maria Salerno's *Anonimo Veneziano* (*The Anonymous Venetian*), Brusati's *Pane e Cioccolata* (*Bread and Chocolate*), Cavara's *La Tarantula del Ventro Nero* (*The Black Belly of the Tarantula*), Cervi's *Il Delitto del Diavolo* (*Queens of Evil*), as well as mondo classics such as Vicario and Margheriti's *Il Pelo nel Mondo* (see chapter four). The towering presence of Alberto Moravia, one of Italy's most famous writers, lent authority and respect to the film; his commentary alternates philosophy, sociology, ethics and poetry throughout. Moravia was no stranger to adapting or having his work adapted for cinema and his commentary for *Ultime grida dalla savana* provided the appropriate mondo blend of poetic-subjective observation, emotion, caution and derision.

And yet, *Ultime grida dalla savana* has many flaws. As Climati's first self-directed film, after working with Jacopetti and Prosperi, his tendency on occasion to hark back to these formative films is obvious. Long before the arrival of the 'compilation film' Climati and Morra were supplementing their original footage shot for *Ultime grida dalla savana* with material from *Africa Addio*: the Acholi tribe's hunting exhibitions are noticeable, sometimes repeated, albeit with 'authentic' sounds applied rather than to Ortolani's complex synchronised orchestration of death created for the original film. Even the original score by Carlo Savina mimics some of the aspects of the *Africa Addio* soundtrack, in particular the use of 'Wild West' style arrangements to signify the supposed freedom of men moving through dramatic landscapes on horseback, jaunty arrangements for comic effect, and the use at the beginning and the end of the film of a highly sentimental ballad as a melancholic device. Climati revisits his brilliant mercenary sequence from *Africa Addio* too when the faces of the Amazonian mercenaries — "the chronically unemployed" — are framed in similar close-range outlaw fashion.

As with all great mondo films the overall presentation of the film material, in this case confined to the various manifestations of 'the hunt' in global culture, is kaleidoscopic, ripping from one scenario to the next with scant regard for narrative continuity. There are some archetypal mondo style image links that recall the revolution of *Mondo Cane* into the documentary panorama some ten years earlier: scenes of a wildlife/nature rally shot at Cape Cod ("a last expression of a neo-romantic return to nature") end with a shot of toy monkey, which then match-cuts to the face of an Amazonian orang-utan; this monkey's clenched fist turns into that of an Australian aborigine; the ceremonial stick held in the hand of a 'skeleton man' of the Black Volta, morphs into that of a French priest blessing a stag hunt), all of which classically serve to blur the differences between the 'modern' and the 'primitive'. Recognisable too is the trick of inserting fabricated simulations of scenarios into the trajectory of the film. In the above mentioned wildlife rally we see placards that bear the traces of being concocted by the film crew (they look too orderly to be real expressions of protest), and the clear presence of Hungarian-born Italian porn star-turned politician, Ilona Staller ('La Cicciolina'), as one of the naked participants codifies the sequence as fake (she appears again, topless, at a record of an Isle of Wight rock festival). A sequence of 'civilised' hunting moves to England (bizarrely signified musically by excerpts from Wagner's *Tannhäuser*) where the ritual is clearly factual but the representation of a sabotage by the 'Wild Fox Association' ludicrously staged (before distracting the hounds with an Afghan bitch they somehow spike the port of the hunters with laxative so that they are forced to halt for regular shit stops, and the WFA's car number plate is foreign). Later we are invited to witness an experiment where the crew try to capture the fastest animal on earth, the cheetah, chasing an ostrich. The 'combi van' where the camera is mounted inside, used to film such scenes, strains to keep up with the speeding animals and eventually the driver loses control and the van crashes, spilling out broken camera parts. The question *who was filming this scene?* may be an obvious one, but the illusion of 'reality' crumbles nonetheless. Such fakery works better when allied to a particular argument, as when the tired myth of firearms as an aggressive virility booster, evident in an American pin-up-festooned shooting gallery, is mocked: "come on and buy a rifle, man… and you'll become a man," a sexy female voice intones over the shots. The sound design, as always created in post-production, comprises a string of heightened audio effects applied to the various processes of carnage on display (the Aboriginal kill of kangaroos with spears and flying foxes with boomerangs being particularly resonant with affecting whips and whooshes and the many shooting expeditions echoing with the cruel smash of bullet ricochets).

There are a number of ways in which *Ultime grida dalla savana* became such an influential mondo film. The fabricated yet convincingly grim 'amateur footage' sequences that occur twice in the film: the Pit Dernitz 'man being attacked and eaten by a lion in a safari park' 8mm footage and the 16mm shots of mercenaries employed to hunt, castrate, scalp and decapitate Amazonian Indios, were the blueprint for the found footage of later shockers such as Ruggero Deodato's *Cannibal Holocaust*. The clever way in which Climati and Morra employ choppy camera movement, jump-cuts, blurred focus and square 'amateur' ratios has been copied ever since as the way to depict 'real' footage within the confines of an existing feature film. Secondly, some of the images from the film became etched in to the consciousness of exploitation film

consumers: the unforgettable sequence on the "ceremony of life" of the 'skeleton men' of the Black Volta, a pogo ritual dance, shot in slow-motion and from below so that their penises flap hypnotically up and down in front of the camera lens has been reused several times in compilation films. Finally, the 'real gore' of many parts of the film (the various slow-motion animal confrontations and a fight between a Peruvian puma, a farmer and his dogs, where one of dogs is disembowelled and has to be sewn up on the spot as the puma is knifed through the heart being particularly blood splattered — these were the scenes that the RSPCA had cut) found its way into the later violent and gory mondo films such as *Faces of Death* before being formally incorporated into a huge variety of Italian zombie and cannibal films. The use and abuse of animals as a device

Savage Man... Savage Beast

for shock and horror may have been augmented in earlier mondo films but in *Ultime grida dalla savana*, it became an art form. Despite this many of the sequences are beautifully filmed and the cinematography undeniably superb: the Aboriginal boomerang hunt, the electrode implanted cormorants skimming the Pampas coastline, display a virtuoso talent for slow-motion framing and movement; the atmosphere and lighting of the opening Patagonian stag hunt are stunning, and all of this elevates the film above many of the tired imitators mondo encouraged and inspired. One can see why Jenny Craven, in *Films and Filming*, was moved to describe the film as a "beautifully executed documentary of death".

But one of the best moments of the film comes when the narrative halts for a consideration on the very act of shooting these kinds of images for entertainment consumption. Over more slow-motion shots, this time of a bear capturing and eating a salmon, Moravia comments:

"Disregarding the cruelty of the scene we smile because certain films have conditioned us to looking at nature in a particular way and these scenes are typical of the animal documentary shot according to the manual. The rules could be summarised as follows: accentuate the romantic aspects of nature; humanise animals making them harmless and lovable; set them in a consumer society paradise, banishing bloodshed of course". A child's voice interjects: "but what about the poor fish?" The commentary resumes. "The child has spoken up and unmasked hypocrisy like her famous counterpart in the Hans Christian Anderson story. Fish also have a right to live but nothing is written in the manual about fish. This is another effect of conditioning by film: the racial discrimination among animal species. Certain animals, fish for example, can be tortured and killed; others can't."

We, the audience for *Ultime grida dalla savana* smile too, because in this moment of poetically expressed, supremely unwitting, postmodern irony, the fraudulent majesty of the mondo film is magnificently exposed.

SAVANA VIOLENTA (THIS VIOLENT WORLD)

Directed by Antonio Climati and Mario Morra
(Italy, 1976)

Fans of mondo films coming at this Climati/Morra effort from one of the many alternative titles, *Mondo Violence* or *This Violent World*, will be disappointed to discover that *Savana Violenta* is largely one of the most beautiful and evocative shockumentary film works. The film is awash with Climati's trademark golden sunsets and sunrises, peoples and animals of the world framed against orange romantic glows and slow-motion shots of both tearing each other into bloody pieces. In this film Climati refines the art of framing cinematographic shock reaching visual heights that sometimes improves on those of *Ultime Grida dalla Savana*, and always surpasses those in the final part of the trilogy, *Dolce e Selvaggio*. It is no surprise that he went on to direct commercials. One of the frames of the film, a shot of an Indian fakir with his head completely buried in the hot sand, has become something of an icon/pin-up of the mondo genre. The opening scenes document dawn at the site of the "primordial" beginning of time (the Lundi savannah of West Africa) where nature's animals, human and non-human, exist in states where "fate decides who is to live and who is to die". Zebra are attacked by lions while cheetahs kill monkeys — all in gorgeous, classically framed slow-motion. A witchdoctor appears framed against the luscious dawn sky waving his magic stick (he is dressed in a long coat

to signify his high status). The film returns to this scenario, albeit with a twist, at the end of the film, emphasising once again Climati and Morra's penchant for circular metaphors and eco-ideologies critiquing a natural world usurped by globalisation and capitalism. The film continues in a strange manner as the next scene depicts the children employed to record the decline of terns by the Great Barrier Reef. The beautiful landscape shots continue as one of the light motifs from the film, Let's Sing A Song (composed by the prolific brothers Guido and Maurizio De Angelis), rings out; a breezy children's choir number that recalls the twisted utopianism of Coca Cola's I'd Like To Teach The World To Sing commercial. This being a mondo film though, such hippy optimism is soon brutally crushed by the ensuing images. The text which rolls over these pictures reads: "The following episodes illustrating the cruel reality of the modern world are presented in the style of cinema vérité

This Violent World

as a means of communicating more vividly the essential truth on which they are based". This serves as a precursor to the fracturing of both the saccharine portraits of lived reality and of film documentary rules. As was proved long ago, any notion of documentary *cinema vérité* was destroyed by mondo aesthetics of which Climati was a lead proponent. Then the shocks come quickly, if at first gently. A sequence reporting on the cult practices of Indian fakirs, who, to test states of insensibility, pierce their faces and necks and contort their bodies into grotesquely ornate shapes and forms, is shown. Two startling images resonate: the first is the above mentioned shot of a fakir with his head buried like an ostrich; the other a man carefully slicing off part of his tongue. Both of these images, like the rest of this sequence are contrived, yet Climati's skill in portraying rituals, the way he pulls focus from one bizarre tableaux to another, recalling the best parts of *Zio Tom*, are visually jolting and induce a mild stomach churning effect. His intrusive, probing camera, goading the subjects to stare at him, also plays a part.

Climati and Morra have never shirked from reusing their own footage and the next sequence, of a perilous Colombian cable car, appeared later in *Dolce e Selvaggio*. The "cinema vérité" promised a few frames back melts away here as the musical accompaniment, a brass and drum march, meant to match the images, just makes it all the more fake; exciting cinema but a very poor simulation of 'truth'.

In addition to the excellent visual style, the film has clearly been a strong influence on subsequent post-mondo cinema. An early section recording the search in New York sewers for discarded or escaped dangerous reptiles, the nightmare of killer animals roaming the streets under our feet, must have influenced the concept behind fellow traveller Franco Prosperi's 1983 eco-horror *Belve Feroci* (*Wild Beasts*). In addition an "authorised footage" account of forbidden child slavery in the Amazon, with its grainy, yellowing film stock, helped shape the vérité aesthetics of Ruggero Deodato's *Cannibal Holocaust*, which perfected the art of simulated 'found film' (the opening airplane shots of the Amazon forest also prefigure the opening shots of the infamous cult shocker). The tribeswomen are sexually fascinated with the white slavers and this interaction also made it into Deodato's film. The film then launches into surreal mode as a group of penguins appear to be singing along to the soundtrack (the stunning close-harmony Dixie number, Anthem) — another violation of cinema 'actuality'. The De Angelis brothers even mimic the tactic begun in *Africa Addio* for matching animals with their musical instrument likeness. The actuality slips even further away in a patently false scene on primal scream therapy in a London clinic where couples excise their sexual frustrations through yelling abuse at each other. Some are encaged in glass booths where they can extend this 'therapy' into a physical 'cure' ("rape therapy" the narrator crassly describes it as). The scenes are fake and loosely pornographic but the presence of a recognisable English character actor as one of the clinicians weakens the credibility further.

The theme of violence against animals, always an essential and distressing element of Climati and Morra's oeuvre, then takes hold. After grim footage of the remains of a girl attacked by a white shark (her face chillingly left intact), a 'revenge' takes place when the shark are hunted for use in fertility drugs. Their

142

THE GREAT HUNTING II

グレート
ハンティング2

2

人喰いライオン▽の
興奮もさめやらぬいま
太陽の返り血を浴びて
登場する衝撃の続篇
今度は何が飛び出すのか！

captured forms are sliced open and mutilated while they are still conscious. A gore shot of one's still pumping heart, visible through the huge gash in its stomach, induces definite queasiness. This violence is cut together with images of human trauma to induce the sense of our own mortality and organic state: shots of suicide corpses washed up by the River Ganges, are picked at by vultures. In the New Hebrides dead fisherman are left out to rot in the heat. The putrefactions that run from the corpse must be sipped by his relatives. Meanwhile in Argentina deer are caught in nets and Nandoo birds are entwined with balls on a rope in a perfectly executed 'ballet of death'. In Papua two tribes fight over a boar hunt. When an angry tribesman smashes Climati's filter holder (the sequence was filmed "against police advice") the arrest of the crew in Zanzibar in *Africa Addio* is recalled. When the camera tips over onto its side and continues to film, another reference to *Cannibal Holocaust* rears up. The ghost of *Mondo Cane* appears in an account of giant turtles, weakened by pollution, are unable to propel their eggs. Naturalist "midwives" move in to help them by extracting the eggs by hand.

There are comic moments in the film, to relieve the slaughter. In a Mozambique national park baboons are used to help 'hunt' the wild boar. The monkeys jump onto the backs of the boar as if they were horses in a Wild West rodeo in order to slow them down and make then easier to catch (the music, predictably, follows the western theme). Two teams of mongoose play 'football' with bittern eggs, while a soccer commentary, rendered in excitable Portuguese ("*Goaaaallll!!!*") emphasises the comedy. Eroticism is also used for 'relief' and in *Savana Violenta*, this takes the form of the unique creation of 'Amazon porn'. We have already peeped in on an Amazonian couple making love in the jungle and now the scene switches to a ceremony by the River Paya where the scales of a large fish are applied to erogenous parts of the body as prelude to the "love season of the firefly". The simulation of sex/fertility rites is shot through soft porn lenses but at least the directors confess their duplicitous intentions: "we waited six days to film the capture of this fish but without this fish the young people of the tribe would not have their festival and we should not be able to film it!". A sequence in the Tropian Islands where women fling themselves from a mango tree to induce miscarriage opens with the kind of close-up, from below, bum shot that Russ Meyer would have approved of. The latter parts of this sequence, where we see the bloody foetus ripped from the woman and buried ritualistically were restaged, equally photogenically, for *Cannibal Holocaust*. The diversion to an English porno film shoot (in Richmond, Surrey for "Hutchinson Studios") with its camp style and appearance by former punk rock icon Jordan is, like the very notion of English erotica, farcical. More hunting absurdity occurs with the account of Peter Thompson's school for 'White Aborigines' in Darwin, Australia where "pale asses" learn to capture crocodiles, drink sap from a tree and spear iguana (again, the 'warrior' music makes the whole thing seem preposterous).

The penultimate scenes are devoted to death in the human sphere. The horrific aftermath of the Guatemalan earthquake of 1976, where 22,000 were killed, is shown. The images of rotting and smashed, fly infested corpses are distressingly real — at one point the camera 'turns away' in mock disgust. The camera does not turn away however from the brutal execution of a young looter whose dog sits forlornly by his machine gun riddled body after the killing. The Rio carnival, where

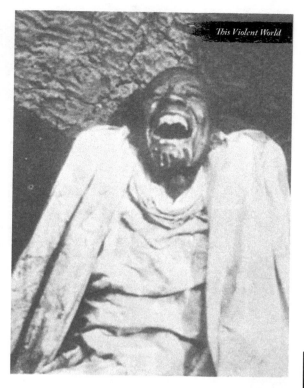

This Violent World

people "sing and dance, copulate and kill" also ends with a bloody shooting in a side street all driven, perversely, by the pulsating, Latin stand out cue from the soundtrack. The film ends back at the start, the Lundi savannah, but as promised with a twist. On this morning the hunted fight back, the" underdog finds the strength to rebel".

Climati and Morra's second film of animal violence is arguably the most beautiful to look at. No matter how hideous the acts we bear witness to, these contributions to the definition of mondo are aesthetically strong and memorable. The shimmering golden orb that ends this, and Climati and Morra's other 'savage' films, offers hope and defines the optimism lacking in subsequent shockumentary cinema.

DAL VERO CIÒ CHE IL CINEMA NON AVEVA MAI OSATO FILMARE

ALESSANDRO FRACASSI
presenta

DOLCE
e
SELVAGGIO

un film di **ANTONIO CLIMATI - MARIO MORRA**

Soggetto e sceneggiatura di **ANTONIO CLIMATI - MARIO MORRA**

Musiche composte, arrangiate ed eseguite da **DANIELE PATUCCHI**

Organizzatore Generale **MAURIZIO ANTICOLI**   Testi di **FRANCO E. PROSPERI**

Prodotto da **ALESSANDRO FRACASSI** per la RACING PICTURES s.r.l.

Colore L.V. di **LUCIANO VITTORI**

SWEET & SAVAGE

DOLCE E SELVAGGIO (SWEET AND SAVAGE)

Directed by Antonio Climati and Mario Morra
(Italy, 1983)

This film represents the third and final segment of Climati and Morra's great mondo trilogy and is a fascinating, yet late contribution to the mondo canon. Although undoubtedly more artificial and unconvincing than earlier mondo efforts, even with Climati and Morra's own contributions, the film has a powerful disquieting quality to it. Moreover, the polarised theme of the movie and its title — the "pendulum swing" between the sweet and the savage — although often laboured as a linking device, epitomises the essential raw elements of mondo aesthetics. There are several odd departures in the film that bear closer scrutiny. Firstly, the device of having 'real' characters in the film speaking directly to the camera (thus to the audience) is a mondo first. The character of Mike Gunn, a bearded Rhodesian gamekeeper, is supposed to embody the sweet and savage concept. We first see him apparently hunting zebra and hippos before it is revealed that he is in fact aiming his rifle at Bulgarian Skoda landmines planted during civil conflicts in the region. We are informed by narrator Robert Sommer that Gunn "fought in a savage war... and you can still see it in his eyes" (this is inter-cut with an ugly scenario from said conflict) and the figure of Gunn appears throughout the film as a motif (he emerges playing with hippos and cheetahs), which actually means very little. Occasionally he offers vague philosophical comments on man's relationship with nature with animals and, inter-textually, reacts to a joke by the narrator. Gunn is coded "an enigma, sweet and savage, a man". Secondly, voice-over is used as a testimony or storytelling device and is 'acted' in place of the standard narration by an expert. The film therefore has a dreamy quality to it, which captivates the viewer for a while.

But there is a cheap and even shoddy quality to many aspects of the film and the horrific 1980s electro sax funk provided by Daniele Patucchi as a musical backing prefigures hideous later mondos, such as Crisanti's *Mondo Cane 2000* (see chapter one) and even Prosperi's own *Belve Feroci* (*Wild Beasts*), which the same composer scored. The hack job is compounded by the fact that Climati and Morra have cannibalised their own films by inserting various scenes recognisable from *Ultime Grida dalla Savana*: the footage of English foxhunting ("sweet is the air of the English countryside... savage are the games people play there") and both the

"The tree of man grew from a seed of the sea. Its roots are birds and iguana, water and naked rock. Its spirit is aloft like a white bird. Its fruit is sweet and savage."
KANADANÉ (INCA POET)

Patagonian conservation footage and the slow-motion African tribe 'pogo' are recognisable). The commentary was written by Climati's former mondo comrade Franco Prosperi, which explains the obsession with the interface between man and the natural world while the literary pretensions of the text, quoting authors and various poets, is an attempt at raising the intellectual plane of the film. Prosperi also tries to add circularity and cohesion to the disparate images, a task in his own films he has proved to be adept at, here from the site of man's beginning to the modern man (Mike Gunn) and back again. Prosperi, being a naturalist at heart fires critiques of the "orgy" of modern consumerism demonstrating that he is also a moralist. Prosperi's long held disgust at the corrosion of naturalism in the modern world emerges with a condemnation of the factory farming of previously 'free' animals. The slow-motion killing of springboks, a Climati/Morra specialism, is presented with the customary aerial photography managing to be stunning and sickening at the same time. The animals "run with the wind and die in the sun" the commentary accuses before quoting Karen Blixen's lament to the passing of the ancient, traditional African way of life.

The common mondo taste for the naked female form, inevitably used here to flesh out the 'sweet' metaphors, include sequences on soft porn photographer Jeff Dumas (said to have shot over 1,000 models "each a fragment of an image of the women of his dreams") which is definitely mocking in tone and some footage of a 'Jane Fonda' workout in an American gym (backed by Josette Martial's absurd eurotrash disco number Ring Ding Dong), which predictably offers stacks of bum and crotch shots. The opening salvo on ostrich meat is constructed from brutal shots of the birds having their necks broken (amplified neck snaps) juxtaposed with photo-shoot images of naked women using the feathers as seductive apparel. There are also the humorous moments of the classic mondo format, this time the grisly sight of a Bolivian slaughterhouse, where the cow's blood is drunk straight from a severed artery 'on tap', and numerous scenes of dolphin training, which, for reasons I have yet to discover, Italian documentary filmmakers find fascinating. This being the mid-eighties and the highpoint

148

of film horror gore and slasher aesthetics there are possibly fabricated, yet nonetheless stomach churning, events represented. One such moment includes a Tibetan funeral rite where the corpses of the dead are lifted to the mountain tops before being hacked to pieces limb by limb and fed to the waiting vultures. The severed head looks very much like a false one. It is the way in which a film like *Dolce e Selvaggio* offers, on the one hand poetic, beautifully composed images representing the awe of nature and lyrical narration (as visioned in the title sequence — waves crashing against Galapagos shores, flamingos, seals — a mondo picture postcard favourite, and the golden sunsets framing animals and people in delicious light) together with gore, violence and carnage (slaughter of seals and dolphins on the Japanese island of Iki where the water is turned red) that illustrates, even in a later mondo, the dimensions which make the films unique. But this balance is a delicate one. Climati and Prosperi stretch the metaphor too far when a scene of Haitian refuges being washed up dead on a Florida beach is turned into a parodic scene as a student lifesaver administers the 'kiss of life', backed by some cheesy piano music. She happens to be attractive and blonde, kisses the boy seductively and softly and giggles when the cameras leave. Strange though it may seem, there can be too much sweet as well as too much savage.

Mondo films of this era usually deliver some haunting material and *Dolce e Selvaggio* is no exception. It may not seem a significant contribution to the central concept of the film, but it is eerie, the way in which the filmmakers have knitted their footage of tightrope walker Philippe Petit — perilously crossing a high-wire to raise money for a church in New York City — with archive of the tragic death of circus patriarch Karl Wallenda, who in March 1978 fell to his death attempting to cross a wire between two hotels at San Juan, Puerto Rico. The two tightrope acts are brilliantly fused by the narration, an imagined voice-over by Petit, reflecting on Wallenda's final act (Phillipe crossed a wire strung between the Twin Towers in 1974). The music used for the excruciating Wallenda tragedy is equally clever, a celestial glass-rim wail of pain. "Being on the tightrope is living; everything else is waiting," Wallenda once opined yet in this distressing, visceral mondo moment being on the tightrope meant death. This scene is followed by another 'real' event with the accidental death of film stuntman A J Bakunas (world record holder for such a jump) while performing a leap from Kincaid tower in Kentucky for the otherwise forgettable action film *Steel*. The insertion of such reality footage into the film, as part of the investigation into the motives behind the man's actions, foresaw the avalanche of 'reality TV' show in the 1990s and beyond. But in this mondo film they act within particular contexts, poetically and so are infinitely more powerful and meaningful. In *Dolce e Selvaggio* the real death of humans and animals still reverberates on the subconscious mind, as it should in the best mondo films.

The sombre and sad end to the film is a portrait of human and animal symbiosis as a paralysed New Yorker is helped to eat, drink and listen to music by a trained monkey. The scene is supposed to be a positive message about the relationship between animal and man and yet the scene feels desperate. This is due to the way that the filmmakers employ music and voice-over to imply sadness and is a fitting end to the last of the great mondo film epics.

FACES OF DEATH

Directed by Conan LeCilaire (John Alan Schwartz)
(US, 1979)

Faces of Death, and the franchise that it begat, has become one of the most famous elements of shockumentary film history, symbolic of mondo, and yet is in essence a cheap facsimile of a mondo film and a clichéd representation of the bizarre and the shocking. Even the name of the director has been hidden, not an unheard of device in the mondo canon, but the nom-de-plume adopted for *Faces of Death* of Conan LeCilaire is tangibly ridiculous. The real director, John Alan Schwartz, was an editor for Leonard Nimoy's 1970s *In Search of...* TV Series where the supernatural and the mysterious were examined. He also wrote for the ludicrous 1980s *Knight Rider* TV crime series (featuring David Hasselhoff and a magical supercar). Once these facts are known about its creator the insincerity and fraudulence of the *Faces of Death* 'language' becomes evident (as does its inevitable serialisation — to date there have been officially four films).

Faces of Death's identikit manifestation of shock aesthetics is evident in the selection and presentation of material, offering a familiar parade of mondo elements: 'primitive' African tribes and Amazonian Indians; violent happenings; strange rituals; animal killings (bullfights, slaughterhouses). The film is carried by a mordant mock-narration delivered by "Dr. Frances B Gröss" who also acts as a 'creative consultant' and who is included to authenticate the film's material and act as an expert on the "many faces of death". Gröss is actually played by actor Michael Carr and his absurd false moustache, wig and ham acting (in the great American expository tradition) falsifies the film before it has barely begun (once Gröss' unconvincing appearance has vanished from the screen, leaving only his voice as an accompaniment, this effect is not quite so intrusive). The introduction to the film is probably the most 'documentary-like', a gruesome montage of open-heart surgery, corpses being sliced open, scalps being peeled back and haunting still shots of agonised dead faces which do deliver, augmented as they are by Gene Kauer's low spooky strings, ghostly electronic 'music' and amplified sound effects (sawing of bones, sloshing organs and tearing skin), sickening shocks to the viewer. This effect is tangible despite the insertion of bloody horror film titles and the massively clichéd use of a pulsating heartbeat effect, exempt from even the crassest student film production, which halts to signify the arrival of mortality.

The following section, a soliloquy on death delivered by Dr Gröss (as he removes his bloody lab coat and surgical gloves, dumping them in the nearest pedal bin) contributes to the kind of presentation favoured by American 'believe it or not' TV programmes; documentary status is not encouraged by some surreal shots of a

woman lying in a coffin which is then lowered into the ground. The angle switches to POV and we see the soil fall over us before the camera goes black and the organ which has accompanied these shots careers wildly out of time and tune. This is supposed to be Gröss' "recurring dream" which "plagues him". There then follows a compilation of Gröss' "library of the many faces of death", many of which are some of the most extreme examples in the mondo canon, others which are some of the feeblest. The contorted faces of exhumed Mexican mummies are certainly terrifying and formed an effective part of the film's promotion (especially in Japan, where the film was a huge success). These recall the hideous death faces shown in the introduction and exemplify the mondo trend for symbiosis effectively and poignantly. Later in the film more mortuary shots, accompanied by a poetic quotation and a plaintive saxophone solo, briefly suggest a (sadly unrealised) *Des Morts*-style discourse on death and dying. After some typical mondo insertions featuring snakes being eaten by Piranha fish and the obligatory severed head rituals of the Ibero "savages" the film launches into its first catalogue of gory animal slaughter, a key aspect of the *Faces of Death* franchise. First a Maasai sacrifice is shown where a cow's jugular is pierced and the blood which pours from the wound is captured and mixed in a pot. Then a chicken is beheaded in a US farmyard to the backing tune of Old McDonald's Farm. The shots of the beheaded animal flapping frantically around the yard are surprising but are made comic by the use of inappropriate silly backing music (this, it turns out, is an irritating feature of the film). The Kosher method of slaughtering is depicted, scenes of immense carnage, accompanied by statistics about massive American meat consumption and the way in which carnivores, through industrialization processes are removed from the process of killing. The pastoral sounds of Greensleeves introduce this scene and more jaunty classical music plays behind the scenes — an awfully crude manifestation of the mondo trend for musical counterpoint. One of the most infamous iconic scenes concerning the killing of animals follows when a group of four tourists in an 'Indian' restaurant enjoy an exotic meal. A monkey is brought to the table and restrained in a special cage, only its head visible. Members of the group then bash its head in with special tools before the waiter carves open the skull and removes the brains. The tourists then eat the raw bloody brains with a mixture of amusement and disgust. Sadly any horror is tempered by the bare fact that the scene is obviously fabricated, the flimsy set and dreadful acting gives it away above all else.

After some shots of alligator poaching ("the murderers of nature"), nature replies with a vengeful attack by a crocodile on some park rangers. This scene is shot as a live news bulletin, complete with reporter (from "Channel 9 Action News") and is another fake, discernible not only by the presenter's very tight casual brown T-shirt and white bell-bottom flares but by the unconvincing limp cries of "Oh my God!" as the reptile chews the man. Hideous scenes of seal clubbing where bloody carcasses stain the ground red are accompanied by more obtrusive backing, this time film noir/chase music. "I decided never to wear the skin of an animal on my back again," claims Gröss in a passable imitation of shockumentary moralising.

The film then switches to human killings by type: the deranged family man (Michael Lawrence is shot dead by police after

Chicken execution in *Faces of Death*

153

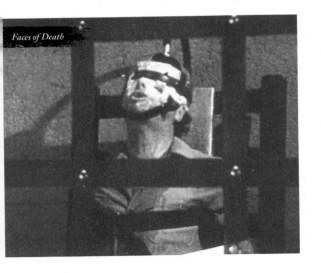

Faces of Death

and lakes of blood are genuinely unsettling. Then the film lurches once again into absurdity with some 'documents' of parapsychology where only the uncanny electronic music is worthwhile. It may seem perverse to associate artistry with mondo but *Faces of Death*, uncaringly compiled, definitely lacks any such reflective qualities. Even the weak pastiches of previous mondos fail. A document on a murderous San Franciscan cult, shot with 'special permission' is a confused blend of Charles Manson and a scene from Scattini's *Witchcraft '70*. The "maniac" leader of the cult, shown removing the heart and organs of a sacrificial victim, is played by the director Schwartz (the young women in the group smear their breasts with blood in the film's only titillatory moment). The section on cryogenics is a *Des Morts* rip-off and the scene where a man is killed by a bear in a safari park after leaving his car to get better shots is terribly realised; at least Climati and Morra's cine-footage of a man being attacked and eaten by a lion requires that you look twice, or even three times, to verify its authenticity. Further mondo clichés are repeated: a woman giving birth and deer leaping in slow-motion before the climax of a freeze-frame red sunset. Yet, *Faces of Death*'s only achievement was to signal the end of the classic mondo period. After this the mondo film lurched into formless perversion and degradation. *Faces of Death* is ultimately so insincere, cheaply commercial and cynically realised that the disclaimer at the end ("exiguous scenes within this motion picture have been reconstructed to document and further clarify their factual origin") is barely necessary.

butchering his family); the suicide (Mary Ellen Wright jumps from a window) and the professional assassin (Francois Girodin shoots dead a political speaker in La Salle). A weak condemnation of American state killings (executions — later to spawn a pseudo-mondo dedicated to this theme) is presented with more reconstructions of death via the gas chamber and the electric chair (once again substandard acting diminishes the credibility). It is after this point that the film should probably end but it drags on with several more disjointed 'faces of death', lacking the originality and the discipline of other (especially Italian) mondo films and confirming Schwartz as a not very good filmmaker. A climber falls down a ravine, natural disasters ensue (volcanoes and nuclear damage) and the inclusion of archive footage of Nazi atrocities and the starving in Biafra all collide and mush together in a hodgepodge of shock images saying nothing and meaning even less. The morbid conclusion to the film is a collection of discernibly 'real' footage of plane disasters and car crashes where the bloody carnage of scattered body pieces

AMERICA COSI NUDA, COSI VIOLENTA
(NAKED AND VIOLENT)

Directed by Sergio Martino
(Italy, 1970)

This mondo film by Sergio Martino, his second foray into the genre after *Mille Peccati... Nessuna Virtù* (1969), reflects a simultaneous reaffirmation of traditional mondo techniques/aesthetics, and a prefiguring of mondo tendencies to come, in what we may like to define as the 'second wave' of mondo films (1969–1980).

Martino was a competent director of genre films, making his name in the giallo field. This in turn is sharply edited, well photographed with a suitably grubby patina, and cleverly constructed in the mondo tradition where contrasting binary opposites are placed side-by-side and subtle (often not-so-subtle) connections between concepts are presented to the viewer (sex masks with kid's toys, for example). Martino's film is worth considering further as is a rare instance of the location-specific mondo film (other examples are Scattini's *Sweden Heaven and Hell* and Arnold Miller's *Primitive London*) concerned here with the vagaries of the most powerful country in the world — then and now — the United States of America. The film has an excellent score by Bruno Nicolai including the requisite overblown ballad (Look Away, delivered by Canadian easy listening singer Shirley Harmer) and the recycling of sections from Jesús Franco's *De Sade 70*, one of Nicolai's best scores.

The film begins by portraying the launch of another NASA rocket at Cape Kennedy, but not as a thrusting and powerful exhibition of US modern power but as a deluded folly that American citizens were even then thoroughly bored with. The commodification of space travel is shown to be moving apace with shots of the 'Lunar Park' amusement wasteland, space toys and porno magazines

America Cosi Nuda, Cosi Violenta

devoted to outer space. The traditional mondo delight in contrasting the ugly and beautiful is in full force. A sequence on homeless 'bums' and the dying in a retirement home district known as the 'Dead End', in New York City's Bowery, is followed immediately by exciting helicopter shots of the Florida coastline and some standard mondo voyeuristic portraits of Miami's beach girls (this section in particular harks back to the Cape Town sequence in Jacopetti and Prosperi's *Africa Addio*). The most amusing instance of the reactionary nature of the middle-aged mondo director occurs with a portrait of the Rolling Stones' free concert at Altamont which notoriously concluded with the stabbing to death of Meredith Hunter by the Hell's Angels employed to police the festival. Naturally, the camera lingers over the many naked girls in the crowd and mocks 'hippy' culture and drug culture in general including a supposed LSD trip captured on film where the youth filmed spouts gibberish. The sonic power of the event is nullified by overlaying Look Away, instead of the actual sound of the bands at the festival. This ridiculous audio substitution is another classic mondo trick, necessitated either by contractual/licensing issues or sheer laziness.

'Strip Joints' and the naked bottoms contained therewith are shown, the haven of "real men" as the narration puts it, and is contrasted with the emerging gay movie houses where "unreal" men hang out. Admiration is expressed for the preposterous empire of Hugh Hefner and his Bunny Girls. Such is 'Naked' America.

Violent episodes are included to demonstrate the aggressive nature of the American (white) soul, including the pointless blasting by cowboys of strung-up dead rabbits and a re-enactment of the JFK assassination. A different form of violence is offered in the guise of Black Power, bizarrely, almost surreally, connected to a sequence on African circumcision rites. Ah yes: the occult rite, another mondo trope. The still fresh atrocities of Charles Manson and his followers are depicted with a recreation of what the narrator describes as an "identical" occult rite leading to murder. Over twisty sitar music, a girl is stripped, drugged and covered in hot wax in a ceremony that even the least adroit Manson follower would recognise as utter tripe. Other reflections on contemporary American culture include female hustling (or, the 'follow up') on Sunset Boulevard, still fresh in the mind from the film *Midnight*

Hugh Hefner and *Playboy* Bunny Girls in *America Cosi Nuda, Cosi Violenta*

Cowboy; LA Swingers; the cult of death as reported in Nancy Mitford's *The American Way of Death*; Vietnam protests (including an absurd ritual where a hairy youth has his fingers amputated so that he can no longer hold a rifle). The Hell's Angels' own particular cult of death is portrayed, the director tracking them in a car and firing questions at them as they roar past. Environmental disaster lurks in the displacement of Native American Indians (Arizona, we are told, is a "graveyard of memories") and the enormous garbage city of Staten Island. We also see folk eating disgusting food (in this case cockroaches) and the painting of naked female bodies by artists, both of which, for reasons that remain unclear, appear in every mondo film.

The fear of race war, fomented by certain elements with the Black Power movements and Manson's twisted logic, is represented in a horrific sequence where a group of 'rednecks' in Mississippi hunt down, repeatedly punch and crush the hand of a black man. This prefigures Jacopetti and Prosperi's shocking

Addio Zio Tom (1971). "Uncle Tom is gone forever", the narrator intones.

The film ends ("inevitably" — James White) with helicopter shots encircling the Statue of Liberty. Mondo films were incredibly popular in the US and yet the European mondo director can't make up his mind whether to admire or reject this brash new culture, a confused state of mind probably reflected quite widely still today.

The lofty aims and disparate range of images and sounds located within this mondo film caused concern for reviewers at the time. Attempts by the director, as James White in the *MFB* put it, to "spread a patina of logic over a series of unrelated scenes" frustrated Anglo-Saxon critics who require at all times the dull logic of rationalism be attached to documentary cinema. Martino's admittedly pretentious claim at examining the "collective unconsciousness" of the violence and perversion of America is nevertheless a largely successful and an important contribution to mondo cinema.

15

WITCHCRAFT
The shocking truth!
The weird world of
UNSPEAKABLE CULTS
OBSCENE RITUALS
EROTIC RITES
as it exists today in
cities and suburbs
of our civilized world!
SEE: Actual Human Sacrifice on The Bloodstained Altar of Baal!
SEE: Weird Demonic Rites of the Cult of Kali!
SEE: Erotic Prayers to the Goddess of the Cloven Hoof!
SEE: Macabre Orgies of a Secret Sect of Evil!
SEE: The Church of Satan celebrate its infamous Black Mass!
SEE: Occult Manifestations in The Coven of the Dead!
SEE: The Sensual Ecstasies of Hippie "Families"!
EXPOSED thru the eye of the HIDDEN CAMERA!
A P.A.C.-CARAVEL PRODUCTION
Witchcraft '70
X NO ONE UNDER 17 ADMITTED
COLOR BY MOVIELAB
DIRECTED BY LUIGI SCATTINI · ADDITIONAL SEQUENCES PHOTOGRAPHED and DIRECTED BY R.L. FROST · A TRANS AMERICAN RELEASE
70/144

CHAPTER 7
"UNSPEAKABLE CULTS, EROTIC RITES"

Mondo Magic and Ritual

In his 1970s African travel book *Which Tribe do you Belong To?* the great Italian writer Alberto Moravia describes witnessing a ju-ju ceremony in Lagos. For Moravia the fascination of such ceremonies lies in the fear it engenders in European tourist-visitors (and before that European colonialists). Despite its move towards neo-capitalism Africa remains, according to Moravia, paradoxically "prehistoric" both in terms of the visual (landscape) and of its devotion still to the various processes of magic. Magic in Africa remains rooted in a fear of the unknown and the irrational. Many of Moravia's considerations, his assessment, for example, that the African is more "unstable", and less "sound" than the European, now seem at best simplistically old-fashioned and at worst offensively racist (what Mary Louise Pratt writing in *Imperial Eyes* calls "a discourse of negation, domination, devaluation and fear"). Yet what the author does capture, both beautifully and lyrically, is the European obsession with viewing, watching and 'experiencing' the 'fear' and 'terror' of such ritual magic. This obsession was previously located in literature and poetry but now crucially and most powerfully, via the film imagination (sections of Moravia's book, his travels to Tanzania, were written while on location for an Italian TV film by Pier Paolo Pasolini — probably the unfinished *Appunti*

per una Orestiade Africana). Moravia, having contributed to Cavara's mondo critique *L'Occhio Selvaggio* (*The Wild Eye*), subsequently went on to become an influential figure in the construction and development of the 'ethnographic' mondo film, contributing commentary to two of the finest examples of such cinematic art: Antonio Climati and Mario Morra's *Ultime Grida dalla Savana* and Alfredo and Angelo Castiglioni's *Magia Nuda*. Moravia produced his scripts for these two films at the same time as these new forms of mondo were being developed and his subjective, poetic and eroticised approach to the anthropological and the ethnographic is stamped all over films dedicated to the expression of 'mondo magic'. The rich language of Moravia ("ju-ju has a very special quality of foulness" and "is a sombre disgusting substitute for science") resonates throughout the disturbing yet often problematic mondo depictions of ancient ritual and occult practices. Like Jacopetti, Moravia sought to update the picture of Africa offered previously by writers such as Kipling and later Hemmingway, into a modern, freeform prose

159

"Magic should serve, through ritual cannibalism, to confirm man's superiority in the face of nature."
ALBERTO MORAVIA

Le Mepris

style, the scripted surreal visions of the mondo film's visual and audio aesthetics. Moravia's observation that the colours of African fashion exhibited a "barbarism" echoed in the "pictorial experiments of the European avant garde" echoes the modernist schemata of many mondo films and their lurid design elements both in terms of the film and its promotion (see *Africa Addio*, *Mondo Magic*, *Africa Segreta* [*Africa Uncensored*]. Andrew Sarris, in a review of Godard's *Le Mepris* (which Moravia scripted) noted that for the Italian writer "sexuality and sensuality are the symbolic currencies of art, history, sociology, politics and economics". The 'mal d'Africa' favoured by the European imagination both on the page and on-screen, can therefore be found articulated through Moravia's travel writing and then his mondo film scripts.

Meanwhile in his own rather dubious account of travels in Africa for his film *Brutes and Savages* American producer and self-styled 'explorer' Arthur Davis recounts a ritualised Sudanese 'love dance', his description of which beautifully captures this mondo voyeuristic fascination with the exotic: "The flickering flames reflected distorted images of the dancers across the ground, shrinking their legs and stretching their bodies in grotesque caricatures of human shapes. I almost felt as if I were possessed by the same wild spirit. I could hardly distinguish reality from insanity. It looked like the witchdoctor was conducting a party in hell."

Mondo films reflect the obsessions of their time and the visual depiction of 'ritual' held fascination for a wide range of directors beyond the mondo canon (Godard, Fellini, Pasolini). For Herman Weinberg this obsession has developed out of a cynical outlook on the modern world and its increasingly complex cultural manifestations. His observation that "the flagrantly explicit depictions of sex and violence so far beyond anything ever depicted before (not even sparing us the sudden frenzy of cannibalism)... is surely a reflection in the cinema of a growing pessimism about the

Mother Joan of the Angels

future of mankind and the absence of ideals and myths on which to peg a more constructive horizon" articulates the spirit of art film excursions into the ritual tableaux as well as more formal shockumentary themes and codes. In his article on *Mondo Cane* Parker Tyler, a long-standing exponent of 'magic and myth in the movies', describes the "hysteria" induced from the "dominant instincts" that the film probes and offers up as souvenirs to its audience. In describing *Mondo Cane*, and the rituals of the 'modern and primitive' as an "unparalleled guidebook to the sacred and the profane" Tyler articulates the correct emphasis of the mondo school: namely to ritualise bizarre customs as filmed entertainment. Let us recall too that the master of the cinema of the unconscious, in an essay entitled 'Cinema, Instrument of Poetry', Luis Buñuel, drew our attention to the 'ritual' of the cinematic experience and the special role cinema plays, above all other arts, in placing the spectator in a "state of ecstasy".

These themes of ritual, magic and witchcraft, present as far back in films such as *Ingagi*, *Island of the Lost Souls*, *King Kong*, *Tabu*, *Goona Goona*, and fuelled the imaginations of other filmmakers in the 1960s and 1970s ("fascinating cannibalism" — the mixture of fascination and horror that 'ethnographic' films evoke — according to Fatimah Tobing Rony). Polish director Jerzy Kawalerowicz's film, *Mother Joan of the Angels/Devil and the Nun* for example, featured scenes of exorcisms (later restyled in Ken Russell's *The Devils*). The pre-mondo film, *L'Impero del Sole*, the third in a series of Italian exploration films (the previous were *Magia Verde* and *Continente Perduto*) was

"Our films were a compromise between spectacular effects and the needs of the ethnographer. Sometimes we got it right, but not always."
ANGELO & ALFREDO CASTIGLIONI

The Devils

composed of ritualised activities including drug rituals, birth customs, death feasts, animal violence, imported Catholic ceremonies and contrasts these with modernised 'ugly' South America (Franco Prosperi and Stanis Nievo began their careers on such exotic missions).

No doubt of equal fascination for Italians was the creation of the Sicilian 'Abbaye de Thélème' in 1920 by English magician Aleister Crowley, a place where 'sacred orgies', drug-fuelled ritualised acts of sexual magic where carried out. Jacopetti and Prosperi certainly found such macabre rituals of interest: the sequel to *Mondo Cane, Mondo Cane No.2*, features an astonishing Mexican 'feast of the dead' sequence where children consume confectionary sculpted into skulls and body parts, or with meticulous detail, into a likeness of Judas and shots of Indian fakirs defying the pain of hot coals and multiple piercings. Meanwhile such 'sinister practices in bright sunshine' became a staple of mondo films with numerous sequences on Catholic exorcisms, incantations, magic spells and rituals in Southern Italy, mostly created out of desperate poverty, a reaction against the failures of the 'natural order' to bring good fortune, inserted for shock effect. The bizarre dance of the tarantella (tarantulas) is symptomatic of this kind of mondo magic appearing again in *Mondo Cane No.2*, the crazy scenes of women under a spell shrieking and flailing in deconsecrated churches being culturally interesting and cinematically shocking. The ritualised killings of animals occurred in many performance art pieces of the 1970s (Austrian Hermann Nitsch in particular) in an attempt at capturing the primitive energy of the occult rituals in a clinical, scientific age. These attracted the attentions of mondo filmmakers too, most famously in the legendary mocking of French artist Yves Klein and his performances in *Mondo Cane*.

In 1930, French dramatist and theorist Antonin Artaud wrote an essay called 'Witchcraft and the Cinema' concerned with the "unexpected" and "mysterious" side of the cinematic arts. "The cinema reveals a whole occult life with which it puts us directly into contact," he inscribes, "but," he continues, "we must know how to divine this occult life". The mondo film, wilfully lacking the "clear thought" of conventional narrative drives and exhibiting instead "dreams in conscious life", a "fantasy which appears ever more real", brings this philosophy right up close to us and in full colour.

16

ANGELI BIANCHI… ANGELI NERI (WITCHCRAFT '70)

Directed by Luigi Scattini
(Italy, 1969)

This mondo film, although never on any levels a movie masterpiece ("scrapings from the mouldering *Mondo Cane* barrel", as one review described it), is an exquisite example of how the unique sensibilities of Italian shockumentary filmmaking can be pathetically wrecked by the interventions of overly commercialised American entertainment practices. Luigi Scattini's later forays into erotic thrillers were admittedly weak. Yet Scattini is a highly competent mondo filmmaker (he also made *Sexy Magico* with Mino Loy, *Questo*

Sporco Mondo Meraviglioso and *Svezia, inferno e paradiso*), and the subject of *Angeli Bianchi…*, that of the occult and witchcraft in the modern age, was ideal for shockumentary fans searching for a new angle on the mondo cane. The American exploitation producer, R Lee Frost, who re-edited the film for the US market, did not violate Scattini's film to the same level as his counterpart Jerry Gross did with Jacopetti and Prosperi's *Africa Addio*, but he certainly made a mess of it. Scattini and his regular mondo team of cinematographer Claudio

A WILD, WEIRD WORLD
OF BIZARRE PRACTICES

Witchcraft '70

EXPOSED thru the eye of the HIDDEN CAMERA!
COLOR BY MOVIELAB
Ⓧ NO ONE UNDER 17 ADMITTED
A P.A.C.-CARAVEL PRODUCTION · A TRANS AMERICAN RELEASE
©1970 Trans American Films

Racca and narrator Enrico Maria Salerno (reading the text of novelist and critic Alberto Bevilacqua) produced a luridly satisfying look at modern witchcraft, despite many of the scenes being staged or restaged events and the film appearing more 'fake' than Scattini's other mondo efforts. The tedious moral certainty of American documentary, the need to 'explain' everything using 'experts', materialised when Frost supplemented Scattini's original footage with bits of his own: lame testimony/interviews and sensationalist, naff horror motifs blighting the original aura (he also re-titled the film with the much less poetic *Witchcraft '70*). Although Scattini's original was driven by a pungently heady mixture of the occult, sex and horror this was needlessly amplified in the American version of the film becoming less of an inquiry and more of a joke. Edmund Purdom's English narration, always veering towards the hammy, achieves hilarious new heights of melodrama and every other word is emoted with Vincent Price-esque camp solemnity. The music also matches the ham of Purdom's narration constantly rising to 'scary' crescendos and drenched in horror

film musical cliché: ascending low single piano or harpsichord notes, vibrato minor chords, slashing discordant strings (this soundtrack displaced Piero Umiliani's original superb rich, psychedelic score, a further corrosion of quality — see appendix i). The unintentionally comical title sequence created by Biamonto and Grisanti sets the scene perfectly, an all-expense-spared compendium of cheap horror signifiers: bulging eyes, rising smoke, flash frames, possessed, convulsing bodies shot from weird angles, and the looming countenance of the Aleister Crowley-wannabe Anton LaVey (the "high priest of Satan") whose trademark piercing and demonic stare alarms until we see his house painted all black like a teenager's bedroom.

The archetypal dishonesty of mondo is, however, inescapable whichever version of the film you enjoy. Several times in the film the narrator informs us that due to a "lack of co-operation" from Satanist groups we are about to witness "home movie 8mm footage" "purchased" by the film's producers and "blown up to 35 millimetres". These sequences, the first depicting a Bahian (Brazilian) ritual cleansing the sins of man through the flagellation of prostitutes, the second of a "stylised folk drama" held in Bali and incorporating a trance-like dance preceding self mutilation with swords, on closer examination are fakes — albeit quite cleverly constructed ones. Scattini has taken care to insert the white dot perforations common to domestic film formats and a convincing grainy drop in quality, but the portraits of the participants in these dramas look far too professionally framed and the silence of the Java footage is eventually impinged upon by the inclusion of sad, eerie flute music, which the viewer is drawn into long before they realise the duplicity of such actions. Similarly contrived moments recording a voodoo ceremony in

Louisiana make a good job of mimicking secret filming activities (one of the participants suddenly looks at up the camera, but, we are reassured, "he is a paid informant"). A sequence at the end of the film on a counterculture satanic ritual, ending with the sexual assault of the initiates, is said to have been filmed from such a distance, using telephoto lenses, that the sound is inaudible. Yet we hear a vague sub-Hendrix wah-wah improvisation (reinforcing the evils of rock music) cutting through the night air and at the end hand-clapped rhythms and screams increase in time with the writhing of flickering flame-lit bare bums.

But does any of this matter?

From the first secretly filmed ritual, that of a black mass held in the dull London commuter land of Bedford, where the camera zooms intrusively in and out of the various stages of the ritual, we know that we are not watching anything that can be defined as 'reality'. The importance of the film instead lies in the

way it represents an exciting synthesis of horror, the occult and the erotic (the opening narration introducing the film as the "naked truth of black art in the modern age", a report on "Satan's unspeakable and yet sometimes erotic rites" makes this abundantly clear). No opportunity in the record of these occult rites to exhibit naked sexuality is passed up, whether this is the constantly photogenic bodies of sexy young girls in 'western' black arts (the occult marriage ceremony of the Church of Satan is wearily illustrated by a naked woman lying on the altar "attended by clutch of bosomy acolytes"), or the sticky, 'primitive' sexuality of those in the developing world (at the occult finale to the inauguration of the "Queen of the Witches" in Rio, a feast of the dead where participants writhe under the influence of drink, drugs and tobacco, it is observed that "the night air carries the stench of flames, food, sex and an acrid, unnatural sweat"). At the voodoo ceremony in Louisiana the 'queen' appears as a Tina Turner look-alike, complete

with flowing red dress, long black wig, and the hot booty-shaking commensurate with the image of the 'acid queen' herself.

The 1960s pop culture obsessions with the occult and with witchcraft, later to find full expression in horror (the productions of Tigon, Hammer etc) and mainstream thriller films (James Bond epic *Live and Let Die*) are glimpsed effectively whether it be through those of the chronically poor of Sicily (a 'witch' 'speaks' through the voice of her dead nephew who has been killed in a car crash, to the families of other motor car accident victims) or the magic of the middle classes (the occult marriage rites of London bankers, salesman and chemist shop assistants) recalls the bourgeois of 'table-turning' cults of nineteenth century Europe.

Inevitably the guilt-ridden rationale for such a catalogue of occult eroticisms is revealed through Frost's hastily inserted interview with Californian cop Lieutenant David Este, who frets on camera about the increase of interest by young people in black magic. As this film was shot and re-shot around the times of the infamous Tate/LaBianca murders carried out by Charles Manson and his followers the inference is clear: social freedoms, drugs and the occult lead to "our greatest danger... human sacrifice". The penultimate sequence on the hippy rite, designed to complement such neurosis, "the most shocking example of modern witchcraft," may be secretly filmed but is stupidly realised. As ever with mondo moralising, what starts out as being an expression of paternalistic concern through fear of the perverse practices of the modern age only produces belly laughs for the audience.

MAGIA NUDA (MONDO MAGIC)

Directed by Alfredo and Angelo Castiglioni
(Italy, 1974)

The first impressions of *Magia Nuda*, or *Mondo Magic* as it is known in the Anglo-Saxon world, are that the film is yet another sensationalist, greasy, exploitation mondo flick. Not least because of the images that accompanied the American video release of the film (a montage of extreme body piercings, ritual scarring and blood drinking overseen by a mystical all-seeing eye) and the tag-line ("A nightmare visit into the world of primitive practices") with the 'warning' message ("contains graphic depictions of shocking, erotic and/or barbaric practices that may offend the viewer"), all of which connote a hard-to-resist concoction of 'sexy magic'. In addition the film is mostly recalled in the hazy memories of (mostly male) exploitation fans who remember the shock effect of these ritual practices on impressionable, if curious minds (for example Patrick McCabe in his novel, *Mondo Desperado*, evokes "the risk of watching all them old tribesman beating each other senseless with poles" while alternative rock band Big Black used to recount this same scene as a between-songs filler). Most viewers of the film remember at least the circumcision rite. Scenes from the film have appeared in underground 'compilation videos', in particular the evocative shots of the Mundawi tribe's war dance and cattle rituals (see *Amok Assault Video* and Guliano Rossi and Luigi Vizzi's shameless mondo hack-compilation *Shocking Africa* for example) and so the film still has a tangible presence as a mondo paradigm.

The reality is that *Magia Nuda* is actually one of the least sensationalist mondo films produced and the nearest to 'ethnographic' that the genre ever got. The film is actually part of a trilogy by the Castiglioni brothers, Milanese twins with a background in scientific research and archaeology, the remaining films are *Africa Segreta (Secret Africa)* shot on 16mm and *Africa Ama*, their most commercially successful film. The shocks that *Magia Nuda* delivers to audiences are only those of the discovery of the bizarre rituals of so-called 'primitive' cultures of the world, codes that the west finds difficult to accept only because of conflicting attitudes towards death, sex, religion and the way in which these life roles intersect. It is the overall

style and look of the film that gives it an air of ethnographic discourse. The shots are flat and well lit; the lighting is only used as an essential aid to securing clear footage and, unlike in most mondos, is never used expressively. The shots are similarly composed with square medium-shot composition and framing only capturing what is essential (the fact that the Castiglioni brothers engaged Eastmancolor rather than Technicolor for their cameras may have also had an impact on this). The other important ingredient is the narration, which in this instance is also understated and dry. The narration, spoken by Marc Mauro Smith, is lent a socio-philosophical quality by nature of the fact it was composed by Alberto Moravia, no stranger to mondo style expositions of African culture and rituals. Even the opening titles lend the film an ethnographic air being simple block white trying to connote factual, scientific objectivity. The opening statements locate the film within the history of travels into the 'dark continent' evoking "the days when Stanley dared cut through the jungle in search of Livingstone". The scene is underscored by tom-tom drums which we are told, as one of the Castiglioni twins moves into view, "announce the arrival of the white man." The film has a very weird opening: while a river boat brings Africans (and one presumes the filmmakers) to the banks of the Nile, the opening notes of Old Man River can be heard. This segues into the tune known in the US and the UK as When A Child Is Born, a sickly Christmas ballad sung by Johnny Mathis (this version is named Soleado by Zacar, arranged by the Daniel Santacruz Ensemble). The sentimentality of the music inaugurates the film's solemn mood, a mood which continues throughout the film. The locations of the film are grouped around four tribal areas — the Dinka and Mundawi tribes of the Sudanese White Nile; the Yanomamö tribe of the equatorial rain forests of the Amazon and sects of the Philippines and Ceylon (now Sri Lanka). The Castiglionis have tried to capture and display the magic rituals and practices, medicinal and sexual, of these locations with a cold calculating eye, partly with success. Music is sparely used. They have even included the occasional topical socio-cultural quote to support what they are witnessing whether it is Marshall MacLuhan's notion of the 'global village' (the narration in the film states: "the fragments of the Koran [the medium] becomes the message") or Sigmund Freud's theories of 'penis envy'. So far so 'ethnographic'. Yet this being a mondo film the veneer of scientific inquiry begins to slip away and the depiction of the rituals becomes energised by recognisable shockumentary attributes. As early as the end of the opening sequence the practices of the Mundawi, covering their children with cattle urine as an insect repellent, puffing smoke into their precious cattle's vaginas to induce fertility, the narrator observes that we are entering a "darker realm where the difference between terror and ecstasy is meaningless and where the lynchpin of all existence is magic"

"The world of magic is none other than the 'African sickness', no longer seen from the point of view of Europeans but from that of the Africans themselves."
ALBERTO MORAVIA

MONDO MAGIC

A NIGHTMARE VISIT INTO THE WORLD OF PRIMITIVE PRACTICES!

(the collection and usage of cattle dung as a mystical substance echoes scenes in Jacopetti and Prosperi's *La Donna nel Mondo*). The famous sequence capturing the pogo-style warrior dance of the tribesmen is presented with the rationale that "only slow-motion does justice to the structured beauty of the race in action". Such aims may be noble and artistic but close-up groin shots with the men's sexual organs flapping freely up and down code the scene from most angles as (s)exploitative. The Castiglionis claim that they only use field recordings for their soundtracks does not hold up either (in this film at least). Aside from the sad musical score by legendary Italian composer Angelo Francesco Lavagnino, which swells accordingly during emotional passages, scenes from the film resonate with splatterings of weird electro phrases (most creepily over a shot of a dead witch doctor's dried corpse lying untouched on the plain). Any 'authentic' diegetic sound recordings appear to have been amplified for effect,

particularly to heighten the more stomach churning gastronomic aspects of these magic rituals (the Dinka drinking fresh cattle blood, Yanomamö munching on roasted caterpillars and spiders, an Ethiopian witch doctor suckling the nipple of an infertile woman, vomiting as part of an exorcism in Cameroon). Many mondo traits gradually emerge: animal slaughter (a giraffe and an elephant are killed and sliced up by razor-sharp spears in "a brutal assassination", birds are skewered in slow-motion), violence (the finger of a Cameroon man is amputated after a demon has been massaged into it), nudity (close-up shots of bouncing breasts during a ritual dance). The uncontrollable urge to discover and display the weird is clear — Yanomamö tribesmen (described as being "lost in a primordial time zone"... "let's search for them" the narrator urges) mete out an adultery punishment which consists of whacking each other over the head with abrushi canes until one of them falls bleeding and unconscious; the psychic surgery of Manila where operations to remove foreign objects are carried out, incredibly without anaesthetic and by hand (in an interview for *Healter Skelter* magazine the Castiglionis admit to being unable to establish the veracity of these rituals); religious flagellations are shown in painful detail, both Hindu (a devotee is suspended by hooks through the skin of his back, a practice that inspired the Australian performance artist Stelarc, or Christian (Philippine penitents flog themselves until they bleed exhorting the flagellation of Christ). This latter scene together with the pictures of a Yanomamö women suckling a pig with her breast, clearly resurrect the spirit, ten years on, of *Mondo Cane*. The mondo devotion to the icon of the human skull continues

Mondo Magic

during "endo-cannibalistic" practices where the bones of the dead are crushed and eaten with mashed banana. The 'magical' theme of the film is exemplified further with the usually gory witchcraft rituals, whether this documents charms made from the tusks of the slaughtered elephant (whose eye is removed so that he does not "see" the native's desecration) or the mutilation magic of Ethiopian Arabs who incise their children's eyebrows and backs to prevent illness. Meanwhile the film's devotion to 'Naked Magic' is the climax and is exhibited through Islamic sexual rituals (vaginal examinations by a Marabou fetishist mother, the brushing of the bodies of a couple having intercourse with aphrodisiac leaves), the masturbatory initiation ceremonies of novice nuns, and the guileless Legba dance rituals where the simulation/initiation to all form of humane sexuality is open and explicit. The pornographic imagination of the filmmakers is manifested throughout all of these scenes.

Magia Nuda is a memorable mondo film that still, even in an age abundant in shock TV and film, packs a punch. But the predictable finale, lamenting the fact that "magic is no longer naked" because "new myths" (planes bringing consumer goods) "dot the Africans' horizon" and that "gadgets are the fetishes of the new generation" is countered with a defiance that "magic will never die — not in Africa". As the Castiglioni's Land Rover and boat leave the African coast whilst natives wave them off into golden sunsets, such laments (as always) ring hollow. When the filmmakers earlier have (correctly) cursed the advent of modern development in the Amazon rain forests, and paraphrased Jacopetti and Prosperi in bidding "Amazonia farewell", they are forgetting that via such planes along such new concrete roads come Italian directors and their crews, exploiting the location for a long series of grisly "uncut!, uncensored!, untamed!" pseudo-ethnographic mondo, horror and cannibal films.

NUOVA GUINEA, L'ISOLA DEL CANNIBALI (GUINEA AMA)

Directed by Akira Ide
(Italy/Japan, 1974)

This unusual addition to the mondo canon has many curious aspects about it, bearing an uncanny resemblance to Barbet Schroeder's odd dream-like journey-into-the-unknown film *La Valée (The Valley Obscured by Clouds)*. With a soundtrack composed by Pink Floyd, *La Valée* is about a group of affluent, bored, bourgeois hippies undertaking a long trek into the centre of New Guinea to find spiritual enlightenment and an earthly paradise — marked on the map as 'obscured by clouds'. The sequences of the film documenting the group's arrival at this place and their necessary if deceitful engagement with the natives of this location, 'played by' genuine tribes people and shot journalistically, are akin to the exploration/exploitation dichotomy of mondo ethics. In one scene the lead character Viviane becomes immersed in a tribal spirit dance, the masked men that gradually surround her are recognisable as those from Akira Ide's film, *Nuova Guinea, L'Isola del Cannibali*. (And also as an image of 'primitivism' — photos of these tribesmen appeared as the sleeve artwork for the first release by British post-punk group Pop Group for example.) Both films explore the drama and danger of such a remote expedition and image the depths of the 'Island of Cannibals' where the modern world collides with mysticism and man's primitive past. Perhaps a better known aspect of the film is that certain sequences were bought and crudely replanted by Italian exploitation director Bruno Mattei, for his *Zombie Creeping Flesh* and *Libidomania* films. The way in which the film brilliantly plays up horror and taboo via a unique European/

UNVORSTELLBAR·NIE GESEHEN
UNBEGREIFLICH
GUINEA AMA ©

Japanese sensibility would influence late mondos, such as *Faces of Death* and *Killing of America* and create a substantial audience in Japan for mondo movies (the film was, like many cannibal films, popular in Germany where the 'real' practice of cannibalism was to become controversial headline news).

The location of New Guinea was an obvious choice for mondo directors searching out primitive rituals and behaviour patterns not yet touched by 'civilised' progress and technological 'advancement'. The island had long held a mythological status as the final place to outlaw the accepted practice of cannibalism (one sequence in the film depicts the authorities' attempts at stamping out such practices). Whichever translation of the title you prefer, man-eating certainly appears to be the theme of Ide's film. Yet despite some opening shocks representing with the taboo of cannibalism (the gruesome title frame with blood-red lettering dripping over a shot

of a human skull; some scenes of a woman simultaneously nursing a baby and a putrefying maggoty corpse which she picks and nibbles from — the baby plays nonchalantly with her necklace), and the recurrence of death, the film pans out to be a broad survey of New Guinea rituals and customs all delivered in the reassuring mondo fashion. The scenes described above create a tangible amount of trepidation and anxiety, yet as with almost all mondo films this is eventually tempered with the queer, the exotic and the ridiculous. Audiences have to wait until the end of film before further cannibalistic shocks are delivered. The unique atmosphere of much of the film is what makes it an important addition to the mondo canon and is that of Japanese horror, where supernatural fear is created out of simple 'everyday' occurrences presented with cold-eyed pathological clarity. Due to the way they are framed and displayed these simple, if perplexing to western eyes, rituals

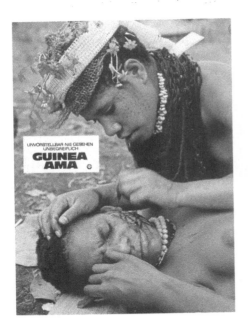

by Corrado Demofonti (the woman picking at the rotting corpse sequence has some eerie flute music and a gong resonating ominously; freeze-frames of tribal members are accompanied by low single piano notes; men bloodletting their noses into the river waters to enrich it, do this in synch with some freaky experimental electronic twinkling — like *The Clangers* on speed). There is the frequent emergence of a 'cannibal island' theme written by mondo veteran Riz Ortolani. This theme has actually been appropriated from one of Ortolani's classic non-mondo scores written earlier for Umberto Lenzi's famous giallo *Così dolce... così perversa*. The booming theme song 'Why?' from that film is used in the finale of *Nuova Guinea*, as is another piece, a slow jazz flute motif. The incongruous use of electric guitar music, one-minute jazz-funk fusion, the next Velvet Underground-style scratching, is also a jaw-dropping feature. But perhaps the most astonishing use of musical backing occurs for a typically lightweight mondo diversion into the dress and adornments of the New Guinea peoples. Shots of women in modern miniskirts and men in other 'western' attire are contrasted with the painful decorations of tribal ritual, in particular use of tattoos, scarification and piercings. While we watch these 'anthropological' studies of ritual in action the soundtrack switches to a gentle organ bossa motif, a superbly breezy luxuriant passage complete with female scat vocals more akin to a hairspray advert than an anthropological study — which may or may not be intentional.

Nuova Guinea is agreeably photographed by an Italian-Japanese team and faithfully mimics the mondo predilection for sudden freeze-frames (the 'secretly filmed' shots of

become creepy and frightening. A key aspect of this atmosphere is the soundtrack, one of the most astounding and intriguing mondo musical accompaniments ever conceived, and one that adds a vital air of unreality to the mood of the film. Fear and shock are created from combining musical instruments, sounds and electronics in a perverse manner and there are two recurring phrases in particular which exemplify this technique. The first, accompanying a trek representing the filmmakers' journey to the centre of the island, is an eerie composition featuring sudden dramatic discordant piano chords and very fast pounding 'ethnic' drumming. The second phrase occurs during sequences depicting the funeral rites of the dead (skeletal remains and recently deceased fleshy corpse) where the music is an astounding collage of avant-electro bleeps, vocal wailing (possibly diegetic), rumbling cymbals building to a crescendo, and strange organ stabs. In addition to other evocative and scary musical themes composed

illegal cannibalism in action) and slow-motion (a dead man, after being wrapped in leaves, is cast into the river waters: this part of the action slows down and then freezes). The killing of animals is notable (bats wings are sliced from their torsos, which are then eaten and made into skirts; crocodiles are sliced; lizards and snakes are cooked). Like virtually all mondo films *Nuova Guinea* is filled with excuses for titillation. Native nudity is natural and as usual is displayed, but cutaway close-ups of bouncing breasts, telephoto glimpses of naked washing, and long pans which linger for no obvious ethno-anthropological purpose over the breasts of young girls as they moan orgasmically at the pain of the tattoo/scarring rituals, fail to be compensated by a short sequence on Koteka (penis gourds). A section on sexual transgressions is similarly exploitative: once the point has been made that homosexuality is accepted in the interior as well as in more modern parts of the island,

it seems crass to introduce some camp, silly backing music. The macho conservatism of mondo directors now emerges: the arrival of "feminist" and "suffragette" concepts in New Guinea is also derided.

Despite this, *Nuova Guinea* is a fascinating and largely original reading of shockumentary filmmaking, certainly one of its most haunting and disturbing treatments. Yet as the film closes and we recall the parts of the film that echo *Mondo Cane* (lyrical aerial shots of landscapes, males being molested by females, the crushing of hogs' skulls before they are feasted on, the recognisable features of some of the natives, the arrival of American tourists wanting to photograph the 'rituals') the viewer is slightly relieved by the shots of the arrival of the island's independent status. Perhaps no longer will white (or brown or yellow) men with probing lenses feel the need to capture on film the culture of the last cannibalistic remnants of the Stone Age.

APPENDIX I :
INTERVIEWS WITH THE JACOPETTI/PROSPERI TEAM

Gualtiero Jacopetti

ualtiero Jacopetti was born on 4 September 1919 in Barga, Tuscany. During the Second World War he was involved in counterespionage with the American forces, and after the war worked as a publicist for the Christian Democrats. He made his name as a journalist in the liberal weekly news magazine *Cronache*, which he helped found. The magazine was the forerunner of *L'Espresso*, launched two years later. After working on newsreels, which Jacopetti tried to make more colourful than the dry, state-sponsored efforts, he teamed up with Franco Prosperi, cameraman Antonio Climati and composer Riz Ortolani, a unit that remained constant for all his feature films.

In addition to *Mondo Cane*, *La Donna nel Mondo*, *Africa Addio* and *Addio Zio Tom* Jacopetti also scripted *Fangio*, the story of the great Argentinian racing driver Juan Manuel Fangio, for Hugh Hudson. *Mondo Candido* (1975) was a satirical tribute to Jacopetti's hero Voltaire, whose most famous work, *Candide*, seemed to echo Jacopetti's own strange traverse through life. As with *Zio Tom*, cinematic parallels were drawn between seemingly disparate continents across random timescales.

Gualtiero Jacopetti died on 17 August 2011. This interview was conducted as his apartment in Rome in 2001.

MARK GOODALL: Can you describe the idea behind your newsreels?

GUALTIERO JACOPETTI: In my opinion there's no difference between journalism, and by that I mean the traditional written one, and the cinematographic one. I started my career as a journalist but I became increasingly fascinated by cinema, by the idea to try to translate a written page into a series of images, a soundtrack, and words; my words, my voice, sound effects which would help in conveying my thoughts.

MG: Can you outline how you began as a filmmaker and who and what were your (cinematic) influences?

GJ: Documentary has been a complete discovery for me. I can't say that I have been inspired by any film maker because before *Mondo Cane* the world of documentaries was something else altogether. This has been my own personal discovery — to realise that with documentary you could do both journalism and entertainment.

Mondo Cane has created a new style, but the reason is that this was unprecedented. I did not know, before its release, how it would have been accepted by the public — the effect and response I would have had by showing it to a paying audience. The things that were astounding me whilst filming are the things that astounded the public too. *Mondo Cane* took a year and a half, almost two years to make, as the nature of the documentary is waiting for the events to happen rather than constructing them. We shot almost two million metres of film as when you're shooting real-life events you push a button and then you have to wait for things to happen. Then, from all of the material filmed you have to edit a story which follows what you set out to narrate.

MG: What do mean by 'shock cuts' (thinking of the 'casa del morte' sequence in *Mondo Cane*)?

GJ: I'd like to make a premise before I answer this question. Having seen this clip now I would edit it differently: I would half it. When I edited it for the first time I was taken by the shock of the novelty and the novelty, at the time, was more interesting than it is today, as many things shown are now taken for granted. Editing a documentary is the most delicate and important stage and it is one that should be done by whoever conceived the film in the

first place. I would relate this to the work of a journalist who goes to report an event and takes many notes in his book. In the case of the documentary, those notes are images. Those images are separate, untied one from the other, and have to be put together just as the journalist puts together his notes into an article and constructs the story, its phrases, its grammar. The editing of a documentary is the equivalent of a grammar, there is a subject, a verb etc... it is a matter of following logic.

MG: Could you talk about your 'team' (Prosperi, Climati etc.)?

"We shot almost two million metres of film as when you're shooting real-life events you push a button and then you have to wait for things to happen."
GUALTIERO JACOPETTI

MG: Did you personally film any sequences?

GJ: Yes I filmed too. The crew is small and everyone in it should be able to do everything; no one should be indispensable. Many times I acted as a cameraman and many shots were taken by me directly.

MG: Can you outline the importance of Riz Ortolani's music in your films?

GJ: When a journalist writes his articles he doesn't need violins. But cinema has a 'space' dedicated to music which is extremely important in emphasising an atmosphere, to help convey the emotions of the images shown to the public. On the track of a film there are four 'voices': the speaker that narrates; the natural sounds; then there is the music and the special effects. The important thing to me is that those voices do not speak simultaneously. There's a time for the narration, a time for the music a time for the effects and so on, otherwise you fall into the trap of being rhetorical — the rhetoric of fiction.

GJ: Making a documentary is not a one-man job. It is very much the work of an team of people that collaborate to achieve one thing. A journalist works with a typewriter, a piece of paper and his experience, his wealth of knowledge. A cinematographer needs collaborators, physical people, not only machines. A camera doesn't work itself, there's a man behind it. Talking about Antonio (Climati), his help was precious. I should explain that when you make a documentary you cannot have numerous people in your crew as you are going to places that are difficult to reach and dangerous, so in one person you need the widest possible variety of skills — and someone who is physically able. Normally a camera moves on a tripod or several mechanical instruments, dolly, track etc. For me, Climati was all of them! I used to stand behind him, by his shoulder, directing him. He was able to do alone what in a studio you would do with lots of machines and many people.

MG: Could you speak about the Yves Klein sequence in *Mondo Cane*?

GJ: To be frank, Klein had been an acclaimed artist, although I did not understand him; or rather I don't think there was much to understand. Anyway, forty years ago to see a man paint a blue canvas and sell it for half a million dollars left me with a few doubts and I wanted to express these. Obviously, there was a bit of irony involved. The satire about his work came to me spontaneously. Today it's all different... a lot of time has passed.

MG: Why do you wish to 'distance' yourself from *Mondo Cane No.2*?

GJ: I was not involved in it. It was entirely an initiative of the producers that wanted to optimise use of the material that had been cut out of *Mondo Cane*.

MG: What do you think of the imitations of *Mondo Cane*?

GJ: Firstly, I have little respect for those people that copy someone else's ideas. Secondly, I reprove the vulgarity of what was produced. *Mondo Cane* shows human situations, reality, there's never a speculation. In trying to copy *Mondo Cane* despicable things have been produced which in the process have also damaged the first and only one (mine).

MG: Why did you make *Africa Addio*?

GJ: I am of a generation who dreamed of Africa, an Africa that's completely different from how it is today — a land of adventure, dreams and freedom — an Africa that I had of course never seen but had learnt to know by reading. Around the time of *Africa Addio* there was a fundamental political process taking place. Colonies were remunerable no longer, they had become increasingly uncomfortable, so the world — Europe — changed its political views and interests in it. This change happened so quickly. The colonial governors in Africa suddenly left and this caused a lot of damage, as Africa became easy prey for dictators. I was there at the time of this happening. I lived this sudden metamorphosis with agony. Still today, Africa is in agony. This is what pushed me to record history, to conduct an inquest.

But the thing that truly pushed me to shoot this movie was the letter from an

"Normally a camera moves on a tripod or several mechanical instruments, dolly, track etc. For me, Climati was all of them!"
GUALTIERO JACOPETTI

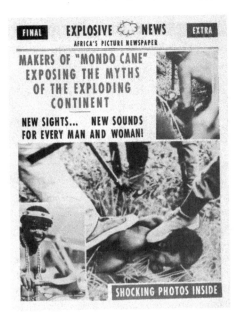

English girl, Carolyn Thompson, to whom I later dedicated the movie. This girl was from a family that lived in what today is called Zambia. She came to study in the UK and on her return back home, after a few years, she sent this letter describing a change so sudden and brutal with such humanity, with such powerful and interesting words that I was inpsired to make *Africa Addio*.

MG: What about the controversy of the film?

GJ: I was accused of slaughter. It was a curious situation, too complicated to explain! The film showed people being shot and a newspaper published an article entitled, "The war fought according to Jacopetti." This article was actually written by a friend, a journalist who was with me in Africa at the time (Carlo Gregoretti). The article was claiming that I was actively staging things, asking for people to be shot not in one place, but rather in another, in order for the scene to be more favourable to

the camera! Following these accusations there was a public investigation. There were a series of articles written by this friend that did not intentionally aim at damaging me, but did.

According to Italian legislation, if and when you are being accused of slaughter there's an immediate arrest. But I managed to convince the judge (in one night) that if he didn't arrest me, the following day I would go back to Africa to gather the evidence to show that I took no part in any massacre and, in fact, contributed in saving many lives. In order not to arrest me the judge had to perform a sleight of hand to make it look as though I had been interrogated as a witness rather than an accused. The following day — Christmas Day — I left for Africa. We went to the various embassies and collected officially stamped papers on which were reported and validated the statements that certified the lives of the several people I helped to save. After a month spent gathering statements, I came back to Italy, presented all the proof we had gathered and was absolved. As often happens though, the papers rush to publish sensational headlines when someone is accused of a crime but not so when someone is proven innocent.

Apart from that I was not really damaged. Also, after *Mondo Cane* 'Jacopetti' had developed the reputation of a cynic. For example, when, in *Mondo Cane*, I show a restaurant that fed people dogs, then it was quite shocking news. Today everyone's aware of it. Jacopetti is the 'bad guy'. It seems as if I am guilty for all this. People always try to assign a personality to what they see.

MG: What drove you on to shoot the dangerous scenes in *Africa Addio*?

Author Mark Goodall interviews Gualtiero Jacopetti at the Bradford Film Festival

GJ: Personal initiative, patience and willpower. I befriended the mercenaries and the commander of the Belgian army in order to be able to get permission, along with the entire crew, to watch and follow them. Naturally they didn't like the idea of having witnesses but it was a matter of overcoming their reluctance. After a while our persistence started to create some irony from their side. When I was asking to follow the war, following was an understatement; to film a war you have to be in front, not behind! So with a bit of irony and malice they gave us a truck that was to precede the entire army. We literally were sitting in front row seats — we were privileged! Though it all went well, the bullets you see coming at us were actually experienced first hand.

The night that we were getting ready to attack Boende we were on a boat, on the river Congo. There was a full moon in the sky. I had the crew around me and I could feel that they wanted to tell me something. Eventually Climati and Nievo told me that their insurance did not cover war risks. As fathers and husbands they were worried and felt the need to tell me this. They were expecting a solution. Under the moon I took a worthless piece of paper and scribbled that I extended their insurance to war crimes. They were fully aware when they took the piece of paper that it had no real value, and happily continued working!

MG: Ortolani told us that Sergio Leone followed the editing of *Africa Addio*?

"I was accused of slaughter. It was a curious situation, too complicated to explain!"
GUALTIERO JACOPETTI

JACOPETTI'S
explosiver Schocker:

ADDIO ONKEL TOM

Atlantic | arabella -Filmverleih

present, with modern technologies, in the past. It was a bit of a hazardous idea, and was not so very well received, but I did it and the result was acceptable. The film was a fake documentary made by a modern crew, with modern technologies shooting in the nineteenth century, reconstructing all of the situations, with actors taken from the streets, with costumes. A reconstruction. On the one side you have the fiction and on the other, fake actuality. It was a hybrid, an unconventional event. An experiment in creating an event that does not exist, a past event.

MG: Why did you choose to act in the film?

GJ: I chose to be in front of the camera because very often there was a lack of actors. When you're making a documentary you have to be ready to be everything: director, cameraman, actor, etc...

MG: How would you like to be remembered?

GJ: I am almost eighty-four-years-old. I doubt I can make many plans. I have a big future in my past. I have many pleasant memories of a life lived, a life which has seen the birth of two, almost three, new generations. I was born when the moon was in its place without people walking on it! When there was no television. The world has changed radically and I have had many experiences. I would certainly like to have several more, providing that fate wants me to...

GJ: Sergio Leone was a friend. I met him whilst we were editing. When I was working on the film we used to meet for breakfast etc. There was a certain feeling between the two of us. He dealt with fiction though. He created situations with several million lira in studios! I did it using reality. We had two different styles: I was a journalist and he was a great film director.

MG: What are your memories of making *Addio Zio Tom*?

GJ: *Addio Zio Tom* was the result of my need to make a compromise. Up until then I had been making documentaries but I was fascinated by the idea to be present in the era that saw the freeing of the African-American slaves. So I thought of creating a fake documentary; to be

Franco Prosperi

Franco Prosperi was born in Rome in 1926 and trained as a marine biologist. This work led to the publication of *Lord of the Sharks* (1952) and *Vanished Continent* (1957) which predated the contemporary obsession with exciting science travelogues. After the spilt with Jacopetti in the mid-1970s, he went on to make his own eco-horror film, *Belve Feroci* (*Wild Beasts*) (1983), and in 2001 published a novel, *Shumba*, based on the true story of a vegetarian lion he befriended. He is often mistaken for another Italian director, who made hugely successful peplum films. Prosperi told me that from time to time he received large tax bills in the other Prosperi's name.

Gualtiero Jacopetti and Franco Prosperi

This interview took place at his home in Formia in 2001.

Mark Goodall: How did you begin as a filmmaker?

Franco Prosperi: Before I started working in mainstream cinema, I had studied zoology. I was a naturalist and worked for the Italian Geographic Society and the geological institute of the University of Rome, doing geographic expeditions. We travelled around the world collecting specimens, both living and dead, that were sent to various museums.

We travelled round making documentaries — these were well received and won awards for being well made. We then came to realise that we could earn more making documentaries than we could from our university salaries, so we had a go at making mainstream films and had some success.

MG: What about your background in marine biology and early projects before *Mondo Cane*?

FP: Yes, I worked in marine biology, but also dealing with land animals. We travelled around virtually everywhere — New Guinea, Australia, Africa — and we made these documentaries that, as I said, won awards. We made loads of them — for RAI (Radiotelevisione Italiana) for example we made over thirty, one or one-and-a-half hours each, and about eighty others. So we were relatively well prepared to enter the world of cinema.

MG: Can you tell us about your collaboration with Stanis Nievo?

FP: Yes, I worked a lot with him. We went to school together and from a young age we both wanted to travel in whatever way we could. So we were ready for these trips. We each had our

A QUESTO "MONDO CANE" CHE TANTO CI PIACE E NEL QUALE CI TROVIAMO TUTTI BENISSIMO

GUALTIERO JACOPETTI
PAOLO CAVARA
FRANCO PROSPERI

CINERIZ   TECHNICOLOR

MONDO CANE

own area of expertise — Nievo specialised in mammals, I in aetiology, and other members of the team in other branches of the natural sciences. Carlo Prola, for example, had already done documentaries for RAI. He and his son Guido were entomologists — in fact his son has two types of butterfly in Tanganyika named after him.

But the big turning point came when I met Gualtiero Jacopetti. We had a mutual friend, Carlo Gregoretti, editor of *L'Espresso*. Gregoretti had made the very first expedition with me to Sri Lanka (Ceylon as it was), and was doing research on sharks and the effects particular substances (like shark repellents) had on them. We had done this expedition together, and Gregoretti knew Jacopetti and introduced us.

Jacopetti then was much better known in the cinema world than me, for not only was he the editor of an important newspaper, but also editor of a film magazine called *Ieri Oggi e Domani* (*Yesterday, Today and Tomorrow*) so

he was already known in the film world. So we met and it was a meeting of minds.

I went to him with the suggestion for a very different film from *Mondo Cane*. I had an idea for a film called *Amore nel mondo* (*love in the world*), that is, love in animals and man the world over. And he suggested we make a sort of 'anti-documentary', and that's how the idea for *Mondo Cane* came about. I already had the experience of travel (more than him). I wrote the screenplay outlining what we were hoping to do, we'd meet at Gregoretti's house and discuss the project, but what was missing was someone to organise everything — so we called Stanis Nievo, who obviously had a lot of experience and understanding, and he became the producer for the film. So that's how we did it — he would go on ahead, seeking out the things we'd talked about, even finding new ones. He would get to know a place, make contacts and do the preparation, then the rest of the gang would join him and while we did the filming there, he would have already gone on to the next place. That's how it was done.

MG: Can you tell us about your collaboration with Jacopetti?

FP: Gualtiero has always had charisma, a unique sort of karma. It's all in his way of filming, we shared the same views — anti-hypocrisy — most films showed the world as a sort of paradise, but we wanted to show what lay behind the façade, the real world. But over and above that he introduced a new take on filmmaking. Usually a documentary would centre on one particular place, like New Guinea for example, but we would go to New Guinea and the piece would last three minutes, then go on to some other spot to get

Mondo Cane

to the essence of the subject. Gualtiero and I were of the same mind-set.

MG: In what way did you work together — were there clearly defined roles?

FP: No, when we were working together — and we weren't always, sometimes certain episodes would take us away from the set — but when we were together, we worked as equals, sometimes he would take the lead, sometimes I would, but he would organise everyone. We were only a small group. There was Gualtiero, Antonio Climati, Benito Frattari, at a later point one of my grandsons (Federico Prosperi) joined us to help and then a lady who helped organise things — so essentially five people. So if we were shooting, for example in *Zio Tom*, the scene with the slave market, with probably 600 people in it — there were five of us to do everything. Each of us had something to do.

MG: Stanis Nievo talked about 'directing an orchestra' rather than being a film director.

FP: I think it's like a good football team, they are successful when they work well together, and we were very fortunate that we had really good individuals (myself apart!) — all brilliant in their own spheres. So Climati, from the photographic perspective, taking daring shots, getting in close, filming with a Steadicam. Then Nievo, so good at organisation, and at gaining acceptance and winning hearts wherever we went. So we had a small team, but we worked well together. And from an administrative point of view, another thing was the honesty — our films actually didn't cost a great deal — *Mondo Cane* cost about 150,000 (lira) for three years' work! *Africa Addio* a few years later cost 300 million (150,000 metres of film) and about the same for *Mondo Cane* and *La Donna nel Mondo*.)

Antonio Climati

MG: What do you think is special about Antonio Climati as a cameraman?

FP: He underpinned the whole thing. Climati was not only a cameraman, but a director — so it was important to have the instinct of what to film and when, without having to be told. We had no rigid divisions between us, I had my own camera too, as did my grandson and Gualtiero, so we would each takes shots from different angles. However, Antonio was the lead cameraman. Also Benito Frattari, whilst perhaps having less flair, was very reliable, in contrast to Climati who was more inspired but more disorganised! Not so much in terms of work, but in his lifestyle.

MG: What was Paolo Cavara's role?

FP: To begin with we all worked together as equals, the three of us. But Paolo was very unlucky, suffering from recurrent pneumonia, then a serious accident in a plane when we came down very quickly and he broke his arm and leg. From that moment he couldn't face flying and, in fact, when we tried to get him on a plane in Singapore to go back to Europe, just before take-off, the plane had to stop and he spent a month recovering in hospital. Then, when he returned to America, there was

another accident in which Belinda Lee died, so sadly our work together only really lasted for the time making *Mondo Cane*.

MG: Can you outline the importance of Riz Ortolani's music in your films?

FP: Yes, Riz Ortolani is another example of having a great team. When he started working with us, he was already close to the world of cinema, full of musical ideas. We would all go to dine at his house, where Katyna Ranieri, his wife, would cook for us, and then he would go to the piano and play us some musical motifs and we'd say 'why don't we put that in this scene' or 'why not highlight this.' For example, with More, which was a famous piece, at the beginning it was a sort of marching tune, but we suggested slowing it down, so it was a collaborative work. But he himself was just bursting with musical ideas.

MG: What was the importance of the music? What does it add to the imagery?

FP: It is very important. Many times we'd ask Riz to give us some music and we would build the scene around it, and then he would say to us that he based the music on the specific scene — it was a case of which came first, the chicken or the egg! But the music was hugely important to us, and also when editing the film, we paid a lot of attention to it. Also his collaboration meant that we had access to a large orchestra.

MG: What do you think is meant by your films being described (around the time of *Africa Addio*) as 'a new form of journalism'? Do you think it's a fair assessment?

FP: Yes, I think it's a fair assessment, I'm proud of the film. However, we came in for some criticism — we were accused of being racist and many other things that took away from the enjoyment of making the film and really upset us.

The Italian left-wing parties accused us of racism and of being romantics, in the sense of being nostalgic, and in Italy nostalgia equates with fascism — and this was certainly not our intention. These stereotypical labels are crazy — but this was the criticism we faced. But there's something else that is also happening at the moment, that's the politicizing of the legal system — a group of judges attacked *Africa Addio*, saying that Jacopetti, Nievo and Climati, who were filming in the Congo (I was with another group in Mozambique) had ordered some mercenaries to kill some people just to provoke a response. This was ridiculous; it's obvious that if you're going to shoot a scene where someone dies, you don't need to kill them. From a filming point of view, you can

'kill' them many times over if the first take is no good. But this censorship was very costly to us, because our film was confiscated, they had to go back and answer questions — the President, the cardinal of the country, all the powers that be — to quash these accusations, because they were on the point of being arrested for murder. So everything ground to a halt.

This mentality stayed until *Addio Zio Tom*, which we were going to film in Brazil, and it was our first work of fiction, a film based on events in the past, but a reconstruction. We did all the preparatory work necessary, went to the Brazilian embassy for permission, we went

"We were accused of being racist and many other things that took away from the enjoyment of making the film and really upset us."
FRANCO PROSPERI

Filing Addio Zio Tom

to New York and we were stopped because Brazil was worried we might film a '*Mondo Cane* in Brazil'. I had to go on my own to Rio de Janeiro, talking to the minister of culture who was called Donatello and originally from Italy, but things didn't go our way.

The rest of the group were stuck in America, with no hope of going on location. In fact, Giampaolo Lomi, who was to organise things in Brazil, because he knew the country well, was left with nothing to do. So we suggested that he join us and we started to film in the southern states of the US. You might have thought this would be easier, but it had its own problems — you can imagine shooting a film about slavery in Alabama or Mississippi was never going to be easy.

I remember we were shooting a scene with some white and black children, and we had put them together — the police arrived because they were together. They were only young, one or two years old. So there were problems even there.

MG: The film was criticised at the time for its negative portrayal of black Africans. Was this justified (now that many of those leaders are discredited)?

FP: Nowadays, as then, there's a kind of inverse racism. That is, just because someone has a black face, whatever he does, he's to be treated with the utmost respect, and we on the other hand, were just telling the truth — you've seen what happened in Rwanda, in the Congo, in Nigeria and at the moment in Sudan and in Rhodesia, and Zimbabwe — millions of people being killed. Why? — because these people had such a strong liberal mentality that prevented them from feeling part of a unified country — for example in Kenya there are seventy-five different tribes, with seventy-five different languages. While the English remained, there was a unifying power keeping them together. The same happened in Yugoslavia. Once the whites had gone, well you've seen what happened. But when we were filming, everyone would have said that independence would be a force for good, would act as a redemption for colonialism, but you've seen that hasn't happened, things have got worse. In Africa now, things have continued deteriorating.

MG: How did *Africa Addio* come about?

FP: It was Jacopetti's idea. He'd received a letter from a girlfriend in Africa, describing events there. I remember we were in the offices of *Ieri, Oggi e Domani* (popular Italian newsreel) and he suggested making a film about the Africa that was disappearing, that he'd loved from a young age. He'd lived there for six or seven years and spoke Swahili well — so we set off straight away, Stanis went on six months in advance, and the great adventure began.

MG: Aerial shots, usually from a helicopter, are a symbolic motif of your films. Why do you favour this?

FP: Well, first of all, in the areas we were filming, there really was no other way to do it. Using a helicopter saved us time — we had the helicopter for six months, and made good use of it. I remember shooting a scene with crocodiles. It was only a small helicopter, with room for the pilot and just one other person, so there was me and the two crocodiles in an aerial sleigh beneath the helicopter. They deposited me and the crocodiles on a leash and left me, and I thought "I must be mad, I'm here in this isolated spot with two crocodiles ona leash" — quite an amusing scenario!

Then the next day, the helicopter broke down, and it was forty days before the spare parts arrived so it could be repaired and we were able to return.

MG: What do you recall of the response to your films in the UK, and elsewhere?

FP: As far as England is concerned, I really can't remember. In France, I remember they were anti, but in America they were received well, and I remember being shown the huge buildings on Fifth Avenue that they said were built with the money from *Mondo Cane*.

MG: The reviews of your films in the British press were quite negative. How do you feel about this — have you been unfairly represented in print?

FP: Critics are free to say what they think, but I think there's a political slant to it, rather than from a filmmaking viewpoint. England was losing her empire, was getting out of Africa and so there was a feeling that we were criticising them for extricating themselves too easily. They did so far too quickly.

MG: Having said that, when *Mondo Cane* was released it was considered avant-garde, not exploitative as it is now. How do you feel about this? Is it accurate?

FP: Yes, in all modesty. It was something new, it broke the mould, both in the way we did the editing, and in the way it was filmed. It was a lot harder in those days, cameras were a lot heavier

"You can imagine shooting a film about slavery in Alabama or Mississippi was never going to be easy."
FRANCO PROSPERI

and if you were trying to shoot unobtrusively it was difficult, because the Arriflex was heavy and noisy. Then there were technical problems — we didn't have video tapes, everything had to be filmed — now you can view what you've shot immediately, but back then you'd have to wait — send the film off to Italy to be developed and printed. So there were practical problems and we were proud to overcome them.

MG: More recently your films have been discussed as exploitation films. Why do you think this has happened, and is it accurate?

FP: I think all modern TV and cinema is like that. It exploits the moment and the situation. There's hardly anything on TV that isn't of the moment. Shooting footage in Afghanistan, for example is like this. If you want something good, it has to be of the moment. It requires courage for people like Nievo, Jacopetti and Climati to place themselves in the front line amongst mercenaries in the Congo — it goes beyond filmmaking, it is physical bravery.

MG: What about the dangerous scenes? What made you do that?

FP: The love of documentary making, to show reality. In Afghanistan we haven't seen much of what's gone on in the Taliban camps, the

decapitations, killing women, mutilating bodies? If we had covered it, we would've shown it in its entirety — not for the spectacle but to show the reality — to show what is really happening. You have to show people, wake them up. It's pointless if you don't show them the reality. It's no use saying traffic is dangerous, there are car crashes unless you show people the mangled car wrecks, you'll see how much greater an impact you'll have. Show the youngsters out in the car on a Saturday night doing 150 miles per hour!

MG: Was *Africa Addio* intended to be political, with an ideological message?

FP: It was, in a way, a painful film to make. If you love someone, or a country like Africa, and you see it disappearing before your very eyes — from the green hills of Hemingway, the creation of various states, especially under the English — every state was an ordered garden, people didn't suffer, weren't starving, it was perhaps the most honest regime that ever existed in Africa — incredibly honest administration. A white person — or should I say European? — could go into any store and could be trusted to pay in a week's time. You could rely on his word. It was a perfect situation, for Europeans it was an incredible paradise that had to disappear sadly.

MG: What about the scenes in South Africa (the beach scenes in *Africa Addio*) — what was their significance?

FP: The scenes with the girls of Durban were purely to show something beautiful: after our experiences in the rest of Africa, being there felt like an explosion of beauty. The girls were indeed very beautiful — and of course from

"They discovered that Climati had hidden a knife that he'd strapped to his leg and they were going to shoot us."
FRANCO PROSPERI

From the makers of "MONDO CANE"

AFRICA ADDIO

THIS IS TODAY'S STORY OF AFRICA AFLAME!

Conceived, Written and Directed by JACOPETTI and PROSPERI

TECHNICOLOR*

RIZZOLI

RAW! Savagery never before seen by human eyes!

RAW! Unbelievable... Women shudder and strong men faint!

RAW! 20,000 Watusi...12,000 Arabs exterminated by wild, brutal modern-day savages!

LEADING CRITICS SAY: "If you could see only one picture this year, this is it! AFRICA ADDIO. There has never been anything like it on the screen — for sheer... searing... shattering impact!"

THEATRE

a racist point of view, we were showing both white and Zulu girls, who were equally lovely. The scenes were a contrast to the darker, crude scenes. An audience needs something uplifting and sunny occasionally.

MG: What are your memories of making *Africa Addio*?

FP: I remember shortly after independence had been declared, there were still English troops in Kenya and Tanganyika and rebel forces were beginning to confiscate belongings and attack women and children, and we rushed to film these scenes as they happened. Of course, the rebels wouldn't distinguish between English and Italian (especially as I'm fair-haired!) They

discovered that Climati had hidden a knife that he'd strapped to his leg and they were going to shoot us. Luckily Nievo managed to talk us out of the situation, remaining totally unphased and calming talking in Swahili.

MG: Jacopetti wishes to distance himself from *Mondo Cane No.2* and *La Donna nel Mondo*. What is your opinion of these films?

FP: They are our productions, but the editing was done by other people. The worst part about it was that these films were commissioned at the same time: we were working on *La Donna nel Mondo* and we encountered censorship problems because we were showing womens' breasts which was deemed to be scandalous, so we had to re-shoot it, then we were asked to do *Mondo Cane No.2*. The problem was it all came at once.

The idea for *La Donna nel Mondo* came from a series of articles by a famous feminist journalist, Oriana Fallaci, whose articles in *L'Europeo* had the same title. We were in Cannes, having been nominated for an award at the film festival. Rizzoli introduced us to Fallaci and we all talked about collaborating in the making of a film. Jacopetti had a great attraction for women, but is also quite mercurial and quick tempered. Fallaci herself was a very strong character and at a certain point, they clashed, and Jacopetti picked Fallaci up... perhaps Fallaci will remember it!

MG: In *Addio Zio Tom*, what did Giampaolo Lomi bring to the process?

It was part of the birth of a nation.

"FAREWELL UNCLE TOM"
A Film Written and Directed by Gualtiero Jacopetti and Franco Prosperi · Music by Riz Ortolani
Techniscope · Technicolor · A Euro International Films S.p.A. Production [X]

FP: Lomi had worked extensively in Brazil, but he also had a huge love of cinema and the desire to make films. He also admired myself and Gualtiero because of the films we'd already made. He brought along his great enthusiasm, he was a good team member and had a wonderful personality — very calm and steady — and we felt a mutual respect and empathy.

MG: What are your views on dubbing in post-production (as in *Mondo Cane* and *Africa Addio*)? Do you prefer subtitles?

FP: In *Africa Addio*, we had a commentary, and I think this is better than subtitles, as it can add something to the mix. If it's not done well, you can remove it but you can also give it a humorous slant — as for example by using the voice of [Stefano] Sibaldi — and people seem to like this humorous vein.

If a commentary is well-written (which I think we were usually able to do), I prefer this. Dubbing, on the other hand, suits fictional films like *Mondo Candido* and *Addio Zio Tom*.

MG: *Mondo Candido* has been reissued in America. Do you think the film should be reassessed? What were the aims and inspirations of the film?

FP: As far as Voltaire's *Candido* is concerned, it has been interpreted in hundreds of different ways. Everyone has their own interpretation of it. However, from the filmmaking point of view, it is really a death warrant, and no one who has tried to do it has ever had a box office success.

MG: How did it come about?

FP: This was also one of Jacopetti's passions. He had read Voltaire when he was young and always remained hugely enthusiastic. One of those things that stays with you until you can actually make it happen.

MG: How do you think your films have influenced modern film and television?

FP: I think mainly our way of filming in an unbiased way and with a certain bravery and courage, also our way of editing and choice and use of soundtrack. These were pivotal things for us.

MG: Did the films you made with Jacopetti influence your own subsequent films?

FP: Obviously, all the choices you've made in the past affect things in the present. I hope perhaps we've left a small mark. Making films is one of the most important jobs there is as

WRITTEN AND DIRECTED BY **JACOPETTI** AND **PROSPERI**

a form of expression. Huge financial success also brings public recognition and popularity and if lots of people have seen our films then they will have left their mark — and perhaps some young person who has seen our films in the past may have been inspired to make a film now.

MG: What do you think of Climati's own films?

FP: Antonio had made some good films, but it was as if there was something missing — and that missing element was our contribution. We worked on *Ultime grida dalla savana* together.

But essentially, we complimented and completed each other. Without him, I wouldn't have been able to do *Mondo Cane* or *Africa Addio*, and the same went for him. And when we did *Addio Zio Tom* without him, we didn't have the same level of success as when we worked together. I didn't want to be on the credits for *Ultime grida dalla savana*, I didn't want to tarnish what felt like our golden period — I didn't believe another was possible. I was wrong; the film was a huge success.

MG: What do you feel about your own films?

FP: *Wild Beasts* (*Belve Feroci*) was a project produced by my grandson and we endured huge ups and downs in the making of it. It was an ambitious project, involving the filming of large herds of animals, and it was to be shot in Rhodesia, with Rhodesian funding.

"I didn't want to be on the credits for *Ultime grida dalla savana*, I didn't want to tarnish what felt like our golden period."
FRANCO PROSPERI

APPENDIX: INTERVIEWS WITH JACOPETTI/PROSPERI TEAM

WILD BEASTS

A Film By Franco E. Prosperi

placed in the context of the history of Italian cinema?

FP: In Italy, they're completely forgotten, we're nowhere. In America and France, we're viewed negatively, but in Germany there has been renewed interest. In Italy we're completely ostracised: I think it's political, because we made enemies.

MG: Have you given up on making films?

FP: Yes, I live very happily in a beautiful place, it's a national park and I've returned to my naturalist interests. I have my animal friends, I'm surrounded by nature — I watch the grass grow!

MG: How do you spend your time?

FP: I paint or write, just to pass the time. I'm currently writing a book, due out soon, called *Shumba*, or *Anche agli Leoni piacciono gli spaghetti* — about a lioness who eats pasta. I do the occasional screenplay. I observe what's going on around me.

MG: How would you like to be remembered?

FP: Like one of my dogs — with great affection! I have my grandchildren, who I've brought up as if they were my own children, and they have followed in my footsteps: one is a film producer and the others works for RAI as a director. So I hope I've done something good!

When war broke out in Rhodesia (this was the time of the independence struggle, and the forming of the Ian Smith 'independence' government) we found ourselves caught up in all of this chaos, there was shooting all around us — we had to watch out for mines, so you can imagine trying to film in such conditions. Which is why we relocated to South Africa. There we were judged on our previous films — *Africa Addio* and *Mondo Cane*. There was certainly a part of the population who were against us shooting the film.

So we had both economic and political problems and we did the best we could under the circumstances. However I think it's a good film; it had something to say about the importance of looking after nature.

MG: Where do you think your films are

Stanis Nievo

tanislao Nievo was born in Milan on June 30 1928. His great uncle was the writer, patriot, follower of Garibaldi and singer Ippolito Nievo. Educated at Rome University, he worked as a marine biologist and then moved into film.

After his work with Jacopetti and Prosperi ended he made his own powerful and controversial mondo film *Mal d'Africa* (1967), influenced by the work of Pier Paolo Pasolini and Frantz Fanon. Nievo loved adventure, and narrowly avoided death in Zanzibar while filming *Africa Addio*. He was only saved when a soldier found his Italian passport and concluded he was 'not white' (i.e. British).

Nievo turned to photography and writing

and became a leading light in contemporary Italian fiction. His *La Foresta di Tarvisio* (1986) and *Le Isole del Paradiso* (1987), like the pioneering mondo films he worked on, contrasted nature and civilisation, myth and reality, adventure and history. He combined his passion for writing and conservation in a guide to what he called '*I Parchi Letterari*' (literary parks). This dealt with sites he catalogued according to literary, scenic and sociological interest. He was co-founder of the Italian branch of the World Wildlife Fund.

Stanis Nievo died on July 13 2006. This interview took place at his apartment in Rome in 2001.

MARK GOODALL: How did you begin as a filmmaker?

STANIS NIEVO: I'd say curiosity was the main reason, whether expressed through photography and filmmaking or writing: these are all ways of gathering images and expressing ideas in a few lines, and this is how you become a journalist — someone who can inform and perhaps even be an artist in today's world.

MG: Have your writing skills influenced your filmmaking?

SN: I'd say that the reverse is true: my film work has influenced what I write, in the sense of having a high degree of visualisation of the situation; that is I still retain a visual image of what I've seen, even though in itself it may not be of anything very specific.

Stanis Nievo

Given my research into extremes, something journalists and writers generally are often drawn to, I think you could say I've made a certain contribution to the films you're interested in.

MG: Can you tell us about your early projects with Prosperi before *Mondo Cane*?

SN: We did a zoological expedition in Africa, to the area between Madagascar and India. In prehistoric times this was a continent known as Lemuria, and we visited various islands to do geological surveys on behalf of the University of Rome. But we weren't just scientists, we were curious, we were journalists, and that's how we began to do the documentaries of that period.

MG: *Africa Addio* was described as a new form of journalism. What do you think about that?

MG: Can you tell us about your role as a writer?

SN: My books are about finding out who we are. The first one was dedicated to my great ancestor, the writer Ippolito Nievo — this was the 'father' book, telling of my family's origins and history. The second book was dedicated to the great Mediterranean sea — the 'mother' in a sense, as in Italy in particular. The Mediterranean is an important part of our psyche.

So gradually I went from looking at the people around me, to looking at what happened to my people, the Friulian Venetians, to looking at large animals like whales and elephants. The blue whale is the largest mammal ever to live on this planet, and if the natural evolution of all animals has reached this size — some thirty metres — this is because that's the maximum form life can exist in.

SN: When filming as an investigative journalist, the more fantastic a scene is, the more you want to show not only the broad picture, but also the particular details — from forests to big cities, and in particular the movements taking place within that setting — people rioting, an uprising when there's a change of regime for example, like in Afghanistan, where journalists went in order to inform the public. Then, as now, journalists want to tell the story.

MG: Can you talk about the team you had and how you met Jacopetti?

SN: I met Jacopetti through Prosperi as they already knew each other. I'd known Prosperi at school, we shared a love of animals and exotic places (especially equatorial), and that's how we came to make our first trips together.

Then I went to the east for six months to discover the origins of the great cultures and religious movements like Buddhism, Hinduism and Islam, and so I travelled from Singapore to Afghanistan to try to gain a better understanding of the world as it was then in 1959.

After that, Prosperi asked me if I'd like to join them in making *Mondo Cane*, and I said yes, as long as it would be done in a witty and entertaining way, and that we would show things as they really were. I think the world is full of variety, and it's always possible to show it in a lively, interesting way. It doesn't matter where you go, whether it's the slums of a city or the desert, you have to be able to seek out the things of interest — there's a wealth of material out there, and a lot of it we filmed thirty or forty years ago!

MG: How did you work with Jacopetti?

SN: I think he was more entertaining than the others in the group. I was doing okay — I had a salary, which was great as before I'd had to fund my own trips — and I did documentaries, newsreel articles, but I really wanted to give it a go, so I went along with them and had a great time.

MG: What do you think of Prosperi's own work? (*Wild Beasts*, etc.)

SN: I've never actually seen his films. I only worked with them up until *Africa Addio*, and then there was my film *Mal d'Africa* which used some of the same material. In total we spent three years in Africa — Climati stayed there for the duration, whereas we would

come and go. Then there was my satirical film *Germania 7 donne a testa* (1970, co-directed with Paolo Cavallina), and since then there's not been much contact. I've seen Jacopetti twice in that time. It's been over thirty years since we all worked together.

The other group of friends I made the first trip with (not Jacopetti) were also school

"It doesn't matter where you go, whether it's the slums of a city or the desert, you have to be able to seek out the things of interest."
STANIS NIEVO

friends, Paolo Umbrelli and Prola — we climbed Kilimanjaro together and thought we'd done really well to reach the summit, until we realised that a group of blind people had managed to do the same!

MG: What was the role of Paolo Cavara?

SN: Cavara was the third friend, a wonderful companion to go around the world with. He perhaps didn't have the brilliance or genius of the other two, but he was more practical and focused and knew exactly how to describe what he wanted to film, just as Climati did with his camera. This was indeed the genius of Jacopetti: he allowed us all to have our own approach, our own ideas and suggestions, which were always listened to and considered in a positive fashion. This undoubtedly helped encourage ideas and increased creativity.

MG: How did you meet Antonio Climati?

SN: I met Climati the same day I met Jacopeti: they were working for the film magazine *Ieri, Oggi e Domani*. It was May 1960 and they had offices nearby. They took me there and told me all about this mad adventure they were planning — to travel around the world making a film. They made films that were controversial, but in a positive way. They were

satirical and undoubtedly had certain flaws and problematic elements.

La Donna nel Mondo, on the other hand, aimed to look at the situation of women around the world. We realised we couldn't make it too explicit or controversial or we wouldn't have got it made. I remember that the actress Belinda Lee came with us, and she was killed in a car crash (I believe *La Donna nel Mondo* was actually dedicated to her). There were other risky events during the making of these films — Cavara and Prosperi were involved in an air accident and another time they were very nearly executed. That was in 1964, during the shooting of *Africa Addio* — it was the time of revolution, and the emergence of the new states, so it's understandable that such things happen. I remember that time, an exchange between rebels and ourselves, one said, "Ah, you're Italians, we thought you were Europeans!" Even as a non-European, I'm happy to be considered a citizen of the world!

MG: How did you feel about shooting the dangerous scenes?

SN: Well, it's the same now in Afghanistan, those poor journalists have to go out there and risk their lives in order to show images that will move a public that has become anaesthetised and a bit blasé, they've seen it all before, so you have to try to ramp it up a bit. When you're young you tend to be rather naïve when it comes to your safety — I remember times when we were surrounded by groups of rebel soldiers, we'd walk along with our hands in the air saying "dar es salaam!" Luckily all went well usually.

That particular time, things weren't going very well — someone shot as us and missed –

"I remember times when we were surrounded by groups of rebel soldiers, we'd walk along with our hands in the air saying 'dar es salaam!'"
STANIS NIEVO

Africa Addio

luckily, because as you know if there had been blood it would've been difficult to put a stop to things then, because of leaving evidence. It all started when a rebel soldier appeared holding a blood-stained shirt (I don't know whose blood it was), and said "If you don't get them out, I'll do it." So then we had a discussion over who should decide, I spoke to them in (albeit simple) Swahili and we managed to intervene in the situation and all ended well.

MG: What made Climati special as a cameraman?

SN: Because he was a good writer, using his camera as a pen. He had the ability to visualise the end result of what he was shooting whilst in the process of filming it. While he was filming, he'd be moving his camera from side to side, zooming in and out, and all the while muttering to himself, talking himself through the process. And more often than not, this would result in great work.

MG: Did you do any filming yourself?

SN: No, never in *Mondo Cane* or *Africa Addio*. I had done some before, when we did the documentaries. I have, however, done some photography work — I had a few exhibitions of my work and published a book of portraits — society ladies such as Mrs Agnelli, famed actresses, etc. I did this for a while after the cinema work. I was attempting to produce my idea of modern art. Then after that, I turned my attention to writing.

MG: What makes a good photographer?

SN: It's not about showing the outward appearance, whether someone is clean-shaven or has a beard, or the expression on their face, but it's about the way they live their life.

IL FILM DALLA FEBBRE ALTISSIMA

CINERIZ
presenta

MAL D'AFRICA

TECHNICOLOR   TECHNISCOPE

STANIS NIEVO · ANTONIO CLIMATI · RIZ ORTOLANI

RIZZOLI

Whether happy of reflective, sad or fiery or cool and collected, and we need to capture these emotions and try to fix them in the images we create via photography.

MG: What do you remember about the response to your films in the UK and other countries?

SN: I don't really remember about the UK, but there was some commotion in Scandinavia, particularly amongst the young, but I don't recall what happened in England. I know we shot something for *Mal d'Africa* in England, but I don't think there were problems, it all went ok.

MG: When *Mondo Cane* was released in the UK, it was considered avant-garde. What is your opinion?

SN: It certainly was avant-garde. In fact, after this interview, I'm going to a theatre in the centre of Rome where they are showing the film *L'attesa* (*The Wait*), which is all about waiting for a ship that never came. It's to celebrate the work of my great uncle Ippolito Nievo, who would have been 170 this year, and it's part of plans to create a sort of museum of his work in a castle where both he and I have written. I wrote a letter to a newspaper saying "how long have you kept us waiting" and I've been happy to have involvement in this project. So today, I'll go and wait for my uncle, who obviously won't arrive!

L'attesa is rather like the waiting room for hell (or it could be for heaven, but if it's a long wait it's definitely for hell). It's about those things we may have wanted, but never had. It's where our dreams come from. But it's not about just sitting and waiting, you have to be pro-active, and ask "what have we managed to save, and what have we lost?"

MG: How important was the music of Ortolani?

SN: I think Ortolani (and others before him working on the films) was a great composer, but the music wasn't the starting point for us: creating a sense of adventure was all-important. If the music was adventurous or evoked images of deserts, for example, it sprang from those concepts. In fact, Jacopetti and Prosperi have been likened to two great musical conductors rather than film directors. Directing was a shared endeavour.

MG: The mondo films have been criticised as exploitative. Do you think the images are too explicit?

SN: When is it not so? It's extreme images that allow us to feel the full impact of something. If you're shooting a love film, then you need to show a proper kiss, it may be sexual or spiritual, depending on the story. If you go into a church and see a statue like 'Il Travaglio di Santa Teresa' it's akin to making love, a sort of divine love.

In the same way, though obviously in a more mundane one, these films were seeking to arouse the interest of the moment. This is the job of the journalist: for example by showing the inside of a library where nothing is happening, you create an impression of something that's fallen asleep, as indeed so many libraries have. Why do we not read so much in Italy nowadays? It's because so much literature is boring today. I've been promoting *parchi letterari* (literary parks), a project with the idea of making culture more entertaining.

In this way, *Mondo Cane* was informative, but in a stimulating, exciting way. Nowadays we have so many gadgets surrounding us, buttons to press, mobile phones that communicate by themselves, computers to take us further into the future. No wonder our spirit is deadened. We have all become dull and bored, and boredom is what we really must avoid at all costs.

If someone remains in the same job for years, working his way up the ladder and increasing his salary, he has security. But if he never takes off his safety belt, it would be like never getting out of the car.

MG: Is this what you all had in common perhaps — the search for new things?

SN: Yes — and discovering life. People become fearful too early in their lives: I am more fearful now than I was in my thirties. But you have to keep going,

The trouble is, we rely on medication far too much, and that can stop us feeling what's inside. We are all capable of so much more than we think, everyone is more intelligent than they believe they are. But we often carry on in our safe lives, doing the same repetitive things. While that can be reassuring, it sends us to sleep.

MG: What was it about Africa that attracted you?

SN: Because Africa was the continent we all loved, each in our own way. When Jacopetti and Prosperi got together, it wasn't that Jacopetti had as many ideas perhaps as we had (he had one, we had quite a few!), but he knew it was time to bring his dream to life.

And then there was Rizzoli, who was making plenty of money from films, but was bored. Money doesn't make you happy necessarily. Every now and then, people need to be shaken. I'm very pleased that you're wanting to interview me now, and to be remembered in this way.

MG: In *Africa Addio*, the criticism was that black Africans were portrayed in a negative way.

SN: It was partly political of course. And in just the same *Mondo Cane* showed whites,

201

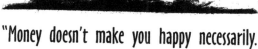

"Money doesn't make you happy necessarily. Every now and then, people need to be shaken."
STANIS NIEVO

way of thinking that was perhaps less logical, but far more mystical. It's difficult to imagine an African staying in love with the same woman all his life. They have a great capacity for passion and music. They are closer to nature.

When you look at certain tribes, it's been a disaster when they've tried to copy Europeans, because we've robbed them of their soul, they needed to carry on believing in their spirits. So revolution was needed — and bound to happen. The first form of written work in Africa was the Bible — great story though it is, it's our story, not theirs. When Picasso and Matisse needed inspiration, where did they go? To Africa. And I went to New Guinea for much the same reason. We need life to lead us to our dreams and adventures.

MG: How would you like to be remembered?

SN: Well, I've chosen to write now, and it's been going well. I think writers are less limited than those in the visual arts. The only problem for writers is selling their books, because here in Italy, television has taken over somewhat. The art of writing became less popular. It seemed more rewarding to be a footballer or a filmmaker.

But above all, I'd like to be remembered as a free spirit, a friend to people I met (I don't need to agree with them, but to have good discussions). Next week I have a book of poetry coming out. So that's how I'd like to be remembered, just as many others have over the past 2000 years.

yellows — even greens, had they existed! — in a negative fashion. But we were telling a story that was true; it was what was happening at the time.

When I was young, I wanted to be a farmer in Kenya, because I thought that was the only way to live in a country with all those wild animals, the wonderful wide skies, the storms — but then I realised there were lots of other countries to explore, like Antarctica and all the other continents.

But to return to your original question about Africa — Africa represented the dawn of the world, it was the place where everything felt closer to their beginnings, and there was so much mythology. African tribes had a

Riz Ortolani

Riz Ortolani

Riziero Ortolani was born on March 25, 1926, in Pesaro. Like his contemporaneous Italian composers, Ennio Morricone and Piero Piccioni, Ortolani worked for RAI, was classically trained and could orchestrate and conduct a wide variety of musical styles from jazz to chamber music and popular songs, including recordings for his wife Katyna Ranieri.

The central theme tune from *Mondo Cane*, Ti Guarderò Nel Cuore, with lyrics by Norman Newell, became the song More, a huge hit for a variety singers from Frank Sinatra to Doris Day by way of Herb Alpert and the Tijuana Brass. The song was nominated for an Academy Award in 1963. Ortolani also worked on a large number of genre pictures including thrillers such as *The Valachi Papers*, giallo such as Umberto Lenzi's *Così dolce... così perversa* and, most controversially, Ruggero Deodato's *Cannibal Holocaust*.

Riz Ortolani died in 2014. This interview was conducted at his villa near Rome in 2001.

MARK GOODALL: Can you tell us how you got together with Jacopetti?

RIZ ORTOLANI: I'm very grateful to be remembered for my part in the films, it was a collaboration that became very successful and was a very happy one. As soon as I met Jacopetti, he realised that I might be a good composer to work on his films. He's a man of great sensitivity and a great lover of both cinema and music, and the films he directed were very well made.

MG: What were your influences in composing film music?

RO: As Jacopetti and I got to know each other, we talked a lot about music, but mainly about creating musical contrasts — that is, when there was a violent scene it required something softer musically, and vice versa. That was more or less how we did it.

I remember when he came here for the first time: he arrived in plaster, transported by the Red Cross. He said to me, "Why don't you play something for me?" There was an Easter parade going on nearby, so I started to play a marching tune inspired by that, and he asked me what it was. I told him I'd just made it up and he told me to get on and finish writing it, as he would base the whole film on it! This was the tune that went on to become More,

Riz Ortolani with Katyna Ranieri

though obviously it wasn't called that at the time, and that theme was used throughout the film in lots of different ways (with different orchestrations, and in different styles).

MG: How did the lyrics come about?

RO: The lyrics came about like this: Katyna (Ranieri) was performing at the plaza in New York and she was already a well known and popular artist. One day we met the distributor of *Mondo Cane* in the States, who suggested using the music in the film for the Yves Klein sequence with Katyna singing it. So, Katyna recorded the Italian version, then all the other versions and the theme became More with words by Norman Newell.

The film went on to be nominated for an Oscar for the music, the theme music became very popular in the States and remains so today — almost as if I'd only written it a year ago. It's become a standard, with recordings by many

different artists — Frank Sinatra, Nat King Cole, Judy Garland, Lena Horne, Count Basie, Quincy Jones, Duke Ellington, Stan Kenton to name a few! It's been done in lots of different styles, like Oscar Peterson's jazz version. It's been a huge success and I don't think there's been another piece like it in the history of film music, in Italy or even world-wide. A few months ago, it reached six million copies recorded, which puts it on par with Yesterday!

MG: You continued to work with Jacopetti after *Mondo Cane*?

RO: Yes, I continued to work with him, and I'm disappointed that he stopped making films. He's a very talented director who has made some great films; the same with Prosperi. The two of them changed the whole style of filmmaking, even though they only made a few films together. Before *Mondo Cane*, films were shot in a different way, and also musically, we changed the way music was used in film. *Mondo Cane* changed everything.

MG: Do you recall scenes you thought particularly effective?

RO: I think this was the case in all their films. But I do remember when working in Los Angeles on an American film, I became interested in the techniques used in Walt Disney cartoons, in particular how the movements of the cartoon characters were synchronised with the music, quite a complex process. So when I returned to Rome to work on *Africa Addio*, all of the movements were based on techniques I'd learned in America, all of the music was in synch with the movements of the animals, the images the directors were focusing on.

For example, there's a scene where some elephants are killed, and even the pauses are in synch, so there's a blow, then a pause, then the music. It was a complicated process, we had to work hard at it and I would often get very tired and have to go and lie down! But I think the soundtrack for that film was one of the most successful.

MG: Sometimes, the choice of music seems ironic — do you feel this is true?

RO: I think it is true, simply because directors are by nature ironic. Jacopetti is very stylish, elegant and ironic, and Prosperi is very different, but these are two very different personalities who understood each other in an incredible way. Prosperi is very organised and very hard-working — he could stay on set for hours and hours. So here you have two huge figures of the cinema world, who sadly now no longer work together, for their own personal reasons.

MG: Have you a personal favourite piece of music from Jacopetti's films?

RO: Oh My Love from *Zio Tom* is a great theme, sung by Katyna who does a beautiful version of it, whether as soundtrack or theme tune. *Zio Tom* was another difficult film to make because I used the same approach as before, so lots of synchronisation and great irony.

MG: How do you see your music in the context of Italian films?

RO: I think things have changed, there's no longer such an interest in film music, no longer the chance to write for a symphony orchestra. Directors don't seem to want to spend as much time or money when making a film. In fact, music seems to come at the back of the queue when it comes to funding. I'm still proud to stand up for my profession, and I choose the films I like and work with those people who allow me to do the music I want.

MG: You combine various different styles of music in your work — does this reflect your own likes and dislikes?

RO: No, I use different styles, but I do try to distance myself from what I write. Obviously the personality of a composer will always be there, but I try not to be repetitive (as some are!). I try to be innovative, and forget whatever

"We changed the way music was used in film.
Mondo Cane changed everything."
RIZ ORTOLANI

I did in the last film. So whilst they are mine, and reflect my personality, I try to keep ringing the changes with the orchestration, harmonisation and construction.

Also, a lot depends on the directors themselves, on their individual tastes and requirements. It must be said that not all directors have the musical background and knowledge of Jacopetti and Prosperi, and some have no experience of this at all. It's important to give a composer the freedom to express themselves musically.

MG: Was this what encouraged you to work with Jacopetti and Prosperi?

RO: I was part of the team, and Jacopetti and Prosperi couldn't have chosen another composer. They couldn't do without me, nor I without them; I had given them so much already. Working with them attracted me because I could write what I wanted and they understood me.

In the recording studio when they'd hear the music for the first time, they'd be overjoyed. While working on *Africa Addio*, I'd asked to have a large orchestra and I was working in the studio on the scene where the elephants are killed and then on the fleeing of the zebra. I was busy doing the synchronisation and looked up to see their reactions and they were full of praise, and came in and hugged me. I've always had a huge affection for the directors I've worked with. Once I went into the studio to find they'd left me a present of a Zodiac, knowing how much I loved the sea. That was such a kind thought.

Another thing to mention is the presence of Sergio Leone, who learned a lot from Jacopetti and Prosperi. Right from the time of *Mondo Cane* and *Africa Addio*, he never deserted us, and was always at our side. He was a big fan of Jacopetti and he learned a lot from us. We didn't have all the technical innovations like reverb — we'd use the microphone in a dustbin to create an echo, and we did it first. Sergio copied a lot of our techniques. A lot of the innovations were ours first.

Sergio Leone went on to become a great director. He and I were very close — in fact I was going to do *A Fistful of Dollars*, but the problem was that I had become too expensive to hire, because of my success. I have always kept in touch with him, and he would often talk about me doing the next film with him, and obviously I'm very proud of this.

MG: In England you're not as well known as other Italian composers. Does this bother you?

RO: I've worked in many different countries and done concerts in Germany, France, Brazil and Mexico for example, and at the moment I'm in Monte Carlo with the philharmonic, but I'd be very happy to do a concert of film music with an English orchestra.

I love being in the recording studio, especially the first time you hear the recording, but even more I enjoy conducting an orchestra, and it would be great if someone were to ask me over to England. I did, it's true, abandon the idea of working abroad to an extent, because I wanted to work on Italian films, and I regret turning down offers from MGM and United Artists. I'm happy that I'm known a little in England. I've done some recording work there in the past, and it's a great place to work. I would be very interested in returning to that beautiful country.

Giampaolo Lomi

Giampaolo Lomi in the set of Addio Zio Tom (1971)

G iampaolo Lomi was born on February 4, 1930, in Livorno, Italy. He began his career in 1956 as an assistant cameraman on the expeditions of adventurer Willy Aureli in the Brazilian Amazon. He worked as an assistant to Adolfo Celi, organised European productions in South America and directed several short films for local television. In the 1960s and early 1970s, Lomi worked with Gualtiero Jacopetti and Franco Prosperi and was location manager for *Addio Zio Tom*.

He directed the giallo film *Tropico nel Cancro* in 1972 and in 1975 a sex comedy, *I Baroni*. Lomi also founded the International Film Festival of Manila.

This interview was conducted at his apartment in Rome in 2001.

MARK GOODALL: How did you get involved in the film industry? Who influenced you?

GIAMPAOLO LOMI: It's a long story! I went to Brazil when I was twenty-three-years-old. I always had a spirit of adventure. I started making documentaries for Brazilian TV. That was in 1953. I always loved movies. Actually, the real reason I went to Brazil was because I saw the Walt Disney film *Saludos Amigos*. Another film that impressed me very much was *Green Hell* where I saw piranhas for the first time. These two films persuaded me to go to Brazil rather than the United States, which was the usual route for young Italian filmmakers. Then, when I came back to Italy, I worked as a production manager on a film by Franco Cristaldi, *Copacabana Palace*.

MG: Can you tell me how you met Jacopetti and what you knew of his work? What was your opinion of him?

GL: Finally, I came back to Italy and that is when I met Jacopetti through a friend who worked with him in Mozambique while he was shooting *Africa Addio*. I had seen *Mondo Cane* because of course it was a huge success in Italy, then later I saw *Africa Addio* when there was a terrible situation because of politics etc.

MG: What are your memories of making *Addio Zio Tom*?

GL: Jacopetti suggested that I went to Brazil because they wanted to shoot big scenes somewhere where there was access to a lot

Der explosive Schocker:
JACOPETTI'S
ADDIO ONKEL TOM

of black extras. I went to Brazil in October 1968 and tried to get permission to shoot the film. The Brazilians didn't say 'no', but they didn't say 'yes'. They kept us waiting for three months... the law of tiring someone! Jacopetti's reputation went before him. When *Africa Addio* was released in Porto Alegre the students set fire to the movie house! So the Brazilians were nervous. Jacopetti was in New Orleans and I called him and told him nothing can be done. So I went around the Caribbean trying to find somewhere else. Whenever they heard the name 'Jacopetti' they said 'no'. Remember this was 1968...

Then, in desperation, I went to Haiti and I must admit I was a little scared because I had seen the movie *The Comedians*, which showed Haiti like everybody imagined with Papa Doc and the Tonton macoute... I finally got in touch with the Italian embassy and the man said, "whatever you do don't come to this country! Go away! Get the next flight out!" Later when I was having my dinner I saw a very smartly dressed man coming towards me, and I recognised him as the Italian ambassador. He told me "don't listen to that bullshit! Jacopetti is Tuscan; you are Tuscan; I am Tuscan — we make the movie here!" So it was agreed. The next day I went to see Papa Doc and he was very nice. He had a very thin voice — you could barely hear it. We spent eighteen months shooting in Haiti, then went back to Miami for the final sequence of Nat Turner. If you have seen *Addio Zio Tom* it looks as if the team was thirty or forty people!

MG: Do you think watching *Africa Addio* and *Addio Zio Tom* today, we view them differently?

GL: *Addio Zio Tom* was not understood at the time it was released. It's a fiction. Jacoppeti and Prosperi simulated two journalists of today immersed into the past. I think it's a good film but *Mondo Cane* was the one that impressed me the most. However, if you look at *Mondo Cane* today it looks a bit passé, the way it was shot, the innocence of it. Now because of TV it looks dated. *Africa Addio* is different; it's still a good movie and what Jacopetti foresaw turned out to be correct. I didn't really work on *Mondo Candido*, although I wanted to. The situation was very tense and the producers wanted the film finished in five or six weeks. Jacopetti gives his best when he's in the mood to give his best. In fact, you cannot put him in a 'regular' movie set up. The crew for *Addio Zio Tom* was about ten people. It took three years to make the film and he wanted to do *Mondo Candido* in the same way. Actually, the script he produced — more like a guide from his head of everything he wanted in the film — would have taken ten years to film! He wanted to shoot in France and in Turkey and they said 'no': you will shoot along the river Tiber! Unfortunately the filming was handed over to a regular film crew suggested by Sergio Leone. I did some casting and went to London and found the actors (Christopher Brown and Michele Miller) and then said goodbye! The film was finished by Franco Prosperi, who turned his back on Jacopetti to finish it quickly. He should have sided with Jacopetti against the producers but he wanted to finish it quickly and it was a flop.

MG: Can you outline some of the working methods of Jacopetti?

GL: The thing that made me — and not just me, but the others working around him —

very nervous was that he is a very scrupulous man and likes to take care of any small details. He does not stay behind the camera shouting 'action' and then 'cut'. No; he comes in front of the camera, talking to the actors, fussing over the lighting, the location etc. He wants to possess the whole thing. He wants to double-check and triple-check everything. This irritates people! It was hard to sense what he wanted because he wouldn't tell you. He would keep his thoughts to himself, even with Prosperi. The combination of the two was fantastic. Prosperi has fewer ideas and less charisma but he was a very active man, very good at practical things. But Jacopetti had the 'flash' of genius, like Fellini. He would say, "now we break and go fishing." So we went fishing for two or three days! This put his mind at rest and allowed him to think. Prosperi was boiling! He wanted to get back to Rome and finish the film, and this in turn irritated Jacopetti even more!

MG: How did you meet Antonio Climati? What was special about him as a cameraman?

GL: (laughs) Well, let us divide the man and the cameraman! As a man, I don't like him, his character or how he lives. As a cameraman, he is perhaps the best I have worked with in my lifetime. He was one of the first to use

"He told me 'don't listen to that bullshit! Jacopetti is Tuscan; you are Tuscan; I am Tuscan — we make the movie here!'"
GIAMPAOLO LOMI

Ultime Grida della Savana

the 9mm lens, getting very close to people. I remember we were in New Orleans shooting the funeral of a famous jazz musician. We went into the funeral parlour before driving to the cemetery. There were a lot of American TV and film crews inside. Climati took this 9mm lens and, in front of everyone, went up to the feet of the widow who was in tears and put it almost inside her mouth shouting "cry, please cry!" I never met another person with such a lack of the minimum human respect. But when he wanted to do something for the movie, it was the best. Climati was a genius; he did things that I never saw anyone else do.

By the way, he was helpful to me because when I went back to Haiti to make *Tropico nel Cancro* I needed to shoot a voodoo ceremony and I remember the cameraman putting the camera on a tripod, in the traditional way, and I said 'no'. I took the 9mm and shot it myself, by hand. You don't get this from traditional cameramen — they are afraid they will get hit!

I did *Ultime Grida della Savana* with him and we fought several times because

of his character. But he had great sense of responsibility for the quality of the thing he produces. He would never say "OK" if the shot was not 100 per cent good. In order to get a shot of wolf kissing the hand of a human we had to stay up to our waist in the snow from sunrise to sunset — but he did it.

MG: What is your view on Jacopetti being awarded the Barga Prize (special award given to significant Tuscan natives)?

GL: I'm happy for him because for many years, because of political stuff, he was erased form the movie world, which he doesn't deserve, because he did invent a new style. Maybe it will lead to other things, to present him in a new light…

The author would like to thank Rosie Clarke and John Thorpe for the translation of these interviews. The interviews were conducted by Mark Goodall and Luca Dicandeloro. The author would also like to thank Leila Thorpe for continuing help and support.

APPENDIX II :
"BITTERSWEET SYMPHONIES OF DEATH"

The Mondo Soundtrack

As the reviews and comments in this book have already alluded, the soundtrack of shockumentary films, in particular the music, forms an absolutely essential component of the overall artistic success of mondo films. It was no accident that the theme tune composed for the foremost shockumentary film *Mondo Cane*, Ti Guarderò Nel Cuore, became an enormous commercial and artistic success. This theme may have originally been improvised for a tiny part of the film (a scene concerning chicks being dyed colours for Italian Easter celebrations) but it became, like so much of the film, an icon for all subsequent mondo films. The basic sound concept, a counterpoint between the shock, brutality and violence of images, and the sweetness and delicacy of the music became a significant 'effect', always copied (sometimes with success) but rarely deployed with the same adroitness as in the films of Jacopetti and Prosperi (Jacopetti's often stated belief that music should never appear at the same time as speech and narration, was usually the fist principal to be ignored). The mondo soundtrack must echo the images. It must be global, violent, savage, lyrical, sentimental, ironic, melodic. It must sometimes complement the scenes and at other times it must counter them. Italian film music in general has become highly regarded, perhaps unsurprising in an age when the film

soundtrack is largely constructed from the latest popular chart music, or retro salvagings from the hits of the past, the dreaded 'compilation score'. The soundtracks have become highly collectible, those from the fifties and sixties being the most desired. This is partly due to the acute scarcity of original vinyl copies of soundtracks from this 'golden age'. An odd Italian tax law decreed that all unsold copies of pressings of 1,000 or under were to be destroyed rather than discounted. Hence, many copies of valuable and great cinematic musical treasures were melted

"Music is the opium of the cinema."
JEAN ROUCH

MONDO EXOTICA

sounds,
visions,
obsessions of
the cocktail
generation

FRANCESCO ADINOLFI

EDITED AND TRANSLATED BY KAREN PINKUS WITH JASON VIVRETTE

Alessandro Casella calls the "Jet Set Soundtrack") and influencing contemporary artists as varied as British groups Portishead, Pulp and DJs Montepulciano Club, American auteur Beck and Japanese combo Pizzicato Five. While understandably it is the 'classic' Italian maestros that have been foregrounded in this rediscovery — Nino Rota's Fellini scores and the immense body of work by Ennio Morricone — there are plenty more masterpieces to discover, treasure and enjoy. Mondo films were one of the pre-eminent genres for this musical revolution incorporating bossa nova, jazz, orchestral, pop and rock styles which expressed, in a repressive social and cultural milieu, taboo forms through music. The lack of 'dialogue' in mondo footage meant there was scope for the composers of mondo music to express, explore and experiment and it is of regret that, of the audio elements, it is the narration that is frequently foregrounded. The following is an attempt at redressing this, an outline of the principal 'mondo maestros' and their work in the context of the shockumentary film tradition. The cliché was that if someone noticed the music in a film, the composer was not doing his job. In the world of mondo movie soundtracks this rule is not so much bent as mangled out of all recognition. Beautifully.

Riz Ortolani

In the UK and US Riz Ortolani is a criminally overlooked composer, arranger and conductor, one of the few Italian composers to be awarded an Oscar (the theme song from *The Yellow Rolls-Royce*, Forget Domani). Born in Pesaro and trained classically at the Rossini Conservatory, Ortolani composed More for *Mondo Cane* (one of the most

down and crushed. The more romantic (and musical) reason for the collectability of these items is down to the fact that the rich variety, invention, experimentation and originality of Italian arrangers, composers and orchestras is second to none (the cover artwork was often beautiful too). As is becoming clear with the help of this scramble for original material and an active reissue market, Italian film musicians were often capable of more originality in a single piece of cinematic score than twenty Anglo-Saxon efforts put together. Original labels such as CAM and Cinevox together with new specialists Dagored, Right Tempo, Cinedelic, Hexacord and publications such as the essential *Il Giaguaro* with websites like italiansoundtracks.com have kept the music alive. Francesco Adinolfi's *Mondo Exotica* is the bible of the movement astutely linking Italian film music with the contemporary lounge/cocktail/ambient generation (what

La Calda Notte from "Mocac..."

covered songs of all time) alluding that his melodic gifts are arguably superior even to Morricone's. Ortolani worked successfully on all of the Jacopetti and Prosperi mondo films, and cleverly advanced Lavagnino's 'exotic' documentary scores, tightly synchronising musical style with location. This was sometimes done in comic ways (the Singapore snake market in *Mondo Cane*, the animal paradises in *Africa Addio*), others dramatic and tragic (the destruction of Congo mission

camps and the animal massacres in *Africa Addio*). His amazing score for *Mondo Candido* resurrected his collaboration with Jacopetti and Prosperi and provides a surreal backing for their odd tale about Voltaire's eternal optimist Candide. Trademark sweeping lush orchestrations are matched with upbeat pop shuffles and fuzz-guitar riffing mixed with sexy grunts and groans echoing the hero's drifts through disasters and a narrative that defies time and space. His work with Jacopetti and Prosperi is notably great in its contrasts between on-screen action and soundtrack, where the concept of underscoring is wilfully ignored. Ortolani made memorable contributions to a range of other Italian genre movies in the 1960s and 1970s. His abstract music for Lucio Fulci's *Una Sull' Altra*, described by the *MFB* as "making the

MONDO CANDIDO

ORIGINAL
MOTION
PICTURE
SOUNDTRACK
COMPOSED,
ORCHESTRATED and
CONDUCTED by
RIZ
ORTOLANI

"Music tells a story. It is not a filler."
GUALTIERO JACOPETTI

APPENDIX: THE MONDO SOUNDTRACK

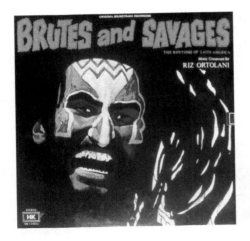

most of otherwise gratuitous sex scenes", is an exemplar of the skill with which Italian film composers raised the level of an otherwise mediocre movie. The offbeat plaintive background offered by the sax driven score is typical of the strong atmosphere created by Italian composers. Ortolani also wrote the music for many other mondo classics (despite his efforts to deny this) including Proia's *Ecco* and *Realtà romanzesca*, parts of Ide's *Nuova Guinea L'Isola dei Cannibali*, Arthur Davis' *Brutes and Savages* where a camp disco backing was entirely appropriate for the absurdity of the film, and even Ruggero Deodato's *Cannibal Holocaust*, which offers one of his most beautiful and morbid themes (when I asked Ortolani personally about the music for this film he claimed he "could not remember it"). In *Africa Addio* Ortolani's superb exoticism of the earlier Jacopetti and Prosperi films is replaced by a more 'tribal' sound that incorporates orchestrations but also intense moments of percussion, driven by what Moravia describes as the tom-tom's "deep monotonous meditative beat" exhorting (perhaps stereotypically) "a rhythm, now an indivisible, ingrained part of industrial

civilisation comes straight from prehistoric archaic times".

Piero Umiliani

Piero Umiliani, if remembered at all by British or American audiences, is noted as the composer of the seemingly banal three-note Mah Nà Mah Nà 1969 hit single combining cheesy female vocal refrains, jaunty organ and the sound of a man singing through his nose (later used on *The Muppet Show*). Umiliani was in fact a brilliant and inventive composer of film and library music with a background — like many Italian film composers — in modern

jazz (see also his tribute to Duke Ellington). Mah Nà Mah Nà originally appeared in the score for one of the best classic period mondos, Luigi Scattini's 'social study' of sexual behaviour in Scandinavia *Svezia, inferno e paradiso*. The tune was improvised at the last minute for the movie by Umiliani's superb orchestra (including Carlo Pes and Alessandro Alessandroni). His score for the film is a typical example of lightweight cinematic fayre being afforded a deep and varied mix of beat, shake, lounge, bossa easy and jazz variations featuring Gato Barbieri on sax. Umiliani's score for Scattini's *Angeli Bianchi... Angeli Neri* was of equal strength combining pulsating 'primitive' rhythms, moody ballads, mysterious easy jazz tunes and the remarkable throwaway song sung by Mark David, Now I'm On My Own. Umiliani's own superb organ playing, with that of Antonella Vannucchi is always at the forefront and the importance of the score (for such a specialist type of film) is underlined by the lineup for the recordings, which as well as including an entire Brazilian ensemble led by Wilson das Neves, included Harmonica player Franco de Gemini, and the choruses of Nora Orlandi, Alessandro Alessandroni and the virtuoso vocals of Morricone regular Edda Dell'Orso. All this was tragically replaced in the American version of the film (*Witchcraft '70*) by a weak and derivative horror score. Umiliani, whose career began when he was hired by the godfather of the modern Italian film soundtrack, Armando Trovajoli, also scored for a vast range of pseudo-mondo films including Joe D'Amato's sex travelogue *Eva Nera*.

"Listen to real music, played with real instruments," Umiliani once advised, a message today's film producers would do well to heed.

ORIGINAL SOUNDTRACK

Piero Piccioni

Piccioni was the son of a Christian democrat MP and as prolific and wide-ranging a film composer as Morricone. He was one of the first Italian composers to employ jazz (rather than classical, ballet, opera) as the background to film scores (there is an astonishing example of this on the compilation, *Barry 7's Connectors 2*), and his original approach began when he improvised music to documentaries by Gian Luigi Polidori, indicating the open, experimental style essential to the free spirit of his mondo film music. Piccioni composed a superb exotic score for Ugo Liberatore's mondo-esque erotic film *Bora Bora* inspired in part by the work of de Falla, Ravel and Debussy, the originators of the exotic mode, integrating Polynesian rhythms and textures

"Think of the simplicity of Riz Ortolani's More or the 'advertisement' style of Umiliani's Ma-nah-Ma-nah: these are truly spontaneous tracks."
AUGUSTO MARTELLI

with sweeping orchestral passages to the film's soundtrack. Piccioni wrote the music for Luigi Vanzi's *Mondo di Notte* incorporating original if standard waltz themes and a fantastical Mike Sammes' style reworking of the standard I'm An Old Cow Hand, which the composer Johnny Mercer would have no doubt winced at.

Angelo Francesco Lavagnino

Lavagnino, classically trained at Milan's Verdi Conservatory, and a composer of over 300 film scores encompassing peplum, Westerns, erotic and sci-fi, is an important figure in the shockumentary tradition, not so much for his scores for mondo films which are rare, but for his introduction to the documentary tradition of the concept of the 'exotic' soundtrack. He wrote the music for *Magia Verde* and *L'Impero del Sole*. A British reviewer crticised Lavagnino's score for *Continente Perduto* (*Lost Continent*) — a pre-mondo collection of symphonically reworked field recordings — for "exploiting the worst kinds of exotic Hollywood cliché as well as adding some of its own such as a choir which combines singing with screaming". Little did he realise he was

articulating precisely one of mondo films' most exciting attributes.

Lavagnino composed the music for Angelo and Alfredo Castiglioni's *Magia Nuda*. The principle theme for the film was credited as Soleado by the Daniel Santatcruz Ensemble but another Italian maestro of the exotic, Augusto Martelli (former arranger and companion of Italian diva Mina), claimed that the Ensemble "took care of copying everything from me". Martelli's *Il Dio Serpente* (*The Serpent God*) is still regarded as a paradigm exotic soundtrack.

Bruno Nicolai

Musical director Bruno Nicolai, the foremost director of film orchestras, was notable for his collaborations with Ennio Morricone (at one time a rumour circulated that 'Bruno Nicolai' was one of Morricone's pseudonyms). Nicolai did indeed work on *Per un Pugno di Dollari/A Fistful of Dollars* and *Il Buono, il Brutto, il Cattivo/The Good, the Bad and the Ugly* as well as countless other spaghetti westerns. But Nicolai is much more than a 'poor man's Morricone'. He worked as musical director on Tinto Brass' infamous *Salon Kitty*

and composed the fabulous score for Jesús Franco's kitsch reading of sadism *Marquis de Sade's Philosophy in the Boudoir*, a kaleidoscope of easy listening, Latin and psycho-pop renditions. It is the weirder commissions that are attracting interest from the re-issuers, in particular Nicolai's demimonde works such as *Femmine Insaziabili* and *Agente Speciale K*, usually featuring the unmistakable voice of Edda Dell'Orso. Nicolai set up his own Gemelli label to issue his vast film, radio and TV commissions from where you can still buy vinyl and CD copies of his varied and beautiful work. Nicolai conceived the superb kaleidoscopic music for *Il Pelo nel Mondo* loaded with as many cues as the film has scenes from the cartoon slapstick of the title theme to New Orleans jazz, sultry jazz-blues, very fast vibe shuffles, cod-Orientalism, cod-Mexicana and the superbly kitsch Alla Mozart which reforms the baroque beauty of *La Belle Epoch* into the accompaniment for a striptease. In directing the score for *Mondo Cane No.2*, derided by one reviewer as "obtrusive chorus and orchestra scoring in the best traditions of the genre", Nicolai cemented his reputation as one of the prominent mondo musicians.

Guido and Maurizio De Angelis

Terence Hill and Bud Spencer, an Italian western fun double act in the spirit of Butch and Sundance, except a lot uglier, were one of the many successful Italian imitations of American genre film. Their adventures were played to a musical backdrop provided by sometime moustachioed brothers Guido and Maurizio De Angelis. This fantastically prolific duo have scored the standard (for Italian musicians) vast range of film styles, most notably police thrillers (Margheriti's *Con la Rabbia agli Occhi/Anger in His Eye*s, for example) and sex comedies (Andrea Bianchi's *La Moglie di Mio Padre/Confessions of a Frustrated Housewife*). Later the brothers operated under the bizarre moniker of Oliver Onions. Working with British songwriter Susan Duncan-Smith (sister of Conservative politician Ian Duncan-Smith) they issued a huge amount of material on their own label, a cottage industry purveying music instead of olive oil and Chianti. Their uncanny ability at combining a vast array of styles and moods is exemplified by the brothers' incredible scoring for Antonio Climati and Mario Morra's *Savana Violenta*, here somehow incorporating acoustic pop, children's choirs

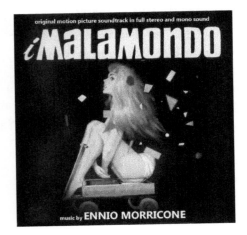

and orchestrations, growled Dixie anthems, 'Ameriarchi', samba and squelching Moog motifs. At times the music veers into the territory of easy listening, against a backdrop of some of the least 'easy' images ever committed to celluloid, and this is no mean feat.

Carlo Savina

Savina was for many years the director of the orchestra for the Italian state television and radio company RAI and provided the fairly standard music for Blasetti's pre-mondo film *Europa di Notte*. However, when Savina received the commission for Climati

and Morra's *Ultime Grida dalla Savana* his powerful sweeping orchestrations were aligned with images both gruelling and elegant. The film's two ballads stand out as typically odd counterpoints to the often troubling images. My Love, sung by Anne Collin, is an acoustic song with a counterculture Woodstock mood typical of Joan Baez, while Leave The Rest To Me rocks along quite convincingly led by wild guitar and a meaty vocal from Gilbert Kopland that is reminiscent of Barry McGuire.

Ennio Morricone

Morricone, born in Rome in 1928 and classically trained, is a legendary figure in the world of film music and one of the few Italians (along with Nino Rota) to enjoy international recognition. His prolific status is as legendary as his scores for Sergio Leone's spaghetti westerns, and those directed by Pontecorvo, Pasolini, Roland Joffe, Giuseppe Tornatore and Brian De Palma.

Given Morricone's ability to score for any type of film or TV production it was inevitable that he would interact with the mondo genre and so he contributed the music for Paolo Cavara's *Malamondo* and this too enjoyed his unique approach — a blend of offbeat vocal effects and orchestrations from the symphonic to the bizarre. His unique melodic and dramatic gifts were lent to this film where reference to a range of musical motifs is made, from trashy spaghetti western to atonal ensemble pieces (the glaring faces of the 'flaming youth' of the film's opening), jazz, twanging guitars, lush romanticism (the main theme), beat, a bossa waltz, tropical (the miscegenation scene) all dedicated to the film's contrasts (barbarism and beauty, mirth and madness).

In addition to the above there have been notable contributions to the mondo musical canon by Gianni Marchetti, for example *L'Occhio Selvaggio* (*The Wild Eye*). Marchetti's music for the film eschews the common practice for one overriding theme to be repeated, offering instead a number of striking motifs from the opening sparse, chilling single piano note and jazz piece, augmented by stabs of shrieking vocal backing, to the swingy romanticism of Barbara's Theme, imbued with bitter tragedy once the listener knows the true fate of the characters. Perhaps the most striking piece is Bali Street — a funky sitar driven number which reviewer Harold Stern could "hardly wait for the jazz boys to get to work on". Notti Di Saigon is a psychedelic riff-driven shake. La Fine Dell'Oriente brilliantly mimics Ortlolani's method while the plaintive reverb guitar of L'Ultimo Appuntamento recalls the Shadows. It is no surprise that the score attracted the interest of British lounge compilers such as Patrick Whitaker and Martin Green. The brilliant Franco Godi, provider of music for the popular fumetti (Italian cartoons) Bruno Bozzetto's *Il Signor Rossi* and Osvaldo Cavandoli's *La Linea*, also scored the music for the Castiglioni brothers *Addio Ultimo Uomo* including the childish song Why and a superbly daft fast guitar/vocal number Qua Qua Qua which also made it into one of the *Il Signor Rossi* cartoon shorts; two more disparate films one would not likely find.

The music that accompanied Italian cinema exotica/erotica is now a staple of lounge/DJ culture. This is understandable as it evokes the free-loving sixties' philosophy epitomised by more open euro attitudes towards sex and sexuality. In the 1970s, renegade director Aristide Massaccesi made the *Black Emanuelle* films, harder copies of Just Jaeckin's legendary 1974 *Emmanuelle*. The remarkable thing about composer Nico Fidenco, the composer of the music for these films, was that he was a successful and respectable crooner in the Modugno/Sergio Franchi mould (his visage appears on posters in early mondo films) before he turned his hand to soft porn or 'exotica-erotica' scores (as well as that of the spaghetti western). His music is effective in creating a fake atmosphere of sensuality dedicated to both director and composer's attraction to an exoticism of the 'other' (naked African, Oriental, Latin American girls) which, common to the period, is really a sneaky use of the anthropological to display sex and nudity for exploitative and titillating means. While the preponderance of 'modern' electronic instruments has reduced the sensuality of this music somewhat, the Come Back! rhythm is a pumping disco track worthy of the modern dance floor. Thus what started with Lavagnino's 'innocent' exotic exploration soundtracks reached its nadir in the sexploitation of 1970s cult cinema. The Italian soundtrack in this field, like the cinema it accompanied, never properly recovered.

APPENDIX III:
CONSIDERATIONS ON THE DOCUMENTARY FILM

by Gualtiero Jacopetti, edited by Mark Goodall

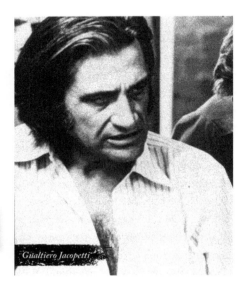

Gualtiero Jacopetti

A documentary film today must keep into account a new mode of expression which has come to the international motion pictures scene, and on this scene I will consider both the professional and amateur experience.*

In short, the 'ugly' documentary is now 'understood' by almost everybody. The documentary 'beautiful at any cost', largely rhetoric, predictable, and only formally correct, is now dead. Today we try to document from a more realistic angle, with quickness of expression. Without pretending to produce work at the level of Grierson, Flaherty or Dreyer, a new school of the young and not so young have applied themselves to an interest,

which is after all, the true essence of the documentary. The documentary is one of the noblest expressions of our era. We want from a documentary truth and sincerity. This is not always possible; in fact, it is very, very difficult.

And why? Because the documentary is a personal and subjective expression and we cannot expect from it the whole truth. It will express a certain truth, it will reflect a slice of life, throw a beam of light on one aspect of the truth. My *Africa Addio* may serve as an example. What counts is that the work be true from the point of view of its author: in its realisation, in its realisation becoming reality, a form of inner truth which determines and shapes spectacular and poetic images.

What is important today is the truth in the individual work, a truth that must of course respect the facts that must be documented (otherwise we would be in the field of 'fiction'), but reflect also the inner truth of its author. The documentary must be free, quick, lively, and speak with a loud, clear, recognisable voice. It fears nobody, it expresses its own truths, it expresses them well, in the best form. It has learned its technique and now it wants to make use of it, wants to live it, in its wholeness, in the new adventure awaiting its directors, its collaborators, its viewers.

The documentary film is, like many other means of cinematographic expression, a way to communicate our ideas — moral, social, political, or simply psychological — to our public. It is sometimes felt that the documentary film, which appears stark, severe, devoid of scenographic tinsels and literary pretensions, lacks ideas and is easy to make. This is not true. Exceptions determined by truly innovative talents are rather frequent: in this case, even if the technique is not regular or a hundred per cent perfect the film may turn out to be beautiful, in fact even better than if the director had been obedient to the accepted rules. The documentary film does not always have artistic pretensions. I feel that the documentary is that much more beautiful, therefore more valid, if it closely and clearly reflects the idea that has determined its origin. In some cases, the various ideas practically blend together: for instance, an inquest on contemporary habits may end up in a sociological inquiry. The success is determined by its author. It is the director who must impose his personal style; suitable, convincing, and above all, which successfully expresses what he wants to say.

I believe that the first step towards the success of a documentary is our interior clearness. In other words, I believe we must, first of all, look inside ourselves and evaluate what we want and can express. Otherwise we risk confusion and uneven work, work that may be beautiful only in part. Chance is sometime a good friend and adviser of the documentary director, but it can also be his worst enemy. It is dangerous to rely on chance too much. What is necessary is dialectic clarity. By this expression however, I do not mean something like political engagement. I mean whatever is clear, neat, precise, both in the memory and in the intellect.

It is obvious that, if I want to make a documentary concerning Christmas celebrations in various places and villages in Italy, I shall have to begin with a long trip throughout the country and 'document' myself thoroughly, otherwise I may do something beautiful, perhaps even very beautiful, but lacking a basic idea and above all, risking to neglect 'this' in favour of 'that'. What has struck me in certain circumstances (situations, external or internal; my mood, the physical, the emotional, all relative to a particular moment) may steal the place of an important detail, much more interesting and compelling for the film. In other words, I may find certain aspects more striking than others. But it is not certain that the more striking aspects are the best, the most exact and appropriate. In order to separate the best from the merely good I must, I repeat, 'document' myself before starting, with books, reports, newspaper and magazine pictures. I must go to the library and there look-up under 'Christmas' the texts that are closer to the idea I have in mind. When I have done all this, I can start my work with some peace of mind. After that I will have to think about the aspects that the books did not consider, aspects which will emerge in light of what I intend to express in my film work. In the meantime I must gradually develop my original idea. It is best, and I do it frequently, to write down an 'outline', a 'story'. All we

"The documentary is a personal and subjective expression and we cannot expect from it the whole truth."
GUALTIERO JACOPETTI

Gualtiero Jacopetti and Franco Prosperi

need are a few pages, a few notes, but these pages and these notes will grow little by little and we will finally obtain an almost complete treatment. That is to say (let's continue with the Christmas example): the initial story, three short pages, will briefly describe Christmas in Milan, Naples, Bologna, in the Friuli hamlet and the Sicilian village. I have now quick notations, rapid images. The actual treatment may start with the reproductions of well known Christmas paintings by the brush of celebrated artists of the past and end on close-ups of children's happy faces, with the human material 'selected' and 'edited' in the screenplay-writing phase.

The actual production will bring more surprises. At this point we must take into account everything: people who do not wish to be photographed, local authorities who may refuse permission to film the scene you have in mind, and so on. The material, now ready for the editor, for the musical score, and for the narration will be perhaps ninety per cent different in its scenario from what we had in mind originally, as we cannot always impose our total will onto social and geographic facts and places far away. Yet the initial determining idea must still exist; or perhaps at this point, it may have been totally reversed. This makes no difference. What counts is that the idea must exist and the documentary must have something to say. Otherwise it will become a useless promenade, a technical exercise.

Before starting to film a documentary I must ask myself this: which aspect of this particular place do I intend to bring out? The ugly or the beautiful? The pleasant or the unpleasant? The traditional or the new? This is the basic question: this defines almost the entire success of my work. I think that the central idea (dialectic, basic, or whichever term you want to use in order to describe it) is not conditioned by a technique; on the contrary the technique is determined by the idea. Only if I have the 'idea' will I be in a position to carry out a free work, and my field of action will widen. I can find and discard many different solutions. I will be able to invent new situations and finally give a personal interpretation to the subject. But in order to do this, a serious and deep knowledge of the subject matter is necessary. Theory, it is true, in the documentary film has often contributed greatly, from Grierson to Rotha. But these are exceptional examples. We must limit ourselves to the average work and, on the basis of our current commonsense, consider what we can do with our own forces, our background, our culture, our artistic sensitivity, our technical knowledge. Without technique it is impossible to produce a good documentary, unless we possess a figurative talent so revolutionary, so new and daring that it is capable of reversing all grammatical and syntactical rules governing this fascinating and subjective means of expression. The master documentarist must possess all these qualities: technical expertise, aesthetic flair, culture, newness of ideas and subjects.

And this is indeed a lot for one person!

In life it is difficult to have everything at once. So we will perhaps have novel ideas and not so much technical background or vice versa. It is important, however, not to be hopelessly mediocre. The documentary cannot be mediocre. It is clear from the very beginning whether a documentary is 'well made' or if it is 'worthless'. It can be clear from the narration, especially if it is inflated and pretentious. It can be evident by its colour, the quality of the photography, even the smallest detail, like repetitious zooms that create discomfort to the viewer, or shots that stay on the screen for interminable lengths, like in some of those boring art documentaries.

The documentary, by its very nature, cannot be totally objective. It could only be so if it were made by a monkey who, operating a camera from a balcony aimed at the street below, for hours and days, came up at the end of the exposure with a thousand feet of film 'document' of what happened in the street. The material filmed by the monkey will have no shape, no meaning. It needs to be put into the hands of an expert to be manipulated, edited, to have a story added, music; in other words to be redone. And while it is being redone, the documentary will have a further ideological development. These 'handlers' will end up with still another documentary which reflects their idea of that particular street.

Saying this, I do not mean that the documentary consists solely of the editing (as some critics were convinced some years ago). It is, however, clear that this 'finishing' work is not at all marginal. It completes the preparation and the production, it does not add useless frills, but instead depth and definition to the original idea of the author.

When my critics say that they do not like my documentaries because they are not objective, they are not merely splitting hairs. They are simply being partisan, or rather, non-

"The material filmed by the monkey will have no shape, no meaning. It needs to be put into the hands of an expert to be manipulated, edited, to have a story added, music; in other words to be redone."
GUALTIERO JACOPETTI

Night and Fog

objective themselves. Because my political ideas are not the same as theirs, they disapprove of my work, using objectivity as an excuse, and in so doing they contribute to, and strengthen the truism that a documentary is documentation. If, on the other hand, the documentary, even if non-objective, reflects their own social and political views, then they will find it nevertheless beautiful and the 'modification of reality' will become for them (rightly so), interpretation, But in my case too there is an interpretation, even if I do not share the ideas of Eisenstein and of Pudovkin. Therefore, if they accept the changes in the work of others, they should accept it also in mine.

Alain Resnais, the great author of *Last Year at Marienbad*, made a documentary on the Nazi concentration camps — *Night and Fog* — very beautiful, very intense. If a director had filmed (provided he could have found the material) a documentary on the Soviet concentration camps, many of those critics who (rightly) praised Resnais' work, would probably have criticised the other director's work, for showing some truths which they,

because of their political ideas, prefer not to show to the public. And this is why information, in the hand of the documentary director, is truly portentous and it is sad that too many documentarists, particularly in the case of the amateurs, who by their very position can do what they want, express what they please, should come up with stories so trite, so common, and useless. Objectivity, whatever the documentary's style and level, is always a convenient excuse for some critics, or even for the public. A totally objective documentary is impossible. If it existed, it would consist of several feet of senseless images. When Cesare Zavattini — who has only written books and screenplays, but never directed a conventional film, or a documentary — theorised on "shadowing" (the following of a person by a detective) he was expressing his views. He thought that all that was necessary to make a beautiful film or documentary was to "shadow" someone during his day, from his house to his office to his return home: the film would appear by itself. His theory seems to me excessively naïve, and also a little gratuitous.

Aside from the fact that when this someone is at home we cannot know what he is doing (and if he takes us home with him, it follows that the "shadowing" is fictitious and artificial), the film imagined by Zavattini lacks that creative synthesis, which alone can give life to the final work.

Similar theories gave birth in France to cinema vérité, which in turn determined the success of the nouvelle vague. However, the French directors have proved to be more creative than their Zavattini-influenced Italian colleagues, and while the latter have produced *I Misteri di Roma* (not particularly incisive or eloquent, with limited spectacular appeal), the French directors, with an eye to the Dziga Vertov theories and another to their changing society, have created elegant, funny, ironic, dramatic works, all extremely realistic. In other words, just because they have transcended the myth of 'realism at any cost', they have been able to create films full of an effective and forceful realism, appreciated by public and critics alike.

Even in the most recent films belonging to the nouvelle vague it is possible to recognise several influences of a healthy and constructive documentarism. Think of that admirable film *Adieu Philipine!* by Jacques Rozier. Several sequences are shot in the street, with a telephoto lens, so that the two young girls, the main characters, were unaware of being filmed. Their strolls through the middle of the Parisian crowds, the chit-chat of these attractive teenagers, are a miracle of fresh documentarist ingenuity. It is not hard to film these scenes: it is difficult to have the basic idea.

Many Italian documentarists instead have an ideological weight and are a little pretentious on account of our culture. In Italy, no offence meant, critics, directors, and people in the business, believe that our movies are, or rather have been, among the best in the world. But if we consider today's average production we have no cause for rejoicing. Nothing appears genuine; there is nothing 'original' in the best sense of the word. We fluctuate between imitation 007 and spaghetti westerns, from third-rate slapstick to exotic documentaries inspired by Quilici, Marcellini, Guerrasio, Jacopetti: a gloomy picture, indeed. I would like to say this: a civilisation, whatever its origin and its development, must feed from a common cultural source, lymph which favours the flowering of the strongest, healthiest, most exuberant forces. If my aim is to conduct polite conversation in a fashionable drawing-room, and expose brilliant ideas and sparkling concepts, I must first of all be conversant in the language, then know the style (good manners, what can be said and what cannot be said, in other words, the code of politeness).

In Italy, the field of documentaries does not have a common cultural basis. This is why we have a few exceptional but isolated works, and a lot of standard production (at low standards, of course). Amateurs indirectly appear to have been conditioned by this influence, in most cases, negatively. This influence can be detected in the choice of subjects, which is the simplest and surest gauge for finding the

"A totally objective documentary is impossible. If it existed, it would consist of several feet of senseless images."
GUALTIERO JACOPETTI

enable him to survive, considering that it is not so easy to survive in this field. The only way to survive is the discovery of a good subject, new, different, unique. I don't mean being different at any cost, but to give some measure of freshness to a fact, a situation, which we have all seen before, but since forgotten, and that we now recall through the images of an unexpected documentary, which pleases us, which will please whoever made it, and whoever commissioned it. Finally, if the choice of a subject can be occasionally a matter of chance (like a tale overheard in a crowd), it is more often the result of conscious research, not motivated merely by a whim, but stemming from an inner need to show that we are alive and present in the world we live in. The documentary language is not simple. Measure, sense of balance, good taste, class: sometimes in ten minutes we must prove what we can do! Without a story, actors, extravaganzas, we must yield a hundred per cent, stop-watch the length of the shots, never forget the rhythm. Boredom is a great enemy of the documentary. Whoever creates boredom in a documentary is not a director, he has no calling for this kind of visual show because making a documentary is indeed an enthusiastic feat, and, in spite of all its difficulties, it is possible to be carried away and improvise forgetting the 'critical' analysis to which I have referred before. By saying critical analysis, I don't mean to imply that you must be a college professor, or pedantically watch all your colons and semicolons. I rather mean to say that once the improvisation season is over, the more mature and proficient season must follow, when one must acknowledge a truth and express its full potential. That is, you can be a poet without writing verses even if you are a bookkeeper.

underlying cultural patterns, the literary and mental attitudes.

What is the best way to develop a taste for the right choice of the subject matter: new, alive, modem, captivating, exciting, amusing, spectacular?

There is only one way, as old as the world: look around, constantly, at any hour of the day. At the same time refine your taste, add to your culture. Read a lot: newspapers and magazines for practical information, but also books of all kinds: poetry, novels, essays. This is what makes us free. Culture makes us free. It opens our mind. It shows life in its different aspects, while ignorance, which breeds commonplace thinking, prefers to leave them dormant, unexplored, dead. The best and newest subjects usually have been found, discovered, invented by people more advanced culturally. So, if chance may be of help once, the second time it is of no use, it will deceive nobody. Whoever lasts in time has the necessary foundations to

To make a good documentary it is important to love the cinema, intelligently and with sensitivity. Love the cinema but recognise its limits, and confronting ourselves with these limits, find within it our liveliest and sincerest aspirations. There are many kinds of love: the conventional, which leads to a state of exaltation and the one that, while loving, can still see the faults and the limitations. This is perhaps the best kind, because it leads to understanding. The documentary cannot tolerate deceits, frauds, betrayals. With the conventional movie it is possible sometimes to deceive the public and critics. This is impossible in a documentary, which is so structured that it is necessary, like in a sonnet, to go over each phrase, each scene, to decant every drop of meaning, to reduce everything to the essential, to its purest expression. And it is well known that, without inspiration, without feeling and participation, it is impossible to synthesise, and I should add that synthesis is the basis of poetic necessity. Those who have something to say must say it right away, without long introductory sequences, without technical affectations, in a simple, direct language. I have noticed for example, the many contradictions existing in a so-called objective documentary *Uccellacci e Uccellini* by Pasolini. You may remember that at a certain point the director has inserted in his film a newsreel section depicting the funeral of Italian Communist leader Togliatti's funeral. It is a beautiful piece — certainly beyond the ability of the one, or several nameless people who filmed it. Yet it is contradictory, because it reflects action while it happens, chaotic, and meaningless, as is always the case when it is not seen through the clear and rational vision of the artist. We see in the film people

behaving irrationally, religiously, irreligiously, in front of Togliatti's bier. There are scenes pathetic and funny, pitiful and laughable. It is an excellent newsreel; objective of course but full of contradictions, of mystery. In fact in the case of the documentary we would have seen the interpretation of the scene by the director and we would have seen the 'right' way (for the director) to behave in front of Togliatti's corpse. We would have seen Jacopetti's way and the anti-Jacopetti way. The best way would have been, certainly, not the one that follows the cultural and political voices of the day, but the most valid and effective from the artistic viewpoint.

I will end with these considerations. I hope that you have followed me to this point and that you see the truth as I see it, namely, that without enthusiasm, without love, it is impossible to create anything that is good and lasting. There can only be attempts, or imitations. The real talent does not consist of a couple of clichés, or a few technical solutions that are fashionable today and ridiculous tomorrow. A true talent can ripen by degrees only, little by little, fed by good readings and by good movies. The most important, the greatest engagement is with oneself, with our own maturity. Whether a documentary transforms itself into a film of social, artistic,

"The best way would have been, certainly, not the one that follows the cultural and political voices of the day, but the most valid and effective from the artistic viewpoint."
GUALTIERO JACOPETTI

Jacopetti on the set of Addio Zio Tom

politic, historical or ethnographic research is not important: what counts is our attitude confronting our subject, our being artists, men, culturally responsible people. If, on the written page, it is at times permissible to be obscure and to play with words then on the screen we must be as clear as light, and understand and make the public understand what we want to say. We must never contraband a touristic film for an ethnographic one, nor align ourselves culturally and politically in one direction when our beliefs are elsewhere. Commitment to ourselves therefore is vital: this means work, work and more work, and a large amount of self-criticism.

In conclusion, what I have said up to now is what I have always practiced while working on my documentaries. I have always looked at the facts with a journalist's curiosity, but later I have registered them according to my personal opinion, my leading idea. Leaving the essential truth unchanged, I have been using the facts like episodes in a screenplay, already carefully thought out before starting the camerawork. In other words, knowing already very well the subject I wanted to deal with. Having my precise, personal opinion, during the filming process I was certainly not objective, impersonal, like a reporter, but an author with a tale to tell, a story, a screenplay, an idea that I wanted to bring into existence. In order to do that, I was using the world as a stage, the crowds as extras, real-life characters as actors. For me, a documentary is a film to be narrated exactly like a conventional film, and as such, it must rely on a director's strong personality and profound preliminary preparation. It has the advantage of the immense fascination coming from contemporary events, of the truth of that which it shows. Documentary, therefore, conceived truly as a spectacle, to be projected in the first-run motion picture halls, with many, many people watching it.

This is the documentary.

* This text was written in 1966.

ACKNOWLEDGEMENTS

This book is dedicated to Luca Dicandeloro and Gualtiero Jacopetti, two individuals whose contributions were essential to its realisation.

Luca Dicandeloro has been involved in almost every aspect of the book as well as the projects predating it. His tireless efforts and gentle drive to get what is required are typical of a great, creative individual. The project is many, many times richer for Luca's involvement and commitment.

Gualtiero Jacopetti assisted with information; with histories and with company; all with the impeccable courtesy one would expect from a great European cinejournalist and auteur. Special thanks also go to Giampaolo Lomi who guards the "vecchio leone" but has always helped out with humour and with passion.

The following friends also helped significantly, professionally and without complaint:

J.G. Ballard (a great writer who responded quickly and beautifully); James Battle; Daniel Becker; Marc Cavazza, Jeremy Dyson (a true polymath); David Kerekes (who as well as supporting the project all along is a rarity amongst publishers — a nice guy); Davide Morena; Stanis Nievo; Alfonso Orsi; Riz Ortolani and Katyna Ranieri; Franco Prosperi; Thierry Zeno. John and Leila Thorpe translated vital material and helped introduce the films to Italians and non-Italians alike, who may have forgotten. Oliver Trenouth did some fine technical stuff. Bill Lawrence and Tony Earnshaw always make my crazy ideas material.

Patrick Eyres and Wendy Frith have always, often against their better judgements and tastes, supported my work and will be relieved to see it finally in print. Now I can get back to Carlos…

Finally, Marie Byatt provided support and encouragement and love — as always.

BIBLIOGRAPHY

There are only two books on film that to my mind are absolutely essential reading. The first is *The Macmillan International Film Encyclopedia* edited by Ephraim Katz which is the ultimate reference tool: detailed, precise and written with immense clarity. The second is Amos Vogel's *Film as a Subversive Art*, a unique and brilliantly written text capturing the thrilling, visceral excitement of great cinema. In an age when the use of film as advertising rather than film as art has massively accelerated, Vogel's words are beautiful, inspiring and essential. The fact that the book is out of print shames all those who profess to love film.

Books

Adinolfi, Francesco. *Mondo Exotica: suoni, visioni e manie della Generazione Cocktail*. Torino: Einaudi, 2000

Ballard, J G. *The Atrocity Exhibition*. San Francisco: RE/Search Publications, 1990

Barber, Stephen. *The Art of Destruction: the films of the Vienna Action Group*. London: Creation, 2004

Barnouw, Erik. *Documentary: a History of Non-fiction Film*. NY/Oxford: Oxford University Press, 1993

Bawden, Lizzie-Anne (ed). *The Oxford Companion to Film*. London: Oxford University Press, 1976

Baxter, John. *Fellini*. London: 4th Estate, 1993

Beckwith, Carol & Fisher, Angela. *African Ceremonies*. NY: Harry N. Abrams, 2002

Bessy, Maurice. *A Pictorial History of Magic and the Supernatural*. London: Spring Books, 1964

Bondanella, Peter. *Italian Cinema: from neorealism to the present*. NY: Continuum, 1997

Braudy, Leo & Cohen, Marshall (eds). *Film Theory and Criticism: Introductory Readings*. NY/Oxford: Oxford University Press, 1999

Bruschini, Antonio & Tentori, Antonio. *Nudi e Crudeli: I Mondo Movies Italiani*. Bologna: Editrice PuntoZero, 2000

Burlingame, Jon. *Sound and Vision: sixty years of motion picture soundtracks*. NY: Billboard Books, 2000

Burt, Jonathan. *Animals in Film*. London: Reaktion Books, 2002

Cameron, Kenneth M. *Africa on Film*. NY: Continuum, 1994

Christoph, Henning & Oberländer, Hans. *Voodoo*. Köln: Benedikt Taschen, 1996

Clover, Carol J. *Men Women and Chainsaws: Gender in the Modern Horror Film*. Princeton: Princeton University Press, 1992

Cohen, John. *Africa Addio*. NY: Ballantine Books, 1966

Davis, Arthur. *Brutes and Savages*. Florida: Valkyrie Press, 1978

Dorfles, Gillo. *Kitsch: an anthology of bad taste*. London: Studio Vista, 1969

Durgnat, Raymond. *Franju*. London: Studio Vista, 1967

Dwyer, Simon (ed). *Rapid Eye 2*. London: Annihilation Press, 1992

Fallaci, Oriana. *The Useless Sex*. London: Michael Joseph, 1964

Firestone, Ross (ed). *El Topo: a book of the film by Alexandro Jodorowsky*. London: Calder

& Boyars, 1974

Forgacs, David & Lumley, Robert (eds). *Italian Cultural Studies: an Introduction.* Oxford: Oxford University Press, 1996

Frayling, Christopher. *Sergio Leone: something to do with death.* London: Faber & Faber, 2000

Furnas, J.C. *Goodbye to Uncle Tom.* NY: William Sloane Associates, 1956

Furness, R.S. *Expressionism.* London: Methuen, 1973

Goldberg, RoseLee. *Performance Art: from Futurism to the present.* London: Thames & Hudson, 1988

Hammond, Paul (ed). *The Shadow and Its Shadow: surrealist writings on cinema.* London: BFI, 1978

Heider, Karl G. *Ethnographic Film.* Austin: University of Texas Press, 1976

Hoare, Mike. *Mercenary.* London: Corgi Books, 1967

Hockings, Paul (ed). *Principles of Visual Anthropology.* Berlin/NY: Mouton de Gruyter, 1995

Katz, Ephraim. *The Macmillan International Film Encyclopedia.* NY: Harper Collins, 1994

Kerekes, David & Slater, David. *Killing for Culture: an illustrated history of death film from mondo to snuff.* London: Creation, 1995

Klocker, Hubert (ed). *Wiener Aktionismus 1960–1971 Volume 2.* Vienna; Ritter Verlag, 1989

Landis, Bill & Clifford, Michelle. *Sleazoid Express: a mind-twisting tour through the grindhouse cinemas of Times Square!* NY: Fireside, 2002

Landy, Marcia. *Italian Film.* Cambridge: Cambridge University Press, 2000

Lindqvist, Sven. *Exterminate All the Brutes.* London: Granta, 1998

Loizos, Peter. *Innovation in Ethnographic Film: from innocence to self-consciousness 1955–1985.* Manchester: Manchester University Press, 1993

Luther-Smith, Adrian. *Delirium Guide to Italian Exploitation Cinema 1975–1979.* London: Media Publications, 1997

McCabe, Patrick. *Mondo Desperado.* London: Picador, 1999

MacDonald, Kevin & Cousins, Mark. *Imagining Reality: the Faber book of documentary.* London: Faber & Faber, 1996

Marcorelles, Louis. *Living Cinema: new directions in contemporary filmmaking.* London: George Allen & Unwin, 1973

Malossi, Giannino (ed). *Latin Lover: the passionate south.* Milan: Edizioni Charta, 1996

Malossi, Giannino (ed). *Volare: the icon of Italy in global pop culture.* NY: Monacelli Press, 1999

Martin, John. *The Seduction of the Gullible: the curious history of the British "video nasty" phenomenon.* Nottingham: Procrustes Press/John Martin, 1993

Moravia, Alberto. *Which Tribe do You Belong To?* NY: Farrar, Straus & Giroux, 1974

Muller, Eddie & Faris, Daniel. *Grindhouse: the forbidden world of "adults only" cinema.* NY: St. Martin's Griffin, 1996

Nichols, Bill (ed). *Movies and Methods Volume 1.* Berkeley: University of California Press, 1976

Nichols, Bill. *Ideology and the Image.* Bloomington: Indiana University Press, 1981

Nichols, Bill. *Representing Reality.*

Bloomington: Indiana University Press, 1991

Palmieri, Luca M. & Mistretta, Gaetano. *Spaghetti Nightmares.* Florida: Fantasma Books, 1996

Pratt, Mary Louise. *Imperial Eyes: travel writing and transculturation.* London & NY: Routledge, 1992

Prince, Stephen (ed). *Screening Violence.* New Brunswick/New Jersey: Rutgers University Press, 2000

Prosperi, Franco. *Vanished Continent: an expedition to the Comoro Islands.* London: The Adventurer's Club, 1959

Renov, Michael (ed). *Theorizing Documentary.* NY/London: Routledge, 1993

Renov, Michael. *The Subject of Documentary.* Minneapolis: University of Minnesota Press, 2004

Rondi, Gian Luigi. *Italian Cinema Today.* London: Dennis Dobson, 1966

Rony, Fatimah Tobing. *The Third Eye: Race, Cinema and Ethnographic Spectacle.* Durham: Duke University Press, 1996

Ross, Jonathan. *The Incredibly Strange Film Book.* London: Simon & Schuster, 1993

Rotha, Paul. *The Film Till Now.* London: Spring Books, 1967

Sarris, Andrew. *Confessions of a Cultist: on the cinema 1955–1969.* NY: Touchstone, 1971

Schaefer, Eric. *Bold! Daring! Shocking! True!: a history of exploitation films, 1919–1959.* Durham & London: Duke University Press, 1999

Shohat, Ella & Stam, Robert. *Unthinking Eurocentrism: multiculturism and the media.* London: Routledge, 1994

Stallybrass, Peter & White, Allon. *The Politics and Poetics of Transgression.* Ithaca, NY: Cornell University Press, 1986

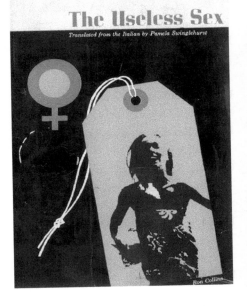

Stephenson, Ralph & Debrix, J R. *The Cinema as Art.* London: Pelican, 1965

Stevenson, Jack (ed). *Fleshpot: cinema's sexual myth makers and taboo breakers.* Manchester: Headpress/Critical Vision, 2000

Stewart, John. *Italian Film: a Who's Who.* Jefferson: McFarland, 1994.

Styron, William. *The Confessions of Nat Turner.* London: Panther, 1970

Swezey, Stuart (ed). *Amok Journal: sensurround edition.* Los Angeles: Amok, 1995

Trevelyan, John. *What the Censor Saw.* London: Michael Joseph, 1973

Tyler, Parker. *Classics of the Foreign Film.* London: Spring Books, 1962

Tyler, Parker. *Underground Film: a critical history.* London: Pelican Books, 1974

Vale, V & Juno, Andrea (eds). *Incredibly Strange Films.* San Francisco: RE/Search Publications, 1986

Vogel, Amos. *Film as a Subversive Art*. NY: Random House, 1974

Voltaire. *Candide*. London: Penguin Books, 1947

Weinberg, Herman G Saint *Cinema: selected writings 1929–1970*. London: Vision Press, 1970

Weldon, Michael J. *The Psychotronic Video Guide*. London: Titan Books, 1996

Williams, Linda. *Hardcore: power, pleasure and the "frenzy of the visible"*. London: Pandora Press, 1990

Yves Klein. *1928–1962: a retrospective*. Houston/NY: Institute for the Arts, Rice University, The Arts Publisher, 1982

Journals & Magazines

Afterimage No.3, Summer 1971. London: Afterimage Publishing

CineAction No.38. Toronto: CineAction collective

Cinema X. London: Top Sellers (various issues 1965–1984)

Ecco: the world of bizarre video. Washington (various issues 1989–1996)

Films and Filming. London: Hansom Books (various issues 1973–1976)

Healter Skelter: Mondo Extremo. Bologna

Il Giaguaro Magazine. Roma (various issues 1999–2005)

Monthly Film Bulletin. London: British Film Institute (various issues 1959–1983)

Nocturno Cinema No.9, March 1999. Torino.

Nocturno Book: Mondorama Speciale, 2002. Milano

Planète 16. Paris: Editions Retz. May/June 1964

Psychotronic Video. NY (various issues 1989)

Selected Filmography

Addio Zio Tom (Farewell Uncle Tom) (1971)
Director: Gualtiero Jacopetti, Franco Prosperi. *Editor*: Gualtiero Jacopetti, Franco Prosperi. *Script/Commentary*: Gualtiero Jacopetti, Franco Prosperi. *Photography*: Claudio Cirillo, Antonio Climati, Benito Frattari. *Music*: Riz Ortolani.

Africa Addio (Africa Blood and Guts) (1966)
Director: Gualtiero Jacopetti, Franco Prosperi. *Editor*: Gualtiero Jacopetti, Franco Prosperi. *Script/Commentary*: Gualtiero Jacopetti, Franco Prosperi. *Photography*: Antonio Climati. *Music*: Riz Ortolani.

Angeli Bianchi Angeli Neri (Witchcraft '70) (1969)
Director: Luigi Scattini. *Editor*: Luigi Scattini. *Script/Commentary*: Alberto Bevilacqua. *Photography*: Claudio Racca. Music Piero Umiliani.

Brutes and Savages (1978)
Director: Arthur Davis. *Editor*: Alan J. Cumner-Price. *Script/Commentary*: Jenny Craven. *Photography*: Jaime Questa, Jorge Ruiz, Antonio Dio, Charles Boyd, Mike Carter. *Music*: Riz Ortolani.

Des Morts (Of the Dead) (1979)
Director: Jean-Pol Ferbus, Dominique Garny, Thierry Zeno. *Editor*: Thierry Zeno, Roland Grillon. *Script/Commentary*: n/c. *Music*: Alain Pierre.

Dolce e Selvaggio (Sweet and Savage) (1983)
Director: Antonio Climati, Mario

Morra. *Editor*: Mario Morra. *Script/ Commentary*: Antonio Climati, Mario Morra, Franco Prosperi. *Photography*: Antonio Climati. *Music*: Daniele Patucchi.

Donna nel Mondo, La (Women of the World) (1964)

Director: Gualtiero Jacopetti, Franco Prosperi, Paolo Cavara. *Editor*: Gualtiero Jacopetti, Franco Prosperi. *Script/ Commentary*: Gualtiero Jacopetti, Franco Prosperi. *Photography*: Antonio Climati, Benito Frattari. *Music*: Riz Ortolani, Nino Oliviero.

Faces of Death (1979)

Director: Conan LeCilaire (John Alan Schwartz). *Editor*: James Roy, Henri Ivon Simoné, Lauri Cushman. *Script/ Commentary*: Alan Black. *Photography*: Michael Golden, Dimetri Fermo. *Music*: Gene Kauer.

Magica Nuda (Mondo Magic) (1975)

Director: Alfredo & Angelo Castiglioni. *Editor*: Alfredo & Angelo Castiglioni. *Script/Commentary*: Guido Guerrasio, Alberto Moravia. *Photography*: Alfredo & Angelo Castiglioni. *Music*: Angelo Franceso Lavagnino.

Malamondo (1964)

Director: Paolo Cavara. *Editor*: Paolo Cavara. *Script/Commentary*: Paolo Cavara, Ugo Gregoretti, Cesare Zanetti/ Guido Castaldo, Franco Torti, Stefano Strucchi. *Photography*: Ennio Guarnieri. *Music*: Ennio Morricone.

Mille Peccati... Nessuna Virtù (Wages of Sin) (1969)

Director: Sergio Martino. *Editor*: Eugenio Alabiso. *Script/Commentary*: Luciano Martino. *Photography*: Floriano Trenker. *Music*: Peppino De Luca.

Mondo Freudo (1964)

Director: R L Frost. *Editor*: R L Frost. *Script/Commentary*: Bob Cresse. *Photography*: R L Frost. *Music*: The Duvals, Bill Wild, Chuck Morgan, Rodney Lee Bermingham.

Mondo Candido (1975)

Director: Gualtiero Jacopetti, Franco Prosperi. *Editor*: Gualtiero Jacopetti, Franco Prosperi. *Script/Commentary*: Gualtiero Jacopetti, Franco Prosperi, Claudio Quarantotto. *Photography*: Giuseppe Ruzzolini. *Music*: Riz Ortolani.

Mondo Cane (1963)

    Director: Gualtiero Jacopetti, Franco Prosperi, Paolo Cavara. *Editor*: Gualtiero Jacopetti. *Script/Commentary*: Gualtiero Jacopetti, Franco Prosperi, Paolo Cavara. *Photography*: Antonio Climati, Benito Frattari. *Music*: Riz Ortolani, Nino

Mondo Cane 2000 (**This is America 3**) (1988)

    Director: Gabriele Crisanti. *Editor*: Cesare Bianchini. *Script/Commentary*: Luigi Mangini/Nick Alexander. *Photography*: n/c. *Music*: Roberto Cimpanelli.

Mondo di Notte 3 (**Ecco**) (1963)

    Director: Gianni Proia. *Editor*: Roberto Cinquini. *Script/Commentary*: Gianni Proia, Francesco Mazzei/Ugo Liberatore, Francesco Mazzei. *Photography*: Gianni Narzisi, Baldo Schwarze. *Music*: Riz Ortolani.

Mondo di Notte Oggi (1975)

    Director: Gianni Proia. *Editor*: Tito Presciutti. *Script/Commentary*: Oreste Lionello, Giancarlo Fusco. *Photography*: Benito Frattari, Claudio Ragona. *Music*: Gianni Oddi.

Mr. Mike's Mondo Video (1979)

    Director: Michael O'Donoghue. *Editor*: Bob Tischler, Alan Miller. *Script/Commentary*: Mitchell Glazer, Michael O'Donoghue, Emily Prager, Dirk Wittenborn. *Photography*: Barry Rebo. *Music*: Sid Vicious, Root Boy Slim & the Sex Change Band, Julius LaRosa.

Nuova Guinea, L'Isola dei Cannibali (**Guinea Ama**) (1974)

    Director: Akira Ide. *Editor*: Koichi Atsumi. *Script/Commentary*: Annibale Roccasecca, Sergio Fiorentini. *Photography*: Isamu Shimakura, Giancarlo Graziano, Shigeru Takana, Etsuo Akutsu. *Music*: Riz Ortolani, Corrado Demofonti.

L'Occhio Selvaggio (**The Wild Eye**) (1967)

    Director: Paolo Cavara. *Editor*: Sergio Montanari. *Script*: Paolo Cavara, Fabio Carpi, Ugo Pirro, Tonino Guerra, Alberto Moravia. *Photography*: Marcello Masiocchi. *Music*: Gianni Marchetti.

Pelo nel Mondo, Il (**Go! Go! Go! World**) (1964)

    Director: Renato Marvi (Marco Vicario), Anthony M Dawson (Antonio Margheriti). *Editor*: Marco Vicario. *Script/Commentary*: Marco Vicario.

HE USED a CAMERA LIKE MOST MEN USE a WOMAN

–and a woman like something you'd keep in a cage!

PHILIPPE LEROY
DELIA BOCCARDO

IN

THE WILD EYE

...it sees things you wouldn't dare look at!

Photography: Giovanni Raffaldi, Giancarlo Lari, Marcello Gallinelli. *Music*: Nino Oliviero, Bruno Nicolai.

Realtà romanzesca (Realities Around the World) (1967)

Director: Gianni Proia. *Editor*: Franco Arcalli. *Script/Commentary*: Gianni Proia, Giancarlo Fusco. *Photography*: Sante Achilli. *Music*: Riz Ortolani.

Savana Violenta (This Violent World) (1976)

Director: Antonio Climati, Mario Morra. *Editor*: Mario Morra. *Script/Commentary*: Antonio Climati, Mario Morra. *Photography*: Antonio Climati. *Music*: Guido e Maurizio de Angelis.

Svezia, inferno e paradiso (Sweden Heaven and Hell) (1965)

Director: Luigi Scattini. *Editor*: Luigi Scattini. *Script/Commentary*: Luigi

Scattini, Lucio Marcuzzo. *Photography*: Claudio Racca. *Music*: Piero Umiliani.

Ultime Grida dalla Savana (Savage Man... Savage Beast) (1974)

Director: Antonio Climati, Mario Morra. *Editor*: Mario Morra. *Script/Commentary*: Antonio Climati, Mario Morra, Alberto Moravia. *Photography*: Antonio Climati. *Music*: Carlo Savina.

INDEX

References in **bold** denote full review or an interview. *Pub* signifies that entry is a publication.

12 Years a Slave (2013) 16
400 Blows (1959) 90

ABC of Love and Sex, The:
    Australia Style (1978) 113
Abraham, Edward Stuart 11
Ackroyd, Dan 47
Act of Seeing with One's Own
    Eyes, The (1971) 15, 34, 70
Addio Ultimo Uomo (1978) 219
Addio Zio Tom (1972) 88,
    105–110, 131, 137, 157, 176,
    182, 187, 193, 207, 208, 209
Adieu Philipine! (1962) 225
Adinolfi, Francesco 212
Africa Addio (1965) 14, 16, 20,
    39, 43, 45, 77, 80, 90, 105,
    107, 115, 118, **119–127**, 131,
    134, 138, 142, 144, 156, 163,
    176, 179, 180, 181, 185, 186,
    189–196, 198, 199, 205–209,
    214, 220
Africa Addio (pub) 115
Africa Ama 167
Africa Blood and Guts. *See also:*
    Africa Addio 14, 127
Africa on Film (pub) 121
Africa Segreta (Secret Africa)
    (1969) 167
Agente Speciale K (1967) 217
Alessandroni, Alessandro 215
All Creatures Great and Small
    (tv) 44
Allen, Gina 113
Alpert, Herb 203
Altavilla, Enrico 65
Amarcord (pub) 14
Ambit (pub) 6
America Cosi Nuda, Cosi
    Violenta (Naked and Violent)
    (1970) 61, **155–157**
American Herald Tribune (pub)
    25
American Way of Death, The

(pub) 157
Amok Assault Video (1989) 15,
    167
Amok Journal (pub) 36
Amore nel mondo (Love in the
    world) (unmade) 184
Angeli Bianchi, Angeli Neri
    (Witchcraft '70) (1969) 65,
    131, **163–166**, 215
Animals in Film (pub) 129
Anka, Paul 49
Anonimo Veneziano (The
    Anonymous Venetian) (1970)
    137
Antonioni, Michelangelo 54
Apocalypse Now (1979) 130
Appunti per una Orestiade
    Africana (1975) 159
Aristotle 90
Arrabal, Fernando 90
Artaud, Antonin 37, 162
Astruc, Alexandre 89
Atrocity Exhibition, The (pub) 6,
    8, 15, 85, 86
Auerbach, Eric 18
Aureli, Willy 207
Australia After Dark (1975)
    111–113
Avanti (pub) 119

Baez, Joan 218
Bailey, Leonard 30
Bakunas, A J 149
Bálasz, Béla 117
Ballard, J G 6–9, 15, 16, 85, 90
Baraka (1992) 135
Barbieri, Gato 215
Barnouw, Erik 24
Baroni, I 207
Bataille, Georges 88
Battaglia di Algeri, La (The
    Battle of Algiers) (1966) 73,
    81, 137
Battle of Algiers, The. *See:*

Battaglia di Algeri, La
Beck 212
Beecher Stowe, Harriet 106
Believe it or Not (Ripley) 8
Belve Feroci (Wild Beasts)
    (1984) 135, 142, 147, 183,
    193
Bertolucci, Bernardo 118
Bevilacqua, Alberto 164
Beyond Evil 37
Beyond the Valley of the Dolls
    (1970) 67
Bianchi, Andrea 118, 217
Birth of a Nation (2016) 16
Bizarre (pub) 9
Black Emanuelle (1975) 219
Black, Joel 11
Blasetti, Alessandro 23, 90, 95,
    96, 218
Blazing Saddles (1974) 5
Blood of the Beasts. *See:* Sang
    des Bêtes, Le
Blowup (1966) 54, 55
Boccardo, Delia 76
Bondanella, Peter 12
Boneschi, Giampiero 100
Bora Bora (1968) 215
Bordwell, David 19
Born, Michael 19
Bozzetto, Bruno 91, 219
Brakhage, Stan 15, 34, 70, 87, 89
Brass, Tinto 67, 216
Bread and Chocolate. *See:* Pane e
    Cioccolata
Brown, Christopher 44, 209
Brown, K H 129
Brusati, Franco 137
Bruschini, Antonio 37, 72
Brutes and Savages (1978)
    39–41, 131, 132, 160, 214;
    film tie-in 39
Buñuel, Luis 88, 161
Buono, il Brutto, il Cattivo, Il
    (The Good, the Bad and the

237

Ugly) (1966) 216
Burn! *See:* Queimada
Burt, Jonathan 129, 134

Cameron, Kenneth M 121
Cannibal Apocalypse (1980) 134
Cannibal Ferox (1981) 4, 134
Cannibal Holocaust (1979) 38, 48, 75, 77, 134, 135, 139, 142, 144, 145, 203, 214
Capone, Al 46
Carmichael, Stokely 106
Carr, Michael 151
Casella, Alessandro 212
Castiglioni, Alfredo 12, 159, 167, 169, 216, 219
Castiglioni, Angelo 12, 159, 167, 169, 216, 219
Cavallina, Paolo 197
Cavandoli, Osvaldo 91, 219
Cavani, Liliana 37, 43
Cavara, Paolo 10, 27, 57, 72, 74, 75, 78, 118, 137, 159, 186, 198, 218, 219
Celentano, Adriano 74
Celi, Adolfo 207
Chiari, Walter 113
Chien Andalou, Un (1929) 88
Cimpanelli, Claudio 29
Cinema as Art (pub) 36
Cinema X (pub) 55
Cirillo, Claudio 108
Citizen Kane (1941) 5
City of the Living Dead (1980) 4
Clangers, The (tv) 174
Clarke, Rosie 210
Climati, Antonio 23, 29, 43, 62, 108, 114, 115, 116, 117, 124, 133, 137, 139, 141, 147, 154, 159, 176, 178, 181, 185, 186, 191, 193, 198, 209, 210, 217, 218
Clover, Carol J 38, 118
Coccinelle 51
Cohen, John 39, 115, 119
Cohen, Norman 11
Cole, Nat King 204
Collin, Anne 218
Colombier, Michel 100
Colombo, Cristofo 46
Colors (pub) 9

Comedians, The (1967) 208
Comerio, Luca 129
Con la Rabbia agli Occhi (Anger in His Eyes) (1976) 217
Continental Cinema (pub) 55
Continente Perduto (Lost Continent) (1954) 161, 216
Cooper, Tommy 96
Copacabana Palace 207
Corner, John 17
Così dolce... così perversa (1969) 174, 203
Count Basie 204
Crash (pub) 6
Craven, Jenny 140
Cresse, Bob 69, 71, 99
Crisanti, Gabriele 29, 147
Cristaldi, Franco 207
Crist, Judith 25
Crockett, Davy 46
Cronache (pub) 176
Crowley, Aleister 162, 164
Crowther, Bosley 25
Cryer, Barry 83
Culloden (1964) 106

D'Amato, Joe 215
Damiani, Damiano 43
das Neves, Wilson 215
David, Mark 215
Davis, Arthur 160, 214
Dawson, Anthony M 91. *See also:* Margheriti, Antonio
Day, Doris 203
De Angelis, Guido 141, 217
De Angelis, Maurizio 141, 217
Debrix, J R 36, 118
Debussy, Claude 215
de Falla, Manuel 215
de Gemini, Franco 215
Déjeuner sur L'herbe, Le (painting) 44
Delitto del Diavolo, Il (Queens of Evil) (1970) 137
Dell'Orso, Edda 215, 217
Demofonti, Corrado 174
Dene, Terry 84
Denis, Armand 41
Deodato, Ruggero 4, 38, 75, 77, 139, 142, 214
De Palma, Brian 218
Dernitz, Pit 139

De Sade 70 (1970) 155
De Sica, Vittorio 17, 118
Devils, The (1971) 161
Dicandeloro, Luca 210
Dio Serpente, Il (The Serpent God) (1970) 216
Disney, Walt 132, 205, 207
Django Unchained (2012) 16
Doctor Who (tv) 51
Dolce e Selvaggio (Sweet and Savage) (1983) 141, 142, **147–149**
Dolce Vita, La (1960) 23, 80
Donna del Mondo, La (1963) 191, 198
Donna nel Mondo, La 46, 55, **57–60**, 78, 170, 176, 185
Dors, Diana 51
Drew, Robert 21
Drowned World, The (pub) 6
Dumas, Jeff 148
Durgnat, Raymond 15, 130
Durniok, Manfred 11
Duvalier, François 'Papa Doc' 108, 208
Duvals, the 71
Dyson, Jeremy 5

Eastwood, Clint 118
Ecco (1963) 53, 214. *See also:* Mondo di Notte 3
Ecco (pub) 14
Edison, Thomas 49
Eisenstein, Sergei 14, 88, 224
Ekberg, Anita 51
Ellington, Duke 204, 215
Emanuelle e gli Ultimi Cannibali (1977) 76
Emanuelle Nera (1975) 76
Emmanuelle (1974) 219
Empire of the Sun (pub) 6
Enter the Dragon (1973) 45
Este, David 166
Ethnographic Film (pub) 115
Eugène Ionesco, Voix et Silences (1987) 32
Europa di Notte (1958) 23, 87, **95–96**, 218
Eurotrash (tv) 9, 63
Eva Nera 215
Evar, Evon 99
Executions (1995) 35

Exterminate All the Brutes (pub) 122

Eyeball: the European Sex and Horror Review (pub) 5

Faces of Death (1978) 10, 132, 133, 139, **151–154**, 173

Fallaci, Oriana 57, 60, 191

Fangio (1981) 176

Fangio, Juan Manuel 176

Fanon, Frantz 195

Faris, Daniel 55

Felicity 113

Fellini, Federico 23, 31, 44, 46, 80, 95, 103, 160, 209

Femina Ridens (1969) 76

Femme Spectacle, La (Paris in the Raw) (1964) 11

Femmine Insaziabili (1969) 217

Ferbus, Jean-Pol 32

Fernandez, Mario Sanchez 34

Fidenco, Nico 219

Film as a Subversive Art (pub) 32

Films and Filming (pub) 140

Fisher, Carrie 47

Fistful of Dollars, A (1964) 206

Fistful of Dynamite. See: Giù la testa

Flaherty, Robert 17

Flint, David 93

Fonda, Jane 148

Foresta di Tarvisio, La (pub) 195

Francesco d'Assisi (Francis of Assisi) 43

Franchi, Sergio 219

Franco, Jesús 155, 217

Franju, Georges 15, 25, 36, 87, 96

Frattari, Benito 29, 43, 51, 65, 79, 114, 185, 186

Freud, Sigmund 69, 169

Fricke, Ron 9, 135

Frost, R Lee 69, 71, 99, 131, 163

Fulci, Lucio 4, 38, 213

Fumetto, Rosa 80

Furnas, J C 106

Furness, R S 101

Gardner, Robert 32

Garland, Judy 204

Garny, Dominique 32

Gascoigne, Dennis 111

Gatto, Il (1977) 76

Gaynor, Gloria 52

Geismar, Ulrich 52

Gell, David 83

Germania 7 donne a testa (1970) 197

Getino, Octavio 121

Giaguaro, Il (pub) 212

Giallo a Venezia (1969) 29

Gigante, Marcello 79, 81

Giraldi, Franco 72

Girodin, Francois 154

Giù la testa (A Fistful of Dynamite) (1971) 43

Godard, Jean-Luc 160

Godi, Franco 219

Gods Must be Crazy, The (1980) 48

Go! Go! Go! World. See: Pelo nel Mondo, Il

Good, the Bad and the Ugly, The. See: Buono, il Brutto, il Cattivo, Il

Goodbye to Uncle Tom (pub) 106

Goodwin, Leonie 112

Goona Goona (1932) 161

Gourager, Alain 100

Grande Colpo dei Sette Uomini D'Oro, Il (1966) 76

Green Hell 207

Green, Martin 219

Green, Milton 59

Gregoretti, Carlo 76, 116, 122, 180, 184

Grierson, John 17, 19

Grindhouse (pub) 55

Gröss, Frances B 151, 152, 153

Gross, Jerry 127, 163

Guerrasio, Guido 225

Guinea Ama. See: Nuova Guinea, L'Isola del Cannibali

Gunn, Mike 147, 148

Halliwell's Film Guide (pub) 13

Hansen, Alan 45

Harmer, Shirley 155

Harris, Hilary 32

Harry, Deborah 47

Hartley, Mark 113

Hasselhoff, David 151

Healter Skelter (pub) 170

Hearts of Darkness: A Filmmaker's Apocalypse (1991) 130

Hefner, Hugh 156

Heider, Karl 19, 21, 115

Hendrix, Jimi 165

Henry, Pierre 100

Hicks, Colin 96

High-Rise (pub) 6

Hill, Benny 53

Hill, Terence 217

Hirst, Damien 74

Hobley, McDonald 83

Hollywood's World of Flesh (1963) 70

Homme et une Femme, Un (1966) 103

Horne, Lena 204

Hudson, Hugh 176

Hull, Rod 51, 52

Hunter, Meredith 156

I Am Curious (Yellow) 65, 87

I Malamondo (1964) **72–74**, 76, 218

Ide, Akira 172, 214

Idi Amin Dada: a Self Portrait (1974) 18

Ieri Oggi e Domani (Yesterday, Today and Tomorrow) (1963) 184, 189, 198

Imperial Eyes (pub) 159

Incredible Film Show, The (tv) 10

Incredibly Strange Films (pub) 15

Ingagi (1930) 161

In Search of... (tv) 151

Introduction to Documentary (pub) 12

Island of the Lost Souls (1932) 161

Isole del Paradiso, Le (pub) 195

Italian Cinema (pub) 12

Jack the Ripper 83

Jacopetti, Gualtiero 6, 7, 8, 10, 14, 16, 23, 43, 57, 77, 91, 95, 105, 119, **176–182**, 184, 196, 204, 207, 209, 211, 213, 220

Jaeckin, Just 219

23

Jaws (1975) 137
Jetée, La (1962) 90
Jodorowsky, Alejandro 45, 87, 88, 109
Jones, Leroy 106
Jones, Quincy 204
Judex (1963) 96
Juno, Andrea 15, 86

Kael, Pauline 105
Kauer, Gene 151
Kawalerowicz, Jerzy 161
Keith, Harvey 131
Kemble, Fanny 106, 108
Kennedy, John F 7, 8, 156
Kenton, Stan 204
Keppeler, Susan 55
Kerekes, David 11, 19, 132, 133
Kermode, Mark 128
Kilgore, Charles 14, 119
Killing for Culture: death in film from mondo to snuff (pub) 11
Killing of America (1981) 173
King Kong (1933) 161
King, Martin Luther 106
Kirchin, Basil 83
Kissinger, Henry 46
Klein, Yves 15, 27, 71, 74, 112, 162, 178, 204
Knight Rider (tv) 151
Kopland, Gilbert 218
Koyaanisqatsi (1982) 16
Kramer, Billy J. 84
Kyrou, Ado 37

Lamond, John D. 111, 112, 113
L'Amore Primitivo (1964) 65
Landis, Bill 13
LaRosa, Julius 48
Last Tango in Paris (1972) 51
Last Year at Marienbad (1961) 224
L'attesa (The Wait) (1992) 200
Lavagnino, Angelo Francesco 170, 216, 219
LaVey, Anton 164
Lawrence, D H 74
Lawrence, Michael 153
League of Gentlemen, The (tv) 5
LeCilaire, Conan (John Alan Schwartz) 151

Lee, Belinda 59, 198
Legend of 1900, The (1998) 51
LeLouch, Claude 11, 103
Lenzi, Umberto 4, 134, 174, 203
Leone, Sergio 43, 118, 181, 182, 206, 209, 218
Leroy, Philippe 76
L'Espresso (pub) 116, 122, 176, 184
L'Europeo (pub) 191
Liberatore, Ugo 215
Libidomania (1979) 172
Libre Belgique, La (pub) 32
Life (pub) 25
L'Impero del Sole (1956) 161, 216
Lindqvist, Sven 121, 122
Linea, La (tv) 219
Live and Let Die (1973) 166
L'Occhio Selvaggio (The Wild Eye) (1967) 72, **75–78**, 118, 159, 219
Lomi, Giampaolo 108, 117, 188, 192, **207–210**
London in the Raw (1965) 11, 84
London Nobody Knows, The (1967) 11
Long, Stanley 83, 84
Lord of the Sharks (pub) 183
Loren, Sophie 59
Lost Continent. See: Continente Perduto
Louw, Ben 116
Love Camp 7 (1969) 69
Loy, Mino 79, 163
Lucas, George 31

MacDougall, David 19
MacLuhan, Marshall 169
Macmillan International Film Encyclopaedia, The (pub) 13
Madame Lash 112
Magia Nuda (Mondo Magic) (1975) 20, 78, **167–171**, 216
Magia Verde (1953) 161, 216
Malabimba (1979) 29
Malamondo 72. See also: I Malamondo
Mal d'Africa (1968) 195, 197, 200
Manet, Édouard 44

Manson, Charles 154, 156, 157, 166
Manzoni, Piero 71
Marcellini, Romolo 225
Marchetti, Gianni 76, 219
Margheriti, Antonio 93, 134, 137, 217
Marker, Chris 90
Marquis de Sade's Philosophy in the Boudoir (1973) 217
Martelli, Augusto 216
Martial, Josette 148
Martino, Sergio 38, 61, 134, 155, 157
Marvi, Renato 91. See also: Vicario, Marco
Massaccesi, Aristide 219
Massi, Stelvio 29
Mathis, Johnny 169
Mattei, Bruno 172
McCabe, Patrick 9, 167
McGuire, Barry 218
Medium Cool (1969) 24, 75
Meek, Joe 48
Mepris, Le (1963) 160
Mercer, Johnny 216
Meyer, Russ 67, 71
Midnight Cowboy (1969) 156
Mike Sammes' Singers, the 52
Mille Peccati… Nessuna Virtù (Wages of Sin) (1969) **61–63**, 155
Miller, Arnold 11, 83, 84, 155
Miller, Michele 209
Miller, Michelle 44
Miracles of Life (pub) 6
Misteri di Roma, I (1963) 225
Mitford, Nancy 157
Modugno, Domenico 96
Moglie di Mio Padre, La (Confessions of a Frustrated Housewife) (1976) 217
Mondo Bizarre. See: Welt Ohne Scham
Mondo Bizarro (1966) 131
Mondo Candido (1975) **43–46**, 176, 192, 209, 213
Mondo Cane (1962) 5–8, 10, 16, **22–28**, 43, 48, 57, 65, 72, 76, 80, 89, 91, 99, 111, 112, 129, 135, 144, 161, 162, 170, 175, 176, 180, 183, 185, 186, 193,

197, 199, 201, 205, 206, 209, 211; *and outtakes* 59

Mondo Cane 2000 (This is America 3) (1988) **29–31**, 147

Mondo Cane No.2 (Mondo Pazzo) (1963) 15, 19, 28, 92, 133, 162, 179, 191, 217

Mondo Cane No.3. *See:* Mondo Cane Oggi: L'Orrore Continua

Mondo Cane Oggi: L'Orrore Continua (Mondo Cane No.3) (1985) 29

Mondo Desperado (pub) 167

Mondo di Notte (1960) 51, 52, 55, 87, 95, 97, 100, 101, 216

Mondo di Notte 3 (Ecco) (1963) 87, **97–100**

Mondo di Notte Oggi (1975) **51–53**

Mondo films *and animals* 128; *and anti-narrative* 85; *and art film techniques* 14, 89; *and comedy* 133; *and danger* 131; *and documentary* 12; *and exploitation* 13; *and fakery* 19; *and framing* 114; *and horror* 132; *and music* 211; *and politics* 131; *and post-mondo* 134; *and ritual and magic* 131, 159; *and the voice of God* 20; *and travelogue* 20; *and violence* 132; *and voyeurism and sexuality* 54

Mondo Freudo (1966) 30, 57, 63, **69–71**, 131

Mondo Magic. *See:* Magia Nuda

Mondo Mod (1967) 11

Mondo New York (1988) 131

Mondo Oscenita (1966) 55

Mondo Pazzo. *See:* Mondo Cane No.2

Mondo Sex (1969). *See also:* Mille Peccati… Nessuna Virtù (Wages of Sin) 61

Mondo Violence. *See:* Savana Violenta

Monroe, Marilyn 46

Montagna del Dio Cannibale, La (1978) 61

Montanelli, Indro 23

Monthly Film Bulletin (MFB) (pub) 13, 24, 105, 113, 124, 135, 157, 213

Moravia, Alberto 20, 78, 88, 121, 127, 137, 140, 159, 160, 169, 214

Morgan, Henry 96

Morra, Mario 87, 91, 133, 137, 139, 141, 147, 154, 159, 217, 218

Morricone, Ennio 72, 73, 74, 203, 212, 215, 216, 218

Morts, Des (Of the Dead) (1979) **32–35**, 135, 152, 154

Mother Joan of the Angels (Devil and the Nun) (1961) 161

Mountain of the Cannibal God. *See:* Montagna del Dio Cannibale, La

Mr Mike's Mondo Video (1979) **47–49**, 134

Muller, Eddie 55

Mulvey, Laura 55

Muppet Show, The (tv) 214

Murray, Bill 47

Naked and Violent. *See:* America Cosi Nuda, Cosi Violenta

Naked North 11

Nanà, Aichè 80, 81

National Geographic (pub) 9

National Lampoon (pub) 47

Natura Contro (1988) 118, 137

Nerosubianco (1969) 67

Newell, Norman 28, 203, 204

New Internationalist (pub) 9

Newman, Kim 12

New Yorker, the (pub) 105

New York Times, the (pub) 25

Nichols, Bill 12, 13, 17, 114

Nicolai, Bruno 92, 155, 216

Nievo, Ippolito 195, 196, 200

Nievo, Stanis 23, 162, 181, 183–185, 191, **195–202**

Night and Fog (1956) 224

Nimoy, Leonard 151

Nitsch, Hermann 38, 162

Nocturno (pub) 14

Nomi, Klaus 49

Not Quite Hollywood (2008)

113

Nude per L'Assassino (1975) 118

Nuer, The (1971) 32

Nuova Guinea, L'Isola dei Cannibali (Guinea Ama) (1974) **172–175**, 214

Nuovo Cinema Paradiso (1988) 87

O'Connor, T P 129

Oddi, Gianni 51

Of the Dead. *See:* Morts, Des

O'Donoghue, Michael 47

Oliviero, Nino 26, 92, 130

Onions, Oliver 217. *See also:* De Angelis, Guido, *and* De Angelis, Maurizio

Orlandi, Nora 215

Ortolani, Riz 26, 28, 40, 41, 43, 45, 48, 99, 102, 103, 108, 125, 130, 132, 174, 176, 181, 186, 200, **203–206**, 212

Otto, Francesco Scarab 102

Our Incredible World (1966) 11

Owen, M.D. (tv) 113

Oxford Companion to Film (pub) 13

Pallottelli, Duiolio 57

Pane e Cioccolata (Bread and Chocolate) (1974) 137

Panigutti, Nico 14

Paris in the Raw. *See:* Femme Spectacle, La

Paris Match (pub) 122

Pasolini, Pier Paolo 37, 43, 89, 159, 160, 195, 218, 227

Patucchi, Daniele 147

Peckinpah, Sam 109

Peeping Tom (1960) 54, 118

Pelo nel Mondo, Il (Go! Go! Go! World) (1964) 87, **91–93**, 137, 217

Penberthy, Wes 112

Per un Pugno di Dollari (A Fistful of Dollars) (1964) 216

Pes, Carlo 215

Peterson, Oscar 204

Petit, Philippe 149

Phillips, Esther 52

Piccioni, Piero 203, 215

Piedone a Hong Kong (1975) 43
Pielke, Eddie 112
Pierre, Alain 34
Pig-fucking Movie, The. *See:*
Vase de Noces
Pink Floyd 172
Pithiou, John 107
Pizzicato Five 212
Platters, the 51
Polanski, Roman 43
Polidori, Gian Luigi 215
Pollock, Channing 96
Pontecorvo, Gillo 43, 81, 137,
218
Pop Group, the 172
Pornography of Representation,
The (pub) 55
Portishead 212
Powell, Michael 113
Pratt, Mary Louise 20, 159
Price, Vincent 20, 164
Primitive London (1965) 11,
83–84, 155
Proia, Gianni 51, 52, 53, 66, 90,
97, 101, 102, 214
Prola, Carlo 184
Prosperi, Franco 10, 14, 23, 43,
57, 59, 76, 77, 105, 119, 135,
142, 148, 162, 176, 183–194,
185, 196, 204, 207, 209, 213
Psycho (1960) 54
Psychotronic Video (pub) 10
Pudovkin, Vsevolod 224
Pulp 212
Purdom, Edmund 20, 21, 61,
63, 164
Pyjama Tops (play) 52
Pym, John 135

Queens of Evil. *See:* Delitto del
Diavolo, Il
Queimada (Burn!) (1969) 43,
137
Questo Sporco Mondo
Meraviglioso (1971) 65, 163
Que Viva Mexico (1932) 88
Quilici, Folco 225

Rabiger, Michael 114
Racca, Claudio 163
Randolph, John 107
Ranieri, Katyna 27, 186, 203,

204
Ravel, Maurice 215
Raymond, Paul 52
Realtà romanzesca (Realities
around the World) (1969) 53,
87, 101–103, 214
Rear Window (1954) 60
Reggio, Godfrey 9, 16, 135
Renov, Michael 13, 19, 114
Resnais, Alain 224
Restany, Pierre 27
Richter, Hans 87
Rizzoli, Angelo 17, 23, 25, 44,
57, 122, 191, 201
Rolling Stones, the 156
Roma Bene (1971) 76
Ronay, Mac 96
Rony, Fatimah Tobing 161
Roots (tv) 16
Rossellini, Roberto 17
Rossi, Guliano 167
Ross, Jonathan 10
Rota, Nino 212, 218
Rotha, Paul 12
Rouch, Jean 17, 117
Rozier, Jacques 225
Rubicon, Jessica 80
Ruggero Deodato 203
Russell, Bertrand 73
Russell, Ken 161
Ruzzolini, Giuseppe 29, 43

Sadismo (1967) 133
Saint-Saëns, Camille 49
Salerno, Enrico Maria 65, 137,
164
Salon Kitty (1976) 216
Salò o le 120 giornate di Sodoma
(Salò, or the 120 Days of
Sodom) (1975) 37, 38
Saludos Amigos (1942) 207
Sammes, Mike 216
Sanders, George 20, 97
Sandokan, Il (tv) 76
Sang des Bêtes, Le (Blood of the
Beasts) (1949) 25, 36, 130
Santacruz, Daniel 169
Saturday Night Live (tv) 47, 49
Savage Eye, The (1960) 7, 24
Savage Man… Savage Beast 132
(1975). *See also:* Ultime Grida
dalla Savana

Savana Violenta 133, 217
Savana Violenta (This Violent
World; Mondo Violence)
(1976) 141–145
Savina, Carlo 96, 138, 218
Savini, Tom 41
Scattini, Luigi 63, 65, 66, 74,
79, 113, 131, 154, 155, 163,
164, 215
Schroeder, Barbet 18, 172
Schwartz, John Alan 151, 154.
See also: LeCilaire, Conan
Searle, Adrian 38
Secret Africa. *See:* Africa Segreta
Serpent God, The. *See:* Dio
Serpente, Il
Sexy al Neon (1962) 95
Sexy Magico (1963) 65, 79–81,
163
Sexy Proibito (1963) 71
Shadows, the 219
Shaft (1971) 41
Shakespeare, William 97, 100
Shock Cinema (pub) 21
Shocking Africa (1982) 167
Shock Xpress (pub) 5
Shohat, Ella 21
Shumba (pub) 183, 194
Sibaldi, Stefano 28, 65, 192
Siegfried and Roy 52
Signor Rossi, Il (Mr. Rossi) (tv)
91, 219
Sinatra, Frank 203, 204
Sjöman, Vilgot 65, 67, 87
Skin of the World, The 92. *See
also:* Pelo nel Mondo, Il
Slater, David 11, 19, 132, 133
Sleazoid Express (pub) 13
Smith, Marc Mauro 169
Solanas, Fernando 121
Sol, Anita 81
Sommer, Robert 147
Spaak, Catherine 74
Spencer, Bud 217
Spielberg, Steven 31
Staller, Ilona ('La Cicciolina')
138
Stam, Robert 21
Staples, Amy J 14
Steel 149
Steele, Tommy 96
Stelarc 170

Steno 43
Stephenson, Ralph 21, 36
Stern, Harold 219
Stevenson, Ralph 118
Stoller, Paul 17
Strick, Joseph 7, 24
Striscia le Notizia (tv) 81
Styron, William 106
Super-Cannes (pub) 6
Sutcliffe, Thomas 102
Svezia, Inferno e Paradiso
 (Sweden Heaven and Hell)
 (1968) **65–67**, 74, 163, 215
Sweden Heaven and Hell. *See:*
 Svezia, Inferno e Paradiso
Sweet and Savage. *See:* Dolce e
 Selvaggio
Swezey, Stuart 36

Tabu (1963) 161
Tarantula del Ventro Nero,
 La (The Black Belly of the
 Tarantula) (1971) 137
Tempo, Il (pub) 119
Tentori, Antonio 37, 72
Teorema (Theorem) (1968) 43
They're a Weird Mob (1966) 113
This is America 3 (1988). *See
 also:* Mondo Cane 2000 29
This Violent World. *See:* Savana
 Violenta
Thompson, Carolyn 180
Thorpe, John 210
Thorpe, Leila 210
Thousand and One Nights, A 43
Three Essays on the Theory of
 Sexuality (pub) 69
Tinti, Gabriele 76
Titicut Follies (1967) 87
Togliatti, Palmiro 227
Topo, El (1970) 45, 88, 109
Tornatore, Giuseppe 87, 218
Towards a Third Cinema (pub)
 121
Trader Horn (1931) 129
Traylor, David 29
Trenet, Charles 15, 130
Trenker, Floriano 62
Trinity Is Back Again (1975) 43
Tropico nel Cancro (1972) 207,
 210
Trovajoli, Armando 215

Truffaut, François 90
Truth (pub) 111
Turnbull, Richard 126
Turner, Nat 106, 109, 110, 208
Turner, Tina 165
Tyler, Parker 25, 56, 87, 88, 89,
 161

Uccellacci e Uccellini (1966) 227
Ultime Grida dalla Savana
 (Savage Man… Savage Beast)
 (1975) 20, 78, 118, 132,
 137–140, 147, 159, 193, 210,
 218
Umbrelli, Paolo 198
Umiliani, Piero 65, 164, 214
Una Sull' Altra (1969) 213
Uncle Si and the Sirens (1938)
 49
Underground Film (pub) 89
Useless Sex, The (pub) 57
Ustinov, Peter 20, 21, 59
Uys, Jamie 48

Valachi Papers, The (1972) 203
Valée, La (The Valley Obscured
 by Clouds) (1972) 18, 172
Vale, V 15, 86
Vanderput, Suzanne 60
Van Dyke, W S 129
Vanished Continent (pub) 183
Vannucchi, Antonella 215
Vanzi, Luigi 90, 95, 96, 216
Vase de Noces (Wedding
 Trough; The Pig-fucking
 Movie) (1974) 35, 135
Velvet Underground 174
Vertov, Dziga 225
Vicario, Marco 76, 93, 137
Visconti, Luchino 17
Vizi Segreti della Donna nel
 Mondo (1972) 65
Vizzi, Luigi 167
Vogel, Amos 32, 35, 37, 56, 90
Voltaire 43, 44, 45, 99, 176, 192,
 213
von Trier, Lars 16

Wages of Sin. *See:* Mille
 Peccati… Nessuna Virtù
Wagner, Richard 138

Wallenda, Karl 149
War Game, The (1965) 105
Watkins, Peter 105, 106
Wedding Trough. *See:* Vase de
 Noces
Weinberg, Herman 85, 160
Welles, Orson 5
Welt Ohne Scham (Mondo
 Bizarre) (1975) 11
Wexler, Haskell 24, 75
What? (1972) 43
Which Tribe do You Belong To?
 (pub) 121, 127, 159
Whitaker, Patrick 219
White, James 157
Wild Beasts. *See:* Belve Feroci
Wild Eye, The. *See:* L'Occhio
 Selvaggio
Winston, Brian 17
Wiseman, Frederick 87
Witchcraft '70 (1970) 154, 164,
 215. *See also:* Angeli Bianchi,
 Angeli Neri
Witchcraft and the Cinema
 (pub) 162
Women of the World (1963) 21
Wright, Mary Ellen 154

X, Malcolm 106

Yellow Rolls-Royce, The (1964)
 212

Zabriskie Point (1970) 110
Zavattini, Cesare 17, 224, 225
Zeno, Thierry 32, 34, 35, 135
Zephyrs, the 84
Zio Tom (1971) 16, 38, 43, 44,
 45, 117, 185, 205
Zombie Creeping Flesh (1980)
 172
Zombi Horror (1981) 29

243

A HEADPRESS BOOK
First published by Headpress in 2006; this revised and updated edition in 2018

[email] headoffice@headpress.com
[web] www.worldheadpress.com

SWEET & SAVAGE
The World Through The Mondo Film Lens

Text copyright © Mark Goodall
'Considerations on the Documentary Film' © Gualtiero Jacopetti estate
This volume copyright © Headpress 2018
Cover design, front: Ganymede Foley; back: Mark Critchell
Book design & layout: Mark Critchell <mark.critchell@googlemail.com>

The moral rights of the author have been asserted.

A CIP catalogue record for this book is available from the British Library

978-1-909394-50-6   ISBN PAPERBACK
978-1-909394-51-3   ISBN EBOOK
NO-ISBN HARDBACK

HEADPRESS.COM
the gospel according to unpopular culture
Special editions of this and other books are available exclusively from Headpress